SHAFTESBU

Richard Turnbull

SHAFTESBURY
THE GREAT REFORMER

RICHARD TURNBULL

LION

Copyright © 2010 Richard Turnbull
This edition copyright © 2010 Lion Hudson

The author asserts the moral right to be identified as the author of this work

A Lion Book
an imprint of
Lion Hudson plc
Wilkinson House, Jordan Hill Road,
Oxford OX2 8DR, England
www.lionhudson.com
ISBN 978 0 7459 5348 9

Distributed by:
UK: Marston Book Services, PO Box 269, Abingdon, Oxon, OX14 4YN
USA: Trafalgar Square Publishing, 814 N. Franklin Street, Chicago, IL 60610
USA Christian Market: Kregel Publications, PO Box 2607, Grand Rapids, MI 49501

First edition 2010
10 9 8 7 6 5 4 3 2 1 0
All rights reserved

Text Acknowledgments
Scripture quotations taken from the *Holy Bible, New International Version*, copyright ©
1973, 1978, 1984 International Bible Society. Used by permission of Zondervan and
Hodder & Stoughton Limited. All rights reserved. The "NIV" and "New International
Version" trademarks are registered in the United States Patent and Trademark Office
by International Bible Society. Use of either trademark requires the permission of
International Bible Society. UK trademark number 1448790.

Picture Acknowledgments:
Pp. I (t), ii, iii: © National Portrait Gallery, London; p. i (b): Classic Image/Alamy; p. iv:
Bettman/Corbis; p. v (t): The Print Collector/Alamy; p. v (b): Mary Evans Picture Library/
Alamy; pp. vi, vii: Image Stage/Photolibrary; p. viii: Image Source/Corbis.

The text paper used in this book has been made from wood
independently certified as having come from sustainable forests.

A catalogue record for this book is available
from the British Library

Typeset in 11/14 Italian Garamond BT

Printed and bound in Malta

CONTENTS

This book is dedicated to my family. Caroline, my wife, and my children – Sarah, Katie, Matt, and Rebecca – have had to live with the Earl of Shaftesbury for a good number of years at the meal table, in family quizzes, and even on holiday. I would also like to thank my eldest daughter, Sarah, and Sam Allen, both history undergraduates at the time, for their help in compiling the index. I am grateful to Lion Hudson for publishing the book and to Kate Kirkpatrick and Miranda Powell, my editors. I am also immensely grateful to the Trustees of the Latimer Trust for financial support of my research. The final writing took place during a period of study leave from my post as Principal of Wycliffe Hall, Oxford. For that privilege I would like to thank both the Council of Wycliffe and my staff colleagues.

Richard Turnbull

Oxford, Summer 2009

ABBREVIATIONS

Bible Society	British and Foreign Bible Society
CMS	Church Missionary Society
CPAS	Church Pastoral Aid Society
LCM	London City Mission
LMS	London Missionary Society
London Society	London Society for the Promotion of Christianity Amongst the Jews
RSU	Ragged School Union

INTRODUCTION

The representatives of some 200 voluntary societies attended the funeral in Westminster Abbey of the Earl of Shaftesbury on 8 October 1885. These institutions ranged from missionary societies to benevolent associations for the poor. They included orphanages, schools, and asylums. There were also some surprises. Alongside those from the London City Mission and the Church Missionary Society were not only the Cab Drivers' Benevolent Association and the Saturday Half-Holiday Movement, but also the London Anti-Vivisection Society and the Royal Society for the Prevention of Cruelty to Animals. *The Times* reported that the gentlemen's clubs and other significant buildings in St James' Street and Pall Mall lowered their window blinds as a mark of respect. Apart from the great and the good, over 1,000 members of the public were able to attend, and to sing Charles Wesley's hymn, "Come, Let Us Join Our Friends Above". This was also the opportunity for those from all sections of society to show "their respect and affection for one who had benefited so many of his fellow countrymen", "the great philanthropist", as the paper described him.[1] The early biographer of the Earl, or, perhaps better, the chronicler of his life, Edwin Hodder, publishing in 1886–87, described the scene. Thousands had gathered in Grosvenor Square from where the funeral cortège departed, "whose hearts were heavy, and whose eyes were red with weeping for the best friend the poor ever had".[2] The streets were lined with people; as the procession neared Parliament there were, on one side of the road, deputations from many of the social and Christian missions associated with Shaftesbury carrying banners with biblical verses. Bands played at regular intervals and those heading the delegations joined the procession as it made its way to Westminster Abbey.[3]

Even allowing for the nature of biography in the late nineteenth century the assessment of the later observer of the Victorian age, G. M. Young, that Sir Robert Peel, who died in 1850, was "the only English statesman for whose death the poor have cried in the streets",[4] requires considerable qualification. What was it that brought together the Archbishop of Canterbury, the Lord Mayor of London, royalty, and members of both Houses of Parliament alongside the committee members and beneficiaries of numerous small and disparate voluntary groups?

Perhaps it seems strange to commence a biography with a description of the funeral of the subject. Shaftesbury himself pointed to observing as a child the funeral of a pauper as one of the formative influences on his compassion in life. Shaftesbury was a complicated and complex figure, but also a towering one. His death marked the end of two eras, not just one. The age which had formed the Earl's character was one of paternalism, aristocracy, deference, and duty. This was already passing when he was born. The age in which he lived, mainly that of Victoria, although the Queen herself had another sixteen years to live when Shaftesbury died, was both a romantic and a religious period. Shaftesbury encapsulated the ideal of the Christian philanthropist and evangelist. That combination was his life's passion. Religion and life were not to be separated but integrated. The state and the voluntary society had equal claims to meet the social and religious needs of the nation. Sadly his death also marked the end, or at least the eventide, of the era of religion's engagement with the public life of the nation in such a unique fashion.

Shaftesbury turned down high office because it would interfere with his calling. As late as 1866 he refused the Cabinet offices of Home Secretary, Chancellor of the Duchy of Lancaster, and Lord President of the Council. To have taken government office would have required him to "withdraw myself from the many and various pursuits which have occupied a very large portion of my life", and there were "yet fourteen hundred thousand women, children and young persons to be brought under the protection of the Factory Acts".[5] This demonstrates his great principle and strength of character. It also shows his single-minded passion and commitment to the pursuit of justice and relief for the poor as well as, of course, to their salvation. Whether Shaftesbury was suited temperamentally and emotionally for high office is another matter. He had a dark, unstable side that ran in the family and indeed does so even to the present day. Within six weeks of the tenth Earl being murdered in 2005, the eleventh Earl died of a heart attack at just twenty-seven years of age. Two years later the tenth Earl's third wife and her brother were convicted of his murder. The seventh Earl throughout his life had endured deep anxiety, mood swings, bouts of depression, even periods in a dark abyss. Others too were only too aware of this darker side to his psychological make-up. As early as 1821 Henry Fox, an Oxford contemporary, sensed a dash of madness in him.[6] Florence Nightingale made the memorable comment that had not the Earl of Shaftesbury been committed to the reform of the asylum, he would have been in one.[7] For much of his life, the burden of debt bore heavily upon Shaftesbury – he was not the best manager of money nor judge of whom to employ on his estate. When this is added to his deep religious understanding of the depravity of human beings, the sense of being alone in much of his campaigning, and his own attitudes to duty and role in life then it is not surprising that he faced such oscillations in mood and sense of worth.

So, let us return to his death and funeral. *The Times* stated that "in Lord Shaftesbury there has passed away the most eminent social reformer of the present century… one of the most honoured figures of our contemporary history… the friend of the poor, the degraded and the outcast". The paper later added, "Nothing is more astonishing in the catalogue of his exploits than their variety and comprehensiveness… Lord Shaftesbury fills and will fill a special place in the annals of this century."[8]

This book explores why.

CHAPTER 1

BORN INTO THE AGE OF REFORM: THE EARLY YEARS 1801–1822

On 23 February 1807 the House of Commons voted through the Bill for the Abolition of the Slave Trade by 283 votes to 16. Shaftesbury was less than six years old. Slavery itself became illegal in 1833, the year of the death of the great campaigner William Wilberforce. At that point Shaftesbury, in the Commons as Lord Ashley, was preparing to embark upon the task of the campaign for children working in factories – exactly what Wilberforce had been criticized for ignoring, at least by the radical William Cobbett. A year earlier the Whig prime minister, Earl Grey, much to Lord Ashley's chagrin, started on the path of transforming the political system itself with the Reform Bill. This was a modest measure. It was designed to remove the historic representation from some scarcely populated towns ("rotten boroughs"), to provide for members of Parliament for the new larger cities, and to extend the franchise slightly. Nevertheless, for later historians this first move of political reform rather characterized the age.

In the years immediately before and after his birth some of the great societies which later formed such an important part in Shaftesbury's life came into being. In 1799 the Church Missionary Society was founded, followed in 1804 by the British and Foreign Bible Society and, in 1807, the London Society for the Promotion of Christianity Amongst the Jews. The first of these was specific to the established church, the other two were early examples of interdenominational societies. This was indeed to be an age of reform, politically, socially, and religiously. Politically and socially, Shaftesbury may have belonged to another age. Yet, through his faith, he sought to transform those realms equally, if not more effectively, than reforming governments, whether Whig or Tory.

Birth and upbringing

Born on 28 April 1801, Anthony Ashley Cooper was the fourth of nine children born to Cropley Ashley Cooper and his wife, Anne, at the family's London home, 24 Grosvenor Square. The family estates were mostly in Dorset around the ancestral seat of St Giles House, near Wimborne St Giles. In 1811 Anthony's father succeeded as the sixth Earl of Shaftesbury. The eldest son's courtesy title of Lord Ashley now passed to Anthony. He was known in this way until he became the seventh Earl in 1851.[1]

Ashley was not born into the Victorian age even though most of his adult life was lived under Queen Victoria. During his childhood and early adult life the Hanoverian dynasty was crumbling. "Mad King George" (George III) died in 1820, succeeded by George IV, who had been regent since 1811. In 1830 he was succeeded by his brother, the Duke of Clarence, as William IV. Royal lifestyle left much to be desired. In outlook and attitude the emerging industrial nation was witnessing the transition from one age to another.

Ashley was an aristocrat, born into an aristocratic family, and the values, attitudes, and thought processes of an earlier era of English society were deeply instilled within him. The society to which he belonged was one of duty rather than rights. Deference within the social hierarchy marked out the relationships within society. Each person knew their place, their duties and responsibilities and it was not for humanity to seek to change what was seen as essentially God's providential provision. The attitudes were basically paternalistic. Nevertheless, mutual obligation and dependency were the hallmarks of this pre-industrial, rural, and agrarian, yet also very personal society. The system was held together by the middle-ranking gentry, the small landowners, magistrates, archdeacons, poor-law guardians, overseers, churchwardens – indeed numerous sub-hierarchies, all of which had a vested interest in the continuing operation of a deferential society. The clergy had a particular role in the promotion of social harmony in this divinely ordered society. Many of the labouring classes felt that they too had a common interest in the preservation of such a system.

Whether a plowman or a bishop, each individual had his function, his place, his protectors, his duties, his reciprocal obligations, and his strong ties of dependency.[2]

Natural rights based upon natural law were rejected. The rights of the landed interest depended upon the performance of their obligations, not least to others within their care. Rights were not inalienable, either for gentry or for labourers. The owners of landed estates were thus expected to have a genuine concern for the social as well as the moral well-being of those working on their estates. This provision included making available not only coal and soup, cottages and allotments, but also schools and perhaps even compassionate winter employment. The principle of "a cottage and a cow" meant that the gentry provided (or bestowed) the means of basic food and shelter and granted a degree of independence, but all within the confines of the accepted hierarchy. In return they received harmony and acquiescence. The links which bonded people together were not class relationships, but ties that ran vertically through the social system. It preserved England from revolution.

This system was both local and rural. It worked best in small spheres of influence, especially the landed estates of the squirearchy. The system depended for its operation upon communication as well as deference. These were real relationships between real people. The chain of hierarchy was matched by the bonds of union in a society which depended upon the land, landed estates, and landowning gentry.

Shaftesbury's view of society closely reflected this paternalistic model. Society was a structured, hierarchical, class society, ordered as such by God, into which all were called to their respective stations and positions in life. This was true whether for watercress girls, factory operatives, or aristocracy. Shaftesbury was adamant that the aristocracy had duties imposed upon them by property as well as privileges. If the landed gentry took more seriously their duties toward the labouring poor then this would lead to improved and harmonious relationships. In his many speeches before Parliament in the cause of factory and industrial reform he appealed to these principles. So, when speaking in the House of Commons in 1843 on the Mines and Collieries Bill, he said "property and station had their duties as well as their rights".[3] Nearly twenty-five years later, in the Lords, while speaking on the Masters and Operatives Bill in 1866, he was again seeking to promote mutual understanding by advocating a Council of Conciliation to prevent disputes and strikes and "to foster a better understanding between employers and employed".[4] Indeed, as Shaftesbury's Evangelical religious beliefs interacted with his traditional, aristocratic paternalism, he concluded that breach of these duties constituted sin. Nevertheless, his acute sense of the duties and responsibilities of those entrusted with land and position did at least mean that he would apply these principles to the emerging world of commerce and industry, not just to the personal moral lives of the poor. Sydney Smith had complained at the beginning of the nineteenth century that Evangelicals were really only concerned with the personal morals of those earning less than £500 per annum.

None of this made Shaftesbury sympathetic in any way to such movements for industrial or political reform in the nineteenth century as Chartism or Trade Unionism. This system of paternalism and the attitudes that flowed from it help explain the paradox of how one of the greatest social reformers of all time remained a high Tory and opposed many reform movements. By the middle part of the nineteenth century society was neither local nor agrarian. Industrialization and commerce threatened the traditional means and methods of encouraging good relationships within the social hierarchy. Huge movements of population had led to the large-scale massing of people in cities with all of the attendant issues of housing, poverty, and employment. In the new urban conurbations anonymity was possible in ways that were not so in the rural economy. Hidden people obscured poverty. Society was now also primarily industrial, based on industrial production rather than agriculture. Shaftesbury sought to apply the paternalistic principles of the society which had formed and shaped him to the society in which he now lived. He did so with remarkable success, but his achievements remained full of paradox.

His early family life was difficult and his relationship with his parents less than congenial. His mother and father displayed little love and affection either for each other or for the children. Shaftesbury later claimed that his mother was guilty of dereliction of duty towards the children, and, bluntly, a lack of kindness. In his autobiographical fragment, written near the end of his life, he noted that he remembered little of his earliest years. What did stand out in his mind was the severity shown to him and his three elder sisters and his constant fear of his parents.[5] In his journal (begun in 1825), looking back to his childhood, he described his mother as "a dreadful woman".[6] Leaping slightly ahead his views remained unchanged. On his birthday in 1826 he noted that "my mother continues in her hardness", and even went so far as to declare

"away with her Memory!"[7] His subsequent very happy marriage to
Emily Cowper (known as Minny) and his intense love and concern
for his own children – some of whom beset him with problems, not
least debt – stood in considerable contrast. His father fared little
better in his estimation and their relationship was always rocky. The
sixth Earl was also typical of his age and involved in the affairs of
public life. Ashley regarded him as honest but commented in 1828,
"I cannot feel any esteem for Lord Shaftesbury" and his "whole
pleasure is in finding fault".[8] He was rarely physically present in the
lives of his children and when he was awe, reverence and, by and
large, silence appeared to be the order of the day. Although the Earl
and Countess of Shaftesbury were themselves widely appreciated,
it seems that they simply did not like their children. Offspring were
certainly not to be allowed to get in the way of the balls and social
occasions hosted by Ashley's mother.[9] As Ashley developed into
adulthood, father and son were often at loggerheads.

One person did have long and lasting influence upon Ashley
from his childhood – more so than his parents. The family
housekeeper, formerly a maid to his mother, was Maria Millis.
Shaftesbury recalled her special care, affectionate and pious
nature. He recorded, "I can even now call to mind many sentences
of prayer she made me repeat at her knees."[10] Maria read to Ashley
from the Bible and on his eighth birthday sent him a poem which
wished upon him blessings both in this life, health and joy, and
also in the life to come. Maria provided Ashley with the love that
was so noticeably absent from his mother and father. As a woman
of not just religious but Evangelical conviction her influence on
his religious development may not have been explicitly recorded
but was undoubtedly deep and enduring. There is a note from
Shaftesbury on an envelope written in 1865, "from Maria Millis, to
whom, under God, I owe the first thoughts of Piety, and the first
actions of Prayer".[11] Maria died while Ashley was at his first school,
the Manor House in Chiswick. In her will she left him her watch,
which, at least according to Hodder, he wore for the rest of his life

and showed off, saying that it had been given to him by the best friend he ever had in the world.

School and university

Ashley hated school. He entered the Manor House at the age of seven and remained for five years. He compared it to Charles Dickens' notorious fictional boarding school, Dotheboys Hall, in the novel *Nicholas Nickleby*, published in 1838–39. It was no fiction for Ashley. "Nothing", he said, "could have surpassed it for filth, bullying, neglect, and hard treatment of every sort." However, he also noted that it "may have given me an early horror of oppression and cruelty".[12] A rather carefree life followed after this particular torment. He went next to Harrow, a somewhat less traumatic experience, though he had a Master who insisted on taking the first class at 4 a.m. on a winter's morning because he was a bad sleeper. Less traumatic, that is, until he witnessed an event that made another lasting impression upon the rather troubled mind of this fourteen-year-old adolescent. He recalled the event and its significance in his later life, and related it, while visiting the school, to the then head teacher of Harrow, Dr Butler, the son of the head from his own time there. Young Ashley observed the chaotic funeral of a pauper. Attracted by the shouting and singing he watched four or five drunken men as they dropped the coffin they were carrying. Other than the pallbearers no other mourners were present. The scene descended into a spectacle of foul and unseemly language. He told Dr Butler in 1884, the year before his death, that this was when he resolved to "make the cause of the poor my own".[13] Undoubtedly, the ageing Lord was more than capable of reading back significance into the events of his earlier years to some degree, but the episode was also clearly etched upon his impressionable mind.

Ashley left Harrow in 1816 and then spent two years in the household of a relative who was a clergyman in Derbyshire. Ashley himself noted that the purpose was to get him out of the way. The clergyman concerned made no claims to be able to teach the young Ashley. There was a horse, some dogs, and a kind and hospitable family near by. By his own admission he hardly ever opened a book and "seldom heard anything worth hearing"[14] during these two misspent years. An army career would have been a serious option for someone of Ashley's standing either instead of, or as a prelude to, entering politics. Ashley indicated that this is what his father had in mind for him. The intervention of a family friend, Lord Bathurst, persuaded the Earl to direct Ashley to Oxford. He entered Christ Church, Oxford, in 1819, having thus narrowly avoided the army, and for Bathurst's judicious intervention Ashley had the deepest gratitude. He entered upon his studies, perhaps ill-prepared, but with diligence. He graduated in 1822 with a first-class honours degree in classics. This was no mean achievement and it cautions us against too swift a dismissal of Shaftesbury as simply paternalistic or narrow-minded or in any way anti-intellectual. He was a highly intelligent man.

Competing tensions were still at work in Ashley's heart and mind. What was to be his calling in life? Faith too was stirring. How were these things going to effect the next stage of Lord Ashley's life and career?

CHAPTER 2

THE CALLING OF
PUBLIC LIFE: 1823–1829

Lord Ashley's diary entry for his twenty-fifth birthday, in 1826,
illustrates the complex mind of the young aristocrat. He laments
his three years since leaving Oxford as wasted.

*What might have been performed in three years? but not a study
commenced, not an object pursued; not a good deed done, not a
good thought generated.* [1]

European tour and love

For most of the preceding three years Ashley had undertaken the
classic European tour, the finishing school for young aristocrats.
The upper classes viewed Europe not with suspicion but as a
place of culture, learning, art, and sophistication. As late as the
Regency period (1811–20) it was unthinkable for a young man of
Ashley's family background and standing not to have immersed
himself for a period in the social, cultural and intellectual milieu
of the European mind. This was easier after the conclusion of the

Napoleonic Wars in 1815. Such a tour would not, however, have been the natural undertaking of an Evangelical Protestant. Precise religious commitments were rare among the "tourist" gentry. As a graduate in classics, however, the tour would have been a natural next step for Ashley as he began his exploration of his life's calling. The weather was an added attraction. A. N. Wilson describes the continuing love affair of the Victorians with Italy, associating the sunniness of the climate with optimism.[2]

The main focus of his attention had been in Vienna. His diary description continues:

> An attachment during my residence in Vienna commenced a course of self-knowledge for me. Man has never loved more furiously or more imprudently. The object was, and is, an angel, but she was surrounded by, and would have brought with her, a halo of hell.[3]

The object of Ashley's desires was Antoinette von Leykam, whose father was a minor aristocrat. She clearly captured Ashley's heart. His mind wandered in the direction of marriage, but with her mother being an Italian singer she hardly matched the expectations either of Ashley himself or of his parents. There was an even bigger, probably insurmountable obstacle. She was, unsurprisingly, a Roman Catholic.

The European story begins on 23 August 1823 when Ashley left for France and then Switzerland. He spent three weeks there in the company of John Denison, who later became the Speaker of the House of Commons. He then travelled to Italy. Now joined by George William Frederick Howard, he spent some time in Naples before a sojourn of several months in Rome. Howard was a contemporary of Ashley at Oxford. He was the eldest son of Viscount Morpeth, heir to the fifth Earl of Carlisle, whose family home was at Castle Howard in Yorkshire. Ashley often visited him at the family seat and held Howard's mother, Georgiana, in much affection and high regard. He corresponded with Lady Morpeth (he had begun writing to her during his time in Oxford), sharing with her his impressions of Rome. He was aware of Rome's reputation for gossip and scandal but noted also the positive impact of the city on his own attitudes of heart. Ashley's father, the sixth Earl, funded the trip. Given the already difficult relationship, Ashley was no doubt relieved that his father seems to have been kindly disposed at this point: thus he was free in both his geographical movements and, more importantly, his expenditure. Throughout his life Shaftesbury was a poor manager of money. A period in Europe freely funded by his parents was unlikely to encourage good habits in this regard. From Rome he went to Vienna, in August 1824, where, once again, he spent several months. Ashley did not really like the Viennese, at least the men; the women were a different story. Although he continued to pour out his affections to his recently commenced diaries even after his return to England in the summer of 1825, the blossoming and fading of love was complete by the time of his twenty-fifth birthday. He confided that he "thought the Deity harsh in the obstacle to our union", but confessed his own doubts and also his trust in God's wisdom and providence.[4]

Calling to political service

A political career was the normal route which a man of Ashley's station would enter upon. He first seems to have discussed the possibility of contesting the parliamentary seat of Woodstock in September 1825.[5] He wrote in his diary in October that "I have a great mind to found a policy upon the Bible", indeed, one based upon justice and active benevolence.[6] His birthday entry on 28 April 1826 refers to his trust that God, "if He wanted me, or knew that I could be useful, would doubtless call me forward".[7] To distinguish between the influence of faith, even Evangelical faith, and aristocratic standing, trust in God and nation, not to mention position in society, is a complex matter in this period. Ashley unquestionably was moving towards a position of seeing his calling, his role in life, to be one of public, even parliamentary service. That was a normal aristocratic position; to the role of faith we will return. He wrote, "Politics seem my career but they demand talents and wisdom far beyond my feeble reach: at present I am preparing for the senate, preparing in the hopeless, unsettled way that cannot be called a plan."[8] In these years before the Reform Act of 1832 parliamentary elections bore little resemblance to those today. Electors were few, often determined by ancient rights of land and property. There was considerable expectation of entertainment of the electorate with food and drink. This made elections an expensive matter. Woodstock had around 160 electors in 1826, growing modestly to 170 by 1830. The greatest influence was exercised by the dominant local aristocratic landowning family, the Dukes of Marlborough at Blenheim Palace. Woodstock was, in effect, the Duke's pocket borough. This did not, however, necessarily mean total control – the influence of non-residential voters and the ebbs and flows of relationships with the Duke provided for lively contests. Ashley's mother, Anne, was the Duke of Marlborough's sister. He was nominated in 1826 alongside his cousin, Lord Blandford, his close familial connection to the Duke being a prominent part of Ashley's platform. There were two seats and a four-cornered contest. The Duke was anxious to restore his family influence which had dissipated under the previous members. The race was expected to be close. J. H. Langton, one of the sitting members, was a wealthy Whig of independent mind. The Tory interest, in which Ashley stood, needed to be restored. Ashley and his cousin were duly returned. The reasons for the victory may well have included the Marlborough influence in the borough, but it also owed a good deal to Ashley's message of "no Popery", that is, his opposition to Catholic emancipation. He noted in his diary on 16 November, "Took the oaths of Parliament with great goodwill; a slight prayer for assistance in my thoughts and deeds."[9]

The Tory prime minister, Lord Liverpool, suffered a stroke just a few months into the new Parliament and the Tory party was plunged into crisis. George Canning succeeded Liverpool in office. Ashley held him in high regard except that Canning supported the relaxation of the political disabilities suffered by Roman Catholics. Ashley's praise perhaps fell into hyperbole, but it was to serve him in good stead. At the end of 1826 Ashley recorded a diary entry that came close to comparing a speech by Canning (in response to Spanish aggression against Portugal) to biblical rhetoric. Ashley went on, "I have never heard nor read such rousing eloquence, such sentiments, such language, such a moment; they almost maddened me with delight and enthusiasm – could not sleep for agitation – feverishly and indistinctly recollecting what I had heard."[10] By the end of January 1827 Ashley, on reflection, regarded Canning's speech as somewhat imprudent. Following Lord Liverpool's enforced retirement in February 1827, Canning sought to form an administration.

In April 1827 Ashley was offered a minor office in Canning's government. Ashley was tempted, not least by the prospect of a salary, but declined. Although he was moderating his own opinions on Catholic emancipation he was conscious of both his promises to his constituents and the implacable opposition of his father to any such move. He was exercised by concessions to Whigs and Radicals, though he acknowledged the Catholic question to be secondary. Several of Lord Liverpool's Cabinet had resigned upon Canning's assumption of office and he had been forced to include some Whigs in his administration as well as to seek parliamentary cooperation from others. Ashley's greatest concern was the absence from Canning's Cabinet of both Robert Peel and the Duke of Wellington – "I care for Peel and Wellington, were they again in the Cabinet I should be satisfied."[11] Ashley was frequently in Wellington's company both at his country estate, Stratfield Saye, in Hampshire and at his London home, Apsley House. He was angry about their treatment and equally concerned that Canning would not seek divine help in running the country. He noted his reasoning for refusing office:

> *I declined in a letter as civil and grateful as I could compose. My own mind reasoned thus: 1st. Catholic question has nothing to do with it... Political opinions neither, for I agree with Canning in nine-tenths of his system. I distrust him somewhat. I think him dangerous at the head of Government, injudicious, hasty, loving show more than substance, aspiring, anxious to keep his situation... fiery and domineering, with flippancy in foreign matters... 2nd. With all these dangers, Peel and the D. of W. have retired from the Cabinet – men who might have checked his extravagance... 3rd. Canning is a friend, and so is the D. of W., there has been a personal dispute between them, and if I went into place, I should apparently espouse the part of Canning, and I am entirely in favour of the Duke. 4th. I have here and there made known my sentiments, and it would be inconsistent to declaim against him and receive his largesses... With me the D. is the chief consideration.*[12]

Ashley showed considerable character and principle here at an early stage of his political career. He was never seduced by the attractions and trappings of office. He lamented his loss (a junior office would be training for a more senior post) and fell almost into introspection in his diary entries, reflecting that depressive trait in his character. Perhaps more than ever, though, Ashley was clearer about his life's calling. After his bout of depression he opined, "Entertained yesterday strong opinion that I ought not to give up public business, or rather the endeavour to qualify myself for it. The State may want me, wretched ass as I am!"[13] A few days later he wrote, "I desire to be useful in my generation, and die in the knowledge of having advanced happiness by having advanced true religion." [14] He had earlier declared, "I want nothing but usefulness to God and my country."[15] His mood oscillated between his self-deprecation at his lack of fitness for service and his increasing sense of call. He remained perplexed that he had not yet been called into a great task.

By the summer of that tumultuous political year of 1827 Canning was seriously ill. He died on 8 August. The coalition administration limped on under Goderich until Wellington became the fourth Tory prime minister to form a government within the space of twelve months in January 1828. Ashley's mind raced with both the possibilities and the perils. On 25 January Ashley was offered a post in the government – "now that office can no longer be avoided, I pray the Heavenly Father to give me the will to discharge my duty and the strength to perform it"[16] – subsequently confirmed as Commissioner of the India Board of Control. In order to assume the post Ashley needed to submit himself afresh to the electors of Woodstock. He was duly returned on 8 February unopposed. Ashley was to be the principal speaker for the Board in the House of Commons and the post carried a salary of £1,500 per annum, a welcome guarantee of an income. India remained a passion and an interest for Ashley throughout his life.

Ashley was diligent in his early work in Parliament and public office. His concern for India was a genuine one, stimulated by both his patriotism and his faith. His maiden speech in 1828 was inaudible. It was on the subject of the treatment of the mentally ill, his first cause on behalf of the weak and oppressed. The combination of self-doubt and divine calling continued to mark his character. His introspection and self-analysis drew upon his emotional instability intertwined with the impact of his Christian faith. He noted that his character was "curious and uncertain", and that his emotional state fluctuated between joy and despondency.[17] Ashley himself retained continued doubts about his own capabilities for the discharge of public office. However, he was admired, if not universally, on both sides of the House. He continued to devote himself to his intellectual interests. He learned Welsh, at least for a period, receiving the honour of appointment as Druid and Bard, and also, somewhat less successfully, Hebrew. He also studied science, becoming acquainted with the astronomer Sir James South, and formed a lifelong friendship with the poet Robert Southey.

Catholic emancipation

Lord Ashley's first few years in Parliament were at a time of considerable economic, political, national and religious ferment. The "no Popery" election of 1826 had contained mixed fortunes for anti-Catholic candidates. The Ultra-Tory national Protestants (see Chapter 3) were more noisy than effective. By the time Wellington had succeeded to the premiership in 1828 it could be noted that his cabinet differed "on almost every question of importance".[18] Two religious tests emerged in quick succession.

The Restoration of Charles II to the throne of England in 1660 had led to the re-establishment of the episcopate of the Church of England, which had been abolished under Cromwell. Among the legislative acts brought in to regulate the church was the Corporation Act of 1661 which, among other things, required holders of municipal office to receive holy communion in the established church. The Test Act of 1673 imposed the same burden on the holders of all Crown offices, civil and military, together with a declaration against transubstantiation (that is, the Roman Catholic understanding of holy communion). These Acts also stipulated that only those who subscribed to the Church of England's Thirty-Nine Articles should be able to graduate from Cambridge, or even to matriculate at Oxford. These two pieces of legislation protected the position of the established church in England against two dissident groupings, Protestant nonconformity and Roman Catholicism. The complexity of the position of nonconformists was that although they desired freedom from such civic disabilities they had no such desire for Catholics to share it. Equally, the main hope for repeal of these Acts lay with the Whigs who generally favoured Catholic emancipation but had little time for Protestant nonconformists' concerns. The national Protestants in Parliament disliked nonconformists but were far more concerned about the threat of Catholicism. Hence, when repeal came, the Whigs tended to support the move because it would make Catholic relief more likely and the Ultra-Tories were generally opposed because they feared the same. Lord John Russell's motion to repeal those parts of the Test and Corporation Acts which required holders of public office to receive communion according to the rites of the Church of England was carried on 26 February 1828 by 44 votes. Ashley was in the minority. The oaths and declarations which excluded Catholics remained.

Rather unexpectedly the leader of the Catholic Association (which campaigned for Catholic rights), Daniel O'Connell, was elected as the member of Parliament for County Clare in a 1828 by-election, even though he would be unable to take up his seat. In May of that year Sir Francis Burdett's motion for the relief of Catholic disabilities had passed the Commons by six votes but was then rejected by the Lords. Wellington's administration was now clear that emancipation was inevitable. After much delay and manoeuvring the Home Secretary, Robert Peel, introduced the relief motion into the Commons on 5 March 1829. The resulting Bill passed the Commons on 30 March by 320 votes to 142. The measure subsequently passed the Lords and received the Royal Assent in April 1829.

Ashley, of course, had been elected at least in part on an "anti-Popery" ticket. At first he opposed Catholic emancipation, but then, as a minor member of the administration, and as Peel and Wellington took up the cause, he saw "that resistance was impossible".[19] This falls short of a change of conviction. Among the last-ditch opponents in the Commons were two members of Parliament who were to become close supporters of Shaftesbury's campaigns, both Ultra-Tory, Evangelical national Protestants: Michael Thomas Saddler, the member for Newark, and Sir Robert Inglis, who represented the University of Oxford. Ashley demonstrated here the same combination of conviction and pragmatism that guided his path throughout his life. His position was somewhat different from that of William Wilberforce. The campaigner against slavery was at this time coming to the end of his parliamentary career and indeed his life. Wilberforce supported Catholic emancipation. He represented a rather different form of Evangelical Protestantism. Although they agreed on issues of doctrine and belief, Shaftesbury – sharpened by his convictions concerning the Protestant nation and by a more partisan application of the faith – stood both within and apart from the Wilberforce tradition. Yet Shaftesbury came to apply his faith in yet more radical ways.

Faith, calling, God, providence, station in life, birth – these were all factors that became closely intertwined in Ashley's life in the early period of his public life. The interrelationship is sometimes complex and not easy to unpack. Ashley was destined to become a significant figure and leader within the Evangelical movement. To the stirring of that faith in his early years we must now turn. Ashley, writing in his diary in October 1828, summarized his call to public life:

Every one chooses his career and it is well if he chooses that which is best suited to his talents. I have taken political life because I have, by God's blessing, many advantages of birth and situation which, although of trifling value if unsupported, are yet very powerful aids if joined to zeal and honesty. It is here, therefore, that I have the chief way of being useful to my generation.[20]

CHAPTER 3

THE STIRRINGS OF FAITH: CONVERSION TO EVANGELICALISM IN THE 1820s

We need a brief pause in the chronology of Ashley's early life to ask some questions about his emerging beliefs. What was the faith stirring in the heart, in the mind, and in the diaries of Lord Ashley in the 1820s? Ashley became an Evangelical but it is axiomatic of Evangelical faith that a person is not born Evangelical. So at some point Ashley decided to adopt this particular expression of Christianity.

Evangelicalism and its development

Evangelicalism is the name given to the movement of popular Protestantism that swept across the English-speaking world, notably England and North America, in the eighteenth century. The phenomenon became known through a series of what were subsequently referred to as Revivals (in England) and Awakenings (in North America). In England the Evangelical Revival is usually dated to 1738, the year of the conversion of John Wesley, though, of course, such dating is the preoccupation of later historians rather than contemporary participants. The movement had considerable influence both within and beyond the Church of England. Methodism was a product of the Revival, first within the established church, and later as a separate denomination. Some of the personalities of the movement are household names: John and Charles Wesley, John Newton, George Whitefield, William Wilberforce. The Evangelical Revival gave stimulation to a significant rise in the spiritual temperature. This was characterized by a renewal and resurgence of hymnody, preaching, the story of conversion, prayer and a move to what was termed "vital" religion or "real" Christianity. The movement also generated opposition. Early critics referred to those that held to its tenets as "enthusiasts" or "saints". Neither epithet was intended as a compliment.

There was a somewhat strange link between the radical embrace of Evangelicalism and a highly conservative view of society and its ordering. William Wilberforce, a hero of the movement, writing in 1797 in the wake of the revolution in France maintained that the Supreme Being had arranged "the constitution of things, as to render the prevalence of true Religion and of pure morality conducive to the well-being of states, and the preservation of civil order".[1] This concern for order spilt over into the acceptance among many Evangelicals of the principles of order enshrined within the established Church of England, despite the tensions and sometimes explicit difficulties created for them. Ashley stood firmly in this tradition.

As the Evangelical tradition grew out from the Evangelical Revival itself and as the eighteenth century came to a close, more attention came to be paid to the content of Evangelical belief. As well as expressing the common spiritual heritage of Evangelicals this was also the opportunity to mark out Evangelical faith from other forms of Christianity.

In 1797 William Wilberforce published his book, known as *A Practical View*. The full title reveals much of the cultural conditioning of the age as well as the timeless content of belief. The title itself contained twenty-four words – an unlikely proposition for any publisher in the modern age, but not entirely unusual at the time. The full description was *A Practical View of the Prevailing Religious System of Professed Christians in the Higher and Middle Classes in This Country Contrasted with Real Christianity*. Wilberforce himself had gone through significant spiritual upheaval in the decade prior to publication from which he had emerged into Evangelical Christianity with the help of the former slave-trader, John Newton. In 1792 the wealthy banker Henry Thornton, who would later become the first treasurer of the Bible Society, suggested to Wilberforce that they should share a residence in Clapham, Battersea Rise House. Clapham at this time was a distinct village on the edge of London. Other prominent lay leaders of Evangelicalism also began to move onto the estate. This group formed the nucleus of what has become known as the Clapham Sect, consisting of Evangelical merchants and politicians prominent in, for example, the campaign against the slave trade.

Wilberforce's book was a combination of powerful assertions of zeal and faith and with a defence of society and its ordering. He protested eloquently against the compartmentalization of religion. To him the Christian faith had to be an all-consuming passion, dictating the whole of life and not restricted either simply to good works or to Sunday duty.

How dexterously do they avail themselves of any plausible plea for introducing some week-day employment into the Sunday, whilst they have not the same propensity to introduce any of the Sunday's peculiar employment into the rest of the week.[2]

Wilberforce drew a distinction between those who professed the Christian faith and real Christianity. Nominal Christians neglected the central doctrines of the faith which Wilberforce spelt out as the corruption of human nature, the atonement of the saviour, and the sanctifying work of the Holy Spirit. The appeal of the Evangelical was to "vital" religion, as he called it, to the precise formularies of doctrine rather than vague generalities, to a faith that influenced the everyday life of the believer and was not just a matter of social duty. Wilberforce's book sold in excess of 75,000 copies over fifteen editions up to 1837. Critics were, of course, scathing. Evangelicals were charged with being overly concerned with the personal morals of others, not least the poor.

There are other contemporary sources for understanding the nature of this faith which was proving increasingly influential in the upper echelons of society. Among these are the meetings of a group of Evangelical clergy and laity in London from 1783 onwards, known as the Eclectic Society. Another source is the writings and sermons of the Reverend Charles Simeon, Vicar of Holy Trinity, Cambridge, from 1782. The key themes were, however, beginning to emerge. These included the authority of the Bible, the Reformation doctrine of justification (redemption) by faith alone, humanity's own depravity and the atonement of Christ for it, the nature of God, the call to ministry, preaching, Christian life, and mission. These were all common elements of the Evangelical faith. So too was the conversion narrative. Evangelicals placed great weight upon the notion of conversion, a supernatural act of God in the heart and mind of the believer, which transformed the life and outlook of the individual. People were expected to be able to recount their own stories and Evangelicals looked for the conversion of others at home and overseas.

However, Evangelical belief was not static. In the 1820s it underwent a number of changes of emphasis that have direct bearing upon the faith to which Lord Ashley was converted and which he embraced with such zeal. Two of these developments are of particular relevance. The first was that an increasing emphasis came to be placed upon the supernatural intervention of God. This led to a particular understanding of one aspect of Evangelical belief concerning the end of time. This point of view had profound impact upon Ashley and his work of evangelism and social reform. In the 1820s Evangelicals pressed for greater reliance to be placed upon prayer, God himself and his supernatural intervention and less upon human means, optimism, and confidence. There was greater anticipation and expectation of Christ's return (the second coming or second advent). To the detailed application of this outlook to Evangelical social reform we will return in a later chapter.

The second area of development within Evangelical theology was a hardening of the Protestant Reformed heritage of the movement. The two were linked. If the Lord were to return soon he would expect to find purity in his church. Indeed, the Bible Society split over this quest for purity. Evangelicals looked for patterns in present-day events, institutions, and even individuals that matched the symbolism set out in biblical books such as Revelation. The more colourful characterizations in the Bible's closing book, the Whore of Babylon and the Beast, came to be associated openly and explicitly, as during the Reformation, with the Papacy. Within the Church of England these emphases were brought into even greater relief with the rise from around 1833 onwards of the Oxford Movement. This group sought to downplay the Reformation and some of the Evangelical emphasis on biblical authority and the sacrifice of Jesus atoning for humanity's sin. In later decades this conflict was played out over matters of ritual as well as belief and the then Earl of Shaftesbury was a prominent player.

One further element of the diverse and complex mosaic of Evangelicalism in the 1820s was the emergence of what has been characterized as Ultra-Toryism or Protestant Constitutionalism or perhaps national Protestantism. The essence of this outlook was that it combined elements of Evangelical faith and a high Tory view of society and its ordering and linked the two. The heart of this tradition was that it "encompassed a sense of Protestantism as the fundamental substance of the British constitution".[3] The 1820s and early 1830s were a time of great political ferment and constitutional challenge which included Catholic emancipation, the repeal of the Test Acts and the Reform Act. This legislation was designed to change the face of the British constitution, not least in respect of citizens who were not members of the established church as well as of the electoral base of government. Any attempt to remove the requirement to subscribe to the Thirty-Nine Articles of the Church of England for members of Oxford and graduates of Cambridge (implicitly closing these universities both to Catholics and to nonconformists – or "Dissenters" as they were commonly known) or to extend the vote beyond the traditional landowning categories was viewed by some with horror. Such moves would imperil the Protestant nature of the constitution and could put the established church itself at risk. There were significant supporters of this point of view in both Houses of Parliament. Some found their expression in the founding of the Protestant Reformation Society by Captain James Gordon in 1827. Others, including a large number of Protestant Evangelical members of Parliament, gathered around *The Record*, a hardline newspaper founded in 1828 to provide an alternative to the more moderate *Christian Observer* established by the Eclectics and Clapham Evangelicals in 1802.

The conversion of Lord Ashley

The question of exactly when the Earl of Shaftesbury became an Evangelical is important for understanding his theological, political, and social views. The two most well-known modern biographies of Shaftesbury, one by Georgina Battiscombe published in 1974 and the more comprehensive work by Geoffrey Finlayson in 1981, opt for 1835 and 1834 respectively. There are good reasons to question these conclusions. Both point to the influence of the Reverend Edward Bickersteth, who had been Secretary of the Church Missionary Society from 1824–30. Bickersteth was a convinced premillennialist (see chapter 4). The mistake which the biographers have tended to make is to associate Ashley's clear embracing of premillennialism through the influence of Bickersteth with his conversion to Evangelicalism as such. In other words the adoption of a particular version of the Evangelical faith has become confused with the acceptance of the faith itself. There are references in Ashley's diaries in this period 1834–35 to gaining a deeper sense of religion and to distinctively Evangelical doctrines such as the corruption of the human heart, justification, and atonement. If Ashley had undergone any sort of explicit conversion process at this point he would undoubtedly have mentioned it as such in his diary. The references to theological concepts are in fact quite unlikely in the immediate aftermath of conversion. They are more likely to reflect the fact that he was seeking, in his own words, "to attain deeper acquaintance with critical theology".[4] This was all the prelude, not to his conversion, but to his adoption of premillennial views. We will return to the meeting with Bickersteth subsequently.

At what point then did Ashley become an Evangelical? It is more likely that the pivotal date in Ashley's process of conversion, a course which started before that date and continued afterwards, was the spring of 1826. The events leading up to that time had a profound influence on Ashley and distinctly affected the type of Evangelical faith he was to adopt and his theology of social action.

The religious and social education of a young English aristocrat would have included a healthy disregard for both Catholicism and Dissent (thus for Christians who did not adhere to the Church of England and its link to the state). The scepticism about the former was on the grounds that it was not English and the latter on the basis that it was inimical to the principle of establishment. Edwin Hodder records the Earl recalling these years. He remarked that reading Philip Doddridge (a noted nonconformist writer of the previous century) "was one of the first things that opened my eyes".

In the same extract from Hodder's conversation with Shaftesbury, the Earl also commented:

> *It was not till I was twenty-five years old, or thereabouts, that I got hold of "Scott's Commentary on the Bible", and, struck with the enormous difference between his views and those to which I had been accustomed, I began to think for myself.*[5]

Opening the eyes, reading the works of the noted Evangelical biblical commentator Thomas Scott in 1826, noting the difference in outlook, and beginning to think for himself: these are much more likely indicators of a course leading to conversion to Evangelicalism. This is reinforced by his diary entry for his twenty-fifth birthday where he noted that he had taken up hard study, repeated in his journal at the end of the year. Similarly, as noted in the previous chapter, prayer and faith surrounded his setting out on a political career in this period. He also told his diary in April 1827 that no one should be prime minister unless deeply imbued with religion, to do good in secret, to advance the interests of the kingdom of God, and to consult Scripture and be shaped by Christian wisdom. This degree of emphasis went beyond what might normally be expected. In early 1827 Ashley noted that the first chapter of Romans demonstrated the "insufficiency of a 'natural religion' ".[6] Ashley seems to have embraced at this point the essentials of the revealed biblical faith of the Evangelical. Despite witnessing to Ashley's depressive tendencies, his diaries reveal a distinct change in the period 1825–27. In 1826 he wrote admiringly of Islamic devotion noting, "I do not intend to fall short of their piety." He then referred to the correction of errors "which began to sprout in younger days and which had they not been pursued by an unsparing Hand might have taken deep root".[7] The next year he noted that "time was when I could not sleep for ambition. Thought of nothing but fame and immortality… But now I am much changed."[8] This change amounted to conversion.

At the exact time that Ashley was studying hard, leading up to his "change of view", in the winter of 1825–26 the financial markets crashed. The crisis arose from over-speculation and excess economic stimulation during booms in foreign trade and in foreign investment. Confidence collapsed in a cycle of inflationary and deflationary fears and from October 1825 bankruptcies soared. The calamity may have contributed to altering Ashley's view of God. The traditional view was of a God of order and regularity operating only through his natural laws. Ashley, along with others in this period, moved to a position of an interventionist God acting, when he chose to do so, by way of supernatural intervention in human affairs. These developments were occurring long before Ashley's formal adoption of premillennialism but were clearly preparing the way for his acceptance of that position. In his diary entry of 12 November 1827 Ashley explicitly embraced the notion of a God who can indeed perform miracle and transcend his natural laws. Later in the year Ashley, looking back, saw "the Finger of God" at work in the death of Canning – which ultimately led the Duke of Wellington into office. The business cycle of boom and depression fitted in very well with ideas of an interventionist God. It also matched the alternation in Ashley's personality of periods of optimism and pessimism, joy and gloom.

In addition to all of this there is considerable evidence in the period 1826–34 of distinctively Evangelical emphases in Ashley's thought, including two occasions on which he was referred to by others as a "saint". Even before these references Ashley was poring over Evangelical sermons and, perhaps in line with his changing understanding of God, was reading the book of Revelation and making anti-Catholic comments. He also declared his trust in divine providence (the active direction of events and of the Christian's life by God) seeming to go beyond the usual statements.

The two references to Ashley as a "saint" came in April 1829 and then four months later – the second from his future mother-in-law, Lady Cowper. On both occasions he rejected the appellation. On the first he had two days previously noted that he was (still) reading the book of Revelation. The second time he acknowledged his high sense of religion while repudiating any suggestion of fanaticism. The designation "saint" had come to be applied to the Clapham Sect in particular and then Evangelicals more generally as a slightly derogatory contemporary nickname rather than as a label used by its intended recipients themselves. Hence, Ashley's modest disavowal of the title would seem quite natural. The fact that others applied the title to Ashley twice in 1829 certainly suggests that he was already displaying sufficient Evangelical characteristics for others to call him one.

The adoption of premillennialist views more formally in 1834–35 certainly continued the process of hardening Ashley's Protestant Evangelical outlook. From this point he began to play a more prominent role in Evangelical societies. Ashley's card was increasingly marked as a "party" Evangelical, with his heightened view of the literal inspiration of Scripture, a concern for supernatural divine intervention, the second advent, and last judgment. This intensified his Protestant position and led him into an involvement in numerous Evangelical societies, both missionary-orientated and directed toward social welfare. His conversion, however, occurred much earlier.

CHAPTER 4

LIFE, POLITICS AND MISSION: 1829–1836

This period saw Shaftesbury setting out on the road of marriage and family life, establishing his parliamentary career and beginning his involvement in Evangelical societies. These were formative years.

Marriage

Ashley, having been once bitten by love, prayed for a companion in life. Once the ideal woman was found, he declared with typical overstatement, "I should love her with a tenderness and truth unprecedented in the history of wedlock."[1] Ashley was linked to numerous women by society gossip and he was attractive personally, for his background, and for his intellect, notwithstanding his mood swings. He prayed for a wife, indeed rather urgently,[2] noting in his diary that he was not suited to the life of a bachelor and that marriage was ordained of God. He added, "I have looked around, I have found many amiable girls, two or three *especially* so, but none entirely satisfactory as companions."[3] He had long lamented his lost love in Vienna, Liebe, as he had affectionately known Antoinette, who died in childbirth in 1828.

Family connections were particularly important in nineteenth-century political life and proved so for Ashley. His marriage brought him into a relationship, by a rather circuitous route, with the future prime minister, Viscount Palmerston. This was to prove of significance in his later life and career. The woman who became Ashley's wife was Lady Emily Cowper, known as Minny since her mother was also Emily. Ashley was soon imploring divine providence to deliver. After some initial contacts earlier in 1829 by August Ashley was declaring to his diary his love for Minny. On 2 August he confessed that his mind had wandered toward marriage as he listened to the Sunday sermon. He declared it "high time I should marry" and that marriage was a "state appointed by God".[4] The next day he reported that he felt "more charmed than ever", adding, "what a Paradise of Ecstasy it could be to share with that lovely girl all the sublimities of Religion!"[5] On 11 August he declared her to be "infinitely delightful", and described her as the "choicest gift" and "a treasure to possess".[6] On 13 August he proposed, only to be rejected on 17 August but with the hope of a final answer in September. Minny found Ashley handsome, enjoyed his conversation, and was attracted to his goodness, but nervous of his intensity. Equally she was not short of suitors. Ashley continued to woo her. Minny's family were not backward in coming forward with their reservations, at least some of which had to do with his financial prospects. In October 1829, after some prevarication, he was rejected again but continued his pursuit of Minny with both tenacity and the aplomb which befitted his standing. By April 1830 the engagement was public and the marriage took place, at St George's, Hanover Square, on 10 June. The marriage was close and successful, as Edwin Hodder describes:

For forty years she shared her husband's struggles, inspired his greater efforts, and was, as he himself has described her, "a wife as good, as true, and as deeply beloved, as God ever gave to man."[7]

Ashley's father, the sixth Earl, refused to attend the ceremony, disapproving of the match and of the Cowper family, and no doubt anxious about the financial implications. After the hesitant courtship Ashley and Minny were devoted to each other, in strong contrast to the dysfunctional nature of both their families. Minny's mother and grandmother both lived with constant suspicion of marital infidelity. Emily, Lady Cowper, was the long-term mistress of Lord Palmerston and, after Lord Cowper died, she married Palmerston in 1839. Hence the future prime minister became step-father-in-law to Ashley, the future Earl of Shaftesbury. Palmerston was very close to Minny; he may in fact have been her father.

There was a series of elections in the period 1830–31. In the customary election following the death of the monarch after George IV died in 1830, Ashley was returned for Dorchester rather than Woodstock. Earl Grey headed a Whig administration and thus Ashley lost his post at the India Board of Control. The initial failure of the Reform Bill led to a further election in 1831. Ashley won the seat again, but this time the Whigs were returned with a significant majority which paved the way for the 1832 Reform Bill. The Tories were then seeking a candidate for a by-election in a county seat for Dorset after the suicide of one of the sitting members. The Whigs were promoting a fierce campaign on the subject of parliamentary reform. Ashley was, eventually, persuaded to contest the election on an anti-reform ticket. County seats carried a certain amount of prestige but elections were more expensive to fight and the larger electorates more independently minded. Ashley was victorious by thirty-six votes. The sum of over £15,000 expended on the election was an enormous amount of money. Ashley was entirely incapable of providing the funding. There was confusion over whether the party had or had not agreed to shoulder the burden. He told the Duke of Wellington that "I have before me, in consequence, the prospect of debts and incumbrances which no economy or exertions on my part will enable me to discharge."[8] Matters had been made worse by Ashley's opponent challenging the election result. Ashley made clear that, following the confusion over whether the election expenses were a party or a personal liability, he could not himself afford to defend the petition against the result. Recognizing the importance of the contest the Tory party itself successfully defended the attempt to overturn Ashley's election.

Family and friends

Ashley's circle was expanding both politically and socially, thanks to his marriage to Minny as well as to his own increasing influence and reputation. The early months of the marriage were intertwined with the elections and electoral disputes of 1830–31. The Cowper family into which Ashley had married were Whigs, which did not make for an easy relationship with Ashley's own family. Nevertheless, following the boycott of the wedding by Ashley's father there were serious attempts at reconciliation by both parties. An invitation from the sixth Earl to the Cowpers seems to have led to a warmer relationship, almost intimate on occasions, with both kisses and notes exchanged. Ashley's mother-in-law, although a Whig – but opposed to political reform – had gone into battle over her new son-in-law's predicament following the Dorset election. There was genuine affection between them. The marriage to Minny was also one of real love and intimacy. Minny lamented their times apart. In 1830 when they were parted for just two days she had begged him to return. She wrote that there "certainly never was such a darling as you are dearest Ashley and I really think I love you more and more every day".[9] She worried about him during the 1831–32 cholera outbreak and continued to express her love for him in her letters. The feelings were reciprocated. In short, he adored her. There is an extensive, warm and loving correspondence between them. The letters abound with affection. They often begin with "my dearest love", "my darling husband", and "my dearest pet". The relationship was certainly also spiritual, Ashley noting in his diary in 1834 that he read the Bible aloud to Minny.

The first child, Antony, was born in June 1831. He was known affectionately as "Sir Babkins". The correspondence shows that his parents were devoted to him. He was "the admiration of the town", according to Minny, and Ashley asked his wife to "give a thousand kisses from me to Sir Babkins – and tell him not to forget me".[10]

During the period 1831–34 Ashley was establishing his parliamentary career. Assuming the chair of the Metropolitan Commission in Lunacy in 1834 (see Chapter 5), he had continued his lifelong calling to the care of the mentally ill with a programme of visits and inspections to asylums. Then in 1832 he had become a member of the Select Committee on the Observance of the Sabbath Day. Although in this period Ashley kept no chronological diary (just a travel journal in 1833) he was far from idle. In 1832 the select committee met on no fewer than seventeen occasions and although we cannot be sure that Ashley attended every session, on the basis of his subsequent commitments to such tasks it does seem likely. The role of this select committee has not been fully recognized in explaining the background to Ashley's adoption of his parliamentary campaigns, especially that concerning the conditions and employment of children in factories. The point is that he was brought into contact with the key players. It was unsurprising that Ashley would be appointed to the select committee. He was a Tory, sympathetic to national Protestantism and now, contrary to the views of some earlier biographers, a practising Evangelical. The chairman of the committee was the Scottish MP Sir Andrew Agnew. He was equally a Tory, an ardent Protestant, and an Evangelical. Both men were sabbatarians – that is, committed to the provision in law of protection for the Christian character of Sunday. There was a similar group of such individuals on Agnew's committee. They included the founder of the Protestant Reformation Society, J. E. Gordon, Sir Robert Inglis, and, significantly, Michael Sadler.

As we will see in chapter 6 it was Sadler's campaign for factory reform which passed to Ashley, and Agnew who effected the introduction.

Ashley voted against the Reform Bill in 1832. This was, of course, entirely consistent with his upbringing and position in society, not to mention his political and religious views. He does not seem to have taken an active part in the debates. He advocated and defended "those great principles which inspirit and regulate our glorious Constitution in Church and State". Fifty years later he had no regrets about his position! He regretted the loss of connection between voting and property and the introduction of the secret ballot for elections.[11] This was not just obscurantism. Rather this view reflected everything that Ashley stood for, including transparency in voting in public and having a stake in the land.

These views endeared Ashley to the Poet Laureate, Robert Southey, a high Tory and incurable romantic, who had a close affinity with him. They never met but regularly corresponded. Ashley held the opinions and principles of the Laureate in high regard. Ashley offered Southey a post at the India Board of Control for a son or nephew. Southey sympathized with Ashley's plight in the Dorset election. The Laureate wrote from Keswick, far from Dorset, but a significant location for the development of romanticism in nineteenth-century England, not least in its religious forms. The lakes and the mountains helped engender thoughts of Blake's *Jerusalem*. Southey supported Ashley's campaigns for the poor. He did so partly from principle, but also on the classic English basis of order – the inhabitants of this land have generally preferred order to revolution. To Southey failure to deal with the conditions of the poor threatened the established order of both church and state. In a letter to Ashley dated 1 December 1832 Southey, blaming a publishing deadline for the lateness of the reply – a matter understood by authors then as well as now – thanked Ashley for forwarding to him reports on both the sabbath and animal cruelty. This was an interesting link, appealing to romantics – the protection and welfare of all God's creatures – a theme which flows also into the industrial and factory campaigns. Ashley remained a campaigner against vivisection for the whole of his life.

A tour of Europe

In March 1833 a second son, Francis, was born. In early August Ashley attended William Wilberforce's funeral in Westminster Abbey. In October of that same year, with Minny, her parents, and Antony (but not Francis) all in tow, Ashley set off on a six-month tour of Europe. He kept a travel diary. The journey fed Ashley's romanticism, religious affections, and his Protestantism. It took eight days to cross France and reach Geneva where the party rested for six days before continuing. In Switzerland he observed the people and their lives. Unsurprisingly he was not backward with his opinions about the religious habits of the people and their consequences. In a comparison which would raise many modern hackles he remarked that Catholic Switzerland was marked out by "the slovenly and negligent habits of the people". By contract the Protestant cantons exhibited "a picture of order, cleanliness, and taste".[12] Nevertheless, while deploring what he considered Catholic misuse of the cross he also lamented the Protestant overreaction and thought the more public display of religion in the Catholic areas to be a positive influence that could lead to piety.

However, his tour led him to experience Catholic worship in both Milan and Rome. Not a happy experience for him, it would continue to inform his opposition to such forms of worship at home, whether within or outside the Church of England. At high mass in the cathedral at Milan – which he attended because there was no Protestant place of worship – he described the ceremonial as "tedious and unspiritual". He bemoaned the "everlasting movement and gesture, with numberless repetitions of robing, candles, incense, and drawling chants". The prayers were "cold and short" and the entire service had the character of a performance.[13] On Christmas

Day 1833 Ashley attended the Vatican in the morning and found the ceremonies lacking in worship, love, humility, and gratitude. In the evening, at another church, he described the occasion as being like an opera, but added:

> *In such rites as these the soul has no share; the Papists have*
> *re-imposed upon themselves the Jewish burdens, and renew*
> *the painful and imperfect worship of the Temple at Jerusalem.*
> *Walked home, read the Bible and all the prayers for the day…*[14]

His views had not changed on a visit to Austria ten years later. He described the cathedral in Vienna – "bells ringing, priest dancing, incense rising, fiddles playing, nothing calm or stationary but the worshippers, who remain there like fellows looking at a balloon. Half the world seems to think that to have seen the priest is an act of acceptable adoration."[15] Nevertheless, he remained moved by the unashamed public devotion, the willingness to leave churches open for casual worshippers, and the availability of houses of prayer.[16]

He was covering much of the same ground as in his European tour in his early twenties. He noted in his travel journal that the years had added to his maturity and not in any way detracted from his happiness. He thanked the providence of God for his desire for a wife and for guidance in a suitable choice. Presumably he would have added thanks for Minny's eventual positive response but he did note that the outcome provided him with "a perpetuity of earthly happiness".[17]

Milan he thought to be dull. Antony was then left in the care of the Cowpers and others for six weeks while Ashley and Minny travelled on to Venice, which, although cloudy and cold, he enjoyed. At Padua he even bought a crucifix, though had to record in the journal that the worship of the material was "senseless, wicked, and idolatrous". However, as a memorial of the Lord's death and passion it was a helpful reminder to us to gaze upon Christ.[18] Ashley's campaigning Protestantism which was already in place through upbringing and conviction would flourish more openly from the 1840s onwards. The combination of conviction and an inability to distinguish some aspects of piety from more questionable practices did mean that Ashley's Protestantism proved to be a double-edged sword throughout his life.

From Padua it was on to Bologna where they admired the art. This was followed by San Marino, whose location he described as sublime, albeit inaccessible. He admired its historic independence. At Loreto he intervened in vain to protect a carriage horse from the ill treatment of its masters. He complained, at first without success, to the postmaster and then to the commissary of police. Ashley was not one to give up. He raised the level of the complaint to even higher officials – the culprits eventually receiving three days' imprisonment.

Further travels led to Rome. We have already described his reaction to the worship, but he enjoyed the visit, the art galleries and the entertainment. Invited to one ball he remarked that Minny looked "heavenly" and added, "Is it wrong to be so entirely proud of, and happy in, one's wife's beauty? But surely there is nothing so pretty and fascinating as my Min."[19] While in Rome Ashley dined with his cousin Edward Pusey, who had aligned himself with the emerging (high church) Oxford Movement in England. Chevalier Bunsen, the Prussian Minister in Rome, was also at the dinner. Just as Ashley and Pusey were destined to be religious opponents, so Bunsen would soon become an ally in the cause of Protestantism.

From Rome they travelled to Siena and then Florence, admiring Michelangelo's art work. Then to Pisa, Lucca, and San Remo before arriving at Nice on 8 February. Ashley and Minny rejoiced at now being reunited with their wider family, not least "our darling child, who knew us again, and showed evident joy at our return".[20] The family enjoyed the carnival, though Ashley, with characteristic seriousness, mused over whether the games were innocent or foolish.

The need to be back in England was not now far removed. Parliament had reassembled. He noted that he had avoided newspapers and conversations concerning politics but that he must now "renew my intercourse with vice and misery".[21] They left Italy on 14 March and travelled via Cannes, Provence, and then via Paris to home on 19 April. He had avoided Paris on the outward journey and described it as the "least profitable portion", after the visit on the return journey. The tour itself had been "very entertaining, and I hope instructive".[22]

Politics and life at home

In Parliament Ashley was occupied not only by the sabbath, but also, as will be more fully described in chapter 6, by factory legislation. The Oxford Movement, the high church campaign to restore and return Anglicanism to its Catholic roots, was beginning to emerge. The movement's theological and spiritual emphases clashed with Ashley's Evangelical Protestantism.

Ashley held Oxford in great affection. Perhaps that is why he interfered so much in its affairs. In June 1834 he attended the Duke of Wellington's installation as Chancellor. He expressed in his diary his warm affections for Oxford, infected, of course, by the usual romanticism – "I humbly thank Him that He has once more permitted me to stand on this sacred ground". He continued to lament any absence from Minny – "I cannot bear the shortest separation from her!"[23] The manner in which he held Oxford in his affections was not necessarily reciprocated. He noted in his diary that while in Oxford for the installation he had been hissed at the theatre. This was probably because of his advocacy of factory reform which was becoming prominent in the Commons. During the remainder of 1834 Ashley deepened his faith through reading the memoirs of an earlier prominent personality of the Evangelical Revival, Hannah More, and reflected on the destruction by fire of the Houses of Parliament.

Then in November the Whig Ministry fell to be replaced by Sir Robert Peel.

Ashley viewed the fire at the Palace of Westminster, which destroyed most of the building, as a national calamity that threatened both the constitution and the empire. Parliament was the seat of history, the centre of Englishness and, of course, of a Protestant constitution. The fire was a moral judgment upon the nation. Political events were also moving with the collapse of Melbourne's administration: Peel was returning from Rome in order to form a ministry. Ashley did not have much hope in Peel. He clashed with him several times over factory legislation and earlier in 1834 had confided to the diary, "I can see nothing worse than that Peel should be called to the helm of affairs."[24] Ashley doubted Peel on matters of faith and religion as well as social and political questions. His only redeeming factor was that he was a Tory. Naturally this was a significant factor for Ashley and he was not beyond musing over whether Peel would offer him a place in government. In fact that is exactly what Sir Robert did, although Ashley was undoubtedly somewhat deflated that the offer of a Lordship of the Admiralty was an effective demotion from his previous post at the India Board of Control. The correspondence demonstrates both Ashley's insecurity and his willingness to serve. Ashley was re-elected for the county seat of Dorset in the ensuing election held in January 1835. In February Peel's administration suffered defeat in the Commons on two occasions and again in April by a large majority. Peel resigned and was replaced by Melbourne's second government.

A third son, Maurice, was born in 1835. Later that same year Ashley was involved with the celebrations of the Tercentenary of the Reformation, events marked by "reverence and sincerity",[25] and much hope in the united witness of those who belonged to the Church of England and those who did not. The early months of 1836 saw Ashley involved with the foundation of the Church Pastoral Aid Society. By the end of the year the government was seeking to weaken the earlier factory legislation of 1833 and so Ashley, as we will see in chapter 6, swung into action.

Meeting with Edward Bickersteth

Edward Bickersteth is a key figure in Ashley's theological development and indeed in understanding how he came to adopt a particular view on the relationship of the missionary imperative and social reform. Bickersteth had first become assistant secretary of the Church Missionary Society in 1816, then secretary in 1824, a position he resigned in 1830 upon his appointment to the living of Watton in Hertfordshire. In line with the classic views expressed through the CMS, Bickersteth adopted the normal Evangelical view of the missionary enterprise. He looked for "the gradual conversion of the world, by the spread of missions".[26] Many questions about the future prospects for the Jewish people, including their conversion, as a whole or in part, and their possible restoration to the Holy Land, became dominant features of the Evangelicalism of the 1820s. The theological basis of this was known as unfulfilled prophecy. In other words the increased emphasis on more literal interpretations of the Bible had to deal with specific expectations there of future events concerning the nation of Israel. As yet these prophecies were unfulfilled. To begin with Bickersteth was unconvinced. He noted that "the immediate work of the Lord is disregarded for an uncertain future".[27] As we will see subsequently, it was this kind of emphasis that led Bickersteth and Shaftesbury to adopt a very particular view of the current Evangelical scheme. By 1832 Bickersteth was a premillennialist. This technical term relates to a distinctive view of the end times and the eagerly awaited return of Jesus Christ to earth. It was linked both to literal interpretations of the Bible and to the prospects for the Jews.

The concept of the millennium was derived from chapter 20 of the book of Revelation, where it is stated that the saints will rule over the earth for a thousand years. The general view of Evangelicals in the eighteenth century was that the millennium would come in gradually through widespread conversion. This would be followed by the return of Christ – the second advent or second coming – and the day of judgment. This outlook was known as post-millennialism (the return of Christ occurring *after* the thousand-year millennium). This viewpoint easily fitted with Enlightenment optimism about human progress. Some considered the millennium to be an exact period of one thousand years. Others viewed the millennium in more symbolic terms. In either case the day of judgment was removed far into the future. The role of the missionary societies and indeed, of the British nation, was to be instruments in the hands of God for the conversion of the world. This would gradually lead into the millennium, bliss, and happiness.

This rather optimistic, even complacent, outlook was challenged by a number of factors in the Evangelical world. First, there was the relative lack of success of the missionary enterprise. The euphoria of the early years of the nineteenth century had not been sustained. Conversion on a worldwide scale seemed so far away that doubts crept in about both the methods employed and the reasoning behind them. Second, the impact of revolution in France led many people in Britain to examine the Bible to try to understand the shattering and extraordinary events that were taking place in the world. Owing to their attachment to the Scriptures, Evangelicals were prominent in this development. Third, the increasing influence of romantic thought was shown by the desire to seek shelter and protection from industrial change. Paradise had always been offered by Evangelicals in heaven but was now desired on earth, and soon.

These concerns and influences led to the development of an alternative view of the millennium. Essentially the thousand years of blessing, peace, and felicity needed to arrive rather earlier than previously suggested. A careful reading and exegesis of Revelation showed that Christ would reign on the earth with his saints for a thousand years. Hence the second advent must occur *before* the millennium itself. Thus this scheme became known as premillennialism. The usual expression of this methodology sought to understand historical and contemporary world events within a biblical chronology leading up to the second advent – "the signs of the times". This scheme was known as historicist premillennialism. Premillennialism was characterized by pessimism. The world was worsening and degenerating into chaos. The only hope lay in the second coming. Missionary societies and missionary committees were merely human attempts at human achievement. What was needed was divine action, divine intervention, and soon.

Thus Edward Bickersteth's Evangelical credentials were impeccable. Ashley's adoption of this premillennial tradition can be traced to his meeting in 1835 with Bickersteth, with whom he subsequently spent several days. His concern for the subject, especially for the second advent, is reflected in numerous diary entries. He also had the words "Even so, come Lord Jesus", taken from the book of Revelation, stamped on the back of his envelopes, in Greek. His concern for the Jewish people, not least for their position in Palestine, was another indicator. Ashley's position was one influenced by Bickersteth's particular understanding of the events connected with the millennium, their relationship to the current dispensation, and their implications for both missionary work and social reform. The importance of placing Shaftesbury accurately within this aspect of Evangelicalism is that it helps explain his dual commitment to evangelism and social welfare. To that we will return.

Early engagement with mission societies

After his meeting with Edward Bickersteth and his adoption of the particular version of the Evangelical faith – premillennialism – Ashley began his period of active involvement with the voluntary societies of Christianity. He had already been involved as noted with the issues of sabbath observance. The place of Sunday, together with other aspects of national Protestantism, was a significant feature of his life. He saw no reason why the faith he had embraced as an adherent should not dictate the national conscience as it had historically done.

A particular structure adopted by the nineteenth-century Christian church generally, and by its Evangelical disciples more particularly, was that of the voluntary society. Missionary, or indeed other, endeavours would be best fulfilled by those of like mind combining together in order to achieve their common objectives. Ashley's early attention was taken by two such societies, although a third with which he was to become closely connected was also founded in this period. The 1830s show Ashley campaigning simultaneously in three areas – social reform (mainly factories and lunacy), Evangelical voluntary societies (evangelism and social welfare), and Protestantism.

Nineteenth-century titles, whether of sermons or societies, were often long, if not incomprehensible. The London Society for the Promotion of Christianity Amongst the Jews had its origins in the first decade of the century. It was to become an iconic society for the Evangelical movement. The society combined many of the emphases that characterized the Earl of Shaftesbury's life. Both the future destiny and the current welfare of God's chosen people was a matter of significant emphasis and concern throughout the century. Increased weight given to the literal interpretation of the Bible and the role of the millennium led to the mission to the Jewish people taking on an urgency in Evangelical thought, combined with national Protestantism's campaign for a bishopric in Jerusalem. The London Society was one of many movements for Evangelical unity in the nineteenth century. However, unity around a single missionary objective often disguised doctrinal disunity on other matters.

In 1835 Ashley was elected Vice-Patron. He became the President of the society in 1848, a post he retained for the rest of his life. He was no figurehead and took an active part in the life of the organization. He served on a committee to consider the training of missionaries, led a delegation to Palmerston concerning Jewish persecution and obtained letters of introduction, the patronage of the Archbishop of Canterbury, and even a statement of the tax-deductibility of subscriptions to the society!

The changing face of England in the period 1800–30, together with the less than startling success of the overseas missionary societies, led to Evangelicals paying greater attention to the needs of mission at home. Evangelicals were theologically committed to mission across denominations. However, there were many within the Church of England who held a significant attachment to the principle of "establishment" – the particular role of the church in state and society – and also to the position of bishops. It is therefore not surprising to see the emergence within the confines of the established church of a home mission agency. The Church Pastoral Aid Society was founded in 1836 and it is no surprise to find Lord Ashley at the very heart of this process.

The reason for the founding of the CPAS was essentially simple. The nation was spiritually destitute. The rapid growth in population meant that large numbers of people were beyond normal methods of Christian outreach. This was a key factor in the setting up of many voluntary Christian societies, both evangelistic and social. There were also many spiritual failings among the clergy and within the church. Even the competent and committed clergy were pastorally overstretched, some seeking to minister to parishes with populations of 14,000 or more. All of this contributed to increase the distance, spiritually as much as physically, between the mass of the population and the church. Set alongside all of this the usual litany of immorality, irreligion, and increasing social deprivation and so the need for a *society* linked to the established *church*, committed to *aid* the clergy *pastorally* in their ministries became clear. Thus emerged the Church Pastoral Aid Society.

On 12 March 1835 a letter from Frederick Sandoz, a clerk in the East India Company and a prominent layman in Islington, appeared in the conservative Evangelical mouthpiece *The Record*.

The appeal was for a home missionary society. He launched a nationwide campaign for the establishment of a "church pastoral aid society". He drew support from the Evangelical Bishop of Chester, John Bird Sumner, and the appeal was strongly promoted by *The Record.*

Sandoz maintained that, in the light of the repeal of the Test and Corporation Acts and of Roman Catholic emancipation, little aid for the church could be expected from the state. Sandoz showed here an early appreciation of the decline of national Protestantism. The state would increasingly neither reflect nor act upon the historic Protestant heritage of the nation so beloved of Sir Robert Inglis, Sir Andrew Agnew, the Recordite MPs and peers (the parliamentary group supporting *The Record*), including of course Lord Ashley himself. Sandoz's perceptive understanding of this decline would inevitably lead to a mission-orientated focus for the new society. It is also an interesting observation upon Shaftesbury's own passion which sought, with varying degrees of success, to hold in tension classic Protestantism, Evangelical mission, and Tory paternalism. The initial appeal was for clergy of missionary convictions and outlook to work under the direction of incumbent clergymen in parishes. It was a modest move.

So on 19 February 1836 a group of laymen and clergy met in the committee room at the headquarters of the Church Missionary Society with Lord Ashley himself in the chair. (The CMS was the original Church of England Evangelical missionary society founded by Wilberforce and others in the Clapham Sect following the Revival.) A wider meeting was held the same day, also under Ashley's chairmanship, at which a formal motion was passed to institute the Church Pastoral Aid Society. The beginnings of the society were not without confusion. There was a parallel commitment to augmenting the number of places of worship as well as the labourers employed. The former was a classic response of the age. By the time of its fourth annual report the purpose, objectives, and aims of the society had clarified.

The salvation of souls, with a single eye to the glory of God, and in humble dependence on his blessing, by granting aid towards maintaining faithful and devoted men to assist the Incumbents of parishes in their pastoral charge.[28]

The aims were spiritual and evangelistic. The emphasis was the provision of parish workers, who might or might not be ordained. The concept of the lay agent did, for some, bring some conflict with church order. The CPAS was at first supported by high churchmen as well as Evangelicals. In 1837, led by the future prime minister William Gladstone, the high church party walked out of the society over this shift away from exclusively ordained workers. They established the Additional Curates Society – the name speaks for itself. Among the bishops only Sumner remained a supporter. Charles Blomfield of London initially opposed the undertaking but later recanted.

Shaftesbury always looked upon the CPAS with great affection and favour. He took pride in attending meetings and of all the May meetings (the month when so many of these societies held their annual meeting) he saw that of the CPAS as "the most interesting and constructive".[29] On one occasion he declared, "I heartily thank God for the day when I first became a member of the Church Pastoral-Aid Society."[30] This was a deeply personal involvement. He recollected on a number of occasions his association with the foundation of the society. He had been one of the original small group that had met to establish it. He was elected President for the inaugural meeting and remained so until his death. He attended every single annual meeting in the intervening period with just one exception. His sense of being called to serve God through the CPAS was strong from the beginning as he noted in his diary in 1838: "I never was called by God's mercy to so happy and blessed a work as to labour on behalf of this Society."[31] On another occasion Shaftesbury referred to the CPAS as "a bright light amid the darkness of the land".[32] He attempted to resign after he addressed the 1873 annual meeting on the topic of church reform, fearing he might lose the society both finance and support. The resignation was not accepted.

The CPAS represented a crucial development in the history of Evangelical mission societies. It represented a mature Evangelical theology within the established church. The concentration on lay agency and Protestant principles appealed particularly to Shaftesbury. Alongside the other societies and together with his campaigning, social and religious, the CPAS was a significant place for the outworking of his passion and vision.

In addition to these two societies the mid-1830s also saw the foundation of the London City Mission in 1835. This was to be a society with which Ashley was to have a very important and close connection from the 1840s onwards. We will return to that part of the story in chapter 9. In 1837 Ashley accepted an invitation to become a Vice-President of the Church Missionary Society. It was in the offices of the CMS that the founding meetings of the CPAS had been held. Ashley remained in office until his death, spoke at several of the annual meetings and was actively engaged on the society's behalf. This included joining a delegation to Sierra Leone in 1837, meeting with the Bible Society in 1842, and presenting a petition to the Commons against the opium trade in 1843.

CHAPTER 5

THE ASYLUM: SHAFTESBURY AND MENTAL HEALTH 1828–1845

The asylum, alongside the workhouse, is one of the enduring symbols of Victorian England. To suffer from mental health problems in eighteenth- and nineteenth-century England left unfortunate individuals at the mercy of an inadequately regulated regime of ill-treatment and brutality. This cruelty was only barely disguised as treatment. Poverty simply compounded the difficulties. This chapter reviews Shaftesbury's involvement in mental health care from the beginning in 1828 to the enactment of the Lunacy Act of 1845.

Shaftesbury's lifelong commitment to the protection of the mentally ill stands as a testament to his faith, public service, perseverance, and fortitude. His first major speech in Parliament concerned the protection of lunatics. He served on and gave evidence to numerous select committees and commissions. His diary entries are full of concern for this particularly unfortunate group within society. He was appointed as a Metropolitan Commissioner in Lunacy on 9 August 1828. He became the chairman of the commission in 1834 and served on it and its successor body until his death in 1885. He was assiduous in the exercise of these unsung and often hidden duties. Industrious and attentive to detail he regularly visited asylums and reported upon conditions to the commission, to Parliament, and to the general public. Perhaps it is ironic that he was so committed, given Florence Nightingale's comment noted earlier and Shaftesbury's own constant struggles with depression. The asylum, the protection and treatment of those confined within its walls, was at the heart of Shaftesbury's passion for the less fortunate. He was no less concerned with the issues of public policy which surrounded the asylum.

The state of mental health provision

Mental health provision in the early nineteenth century was diverse in both quantity and quality. There were differing levels of both provision and regulation. Private asylums ranged in size from those with a single inmate to large and extensive establishments. They received both private patients (placed by families) and, for an agreed fee, poor patients from parishes, perhaps where there was no provision of a county asylum. The private asylums were the most difficult to regulate. Some counties, but by no means all, now had their own asylums, mainly to ensure more uniform provision and regulation for pauper lunatics. Borough asylums were less orderly. There were numerous vested interests throughout the system. These ranged from the undue influence of families over the detention of relatives and budgetary pressures in parishes to the disincentive for a private provider to agree to the release of an inmate. In addition, in London, there was the Bethlehem Hospital (known as Bethlem or Bedlam), an independent hospital for the treatment of the mentally ill.

In 1827 the House of Commons established a select committee to investigate the failings of the existing system of asylums and the well-being of the inmates. Ashley was appointed as a member of this Select Committee on Pauper Lunatics in the County of Middlesex, and on Lunatic Asylums. Although limited in scope, not least geographically, the select committee was an important milestone. The report, in June 1827, began with a list of abuses highlighted by a previous committee in 1815. These included, among other things, overcrowding, insufficient staffing, a lack of medical assistance, and the over-zealous detention of patients. There was also concern over poor procedures in respect of certification and visitation. The issue of certification concerned the requirements over who might sign a certificate confining a person to the asylum. The matter of visitation concerned the regulation of the asylums. Regular visits by either magistrates or others were designed to ensure standards were maintained: however, the law was more often broken than observed. The inquiry concluded that these various abuses still existed and no improvement had taken place.

The evidence presented to the committee was devastating. Much of it concerned a private establishment called the White House in Bethnal Green, under the control of a Mr Thomas Warburton. This was the place where most of the pauper lunatics from the parishes which were the subject of the report were placed. The poor-law guardian for the parish of Marylebone, John Hall, reported on the condition of the patients:

> … *they were sitting on benches round the room, and several of them were chained to the wall. The air of the room was highly oppressive and offensive, insomuch so that I could not draw my breath… the room was exceedingly oppressive, from the excrement and the smell which existed there.* [1]

Hall also reported that many patients were manacled in cribs from Friday to Monday. The inmates were only cleaned on the Monday morning and made to stand in tubs of cold water and mopped down.

The report also dealt with the aims of the institution. The apothecary (dispenser of drugs) for the parish of Marylebone was William Goodger. His responsibility was to attend to the pauper lunatics. He commented in his evidence, "I do not think that [it] is the chief aim of the institution to attend to the mental disease."[2] Patients with varying degrees of severity of illness were confined together in a small space. Some were chained. Patients were left entirely to their own devices as there was no attempt to provide employment of any sort. Other witnesses, including former inmates, also provided additional evidence of the most horrific conditions. One described 170 men sharing one towel for a week. Another former patient, John Nettle, described being chained naked on a bed of straw in a crib without any utensils for eating and seeing other cribs infested with maggots and inmates not even let loose to relieve themselves.[3] Treatment was clearly not part of the purposes of these institutions. Containment appeared the main motivation.

Early legislation and the Lunacy Commission

As a member of the committee Lord Ashley sat through this evidence. On one occasion he visited the White House and it undoubtedly had a significant impact upon him. In February 1828 Robert Gordon, the chairman of the select committee, moved in the Commons for leave to bring in a "Bill to Amend the Law for the Regulation of Lunatic Asylums". In his speech he dealt with the abuse of certification and then turned to the question of the treatment of those detained. He referred to his select committee's investigation of Mr Warburton's White House. He cited the lack of medical care and the state of the accommodation. It was clear that the committee had rejected the evidence of Mr Warburton and his own witnesses. Gordon went on, "It was impossible with the strongest language to describe the horrors of this place."[4] He then proceeded to set out the general needs in law for the protection of those of unsound mind. The key issues were certification, treatment, and the difficulty of regaining freedom – not least with so many vested interests in continuing a confinement. Equally there needed to be a proper system of visitation and regulation.

Lord Ashley seconded the motion. As noted earlier this was his first significant parliamentary contribution. It was an opportunity for him to demonstrate his command of the issue, to harness his experience on the committee, and to make a weighty speech in the national interest. Perhaps it was nerves, but Ashley's speech was so inaudible that the parliamentary recorder simply could not hear what was being said. The official report continued:

> *He alluded to the evidence given before the committee, to prove that it was highly necessary that something should be done relative to the treatment of Pauper Lunatics; and he cited several cases that had come within his own knowledge, which clearly proved that the present system was greatly defective.*[5]

Ashley told his diary that his speech had been "far from glorious". Nevertheless he stated that he "felt unusual sympathy for those whom the Bill is intended to protect". He went on, "so, by God's blessing, my first effort has been for the advancement of human happiness. May I improve hourly!"[6] Ashley referred to cases within his personal knowledge. This may have been from witnesses to the committee, or the visit to the White House in Bethnal Green, or other sources. However, it set a pattern which he was to follow in his campaigns for social reforms. Ashley was always committed to gaining first-hand evidence on the ground, much of it, in later years, from the London City Missionaries, which he then presented to Parliament.

Two Acts of Parliament resulted from this select committee report and enquiry. The first, the County Lunatic Asylum Act, provided for the building of county asylums so as to ensure the proper provision for the poor. The Act suffered from the same problems of non-implementation as its predecessors. The second, the Madhouses Act, provided for more effective safeguards on licensing, admission, release, and visitation. This Act was aimed at the regulation of private asylums. The legislation provided for fifteen commissioners, five physicians, who were to be paid, and ten others, unpaid. Prior to the granting of licences each establishment would be visited by at least two commissioners. The plan was to visit each asylum four times a year to monitor the conditions. The inspections would be unannounced and could be at any time of day or night. Certificates for detention would require the signatures of two physicians. Every death would prompt an inquest. The formal powers of the commissioners extended to the Metropolitan area only (in effect Middlesex and certain adjoining parishes in other counties). Elsewhere provision for visitation was made through the justices of the peace acting in quarter sessions. Hence a two-tier system was enshrined at the beginning of this process of reform. This was a long-term obstacle to effective reform. This was unchanged from the previous provision and illustrates the power of locality in English history. The counties and the county magistrates were fiercely protective of their independence. Even with these reforms mental health provision for most of the country would remain a local rather than a national responsibility: but, despite its inadequacies, this legislation was an important advance. The formal name, the Metropolitan Lunacy Commission, was adopted in amending legislation in 1832. In practice the name was used from the beginning, appearing on the first annual report in 1829. As a member and subsequently chairman Ashley guided this work over a period of nearly sixty years, a programme of visiting and reform which led to numerous reports to Parliament, including the important Lunacy Act of 1845.

Ashley's passion, as well as his sense of duty and service, came out in his diary on 13 November 1828. He praised the empire of which he was proud to be a citizen and his popularity (clearly a matter of importance to him) across classes and political divides.

He commented on his activities at the Lunacy Commission: "Yesterday, at our Lunatic Commission; there is nothing poetical in this duty; but every sigh prevented, and every pang subdued, is a song of harmony to the heart."[7]

The language seems to the modern ear to belong to a different era. In the wider debate words such as "lunatic", "madhouse", and "asylum" can grate against and even offend the sensibilities of the contemporary mind. Nevertheless it illustrates the impact that Ashley's first encounters with the complex questions of mental health had upon him. His concern was for the individual, that proper provision and humane treatment should mark society's concern for the insane. Pre-Victorian language and attitudes should not detract from the extraordinary commitment of Ashley to this cause. Characteristically he slipped this work into his diary entries simply as an ordinary part of his daily routine. So, in February 1829: "Went on a visitation of madhouses. I can do good that way if no other."[8] He wrote an extended entry in his diary on 3 October 1838. This is all the more remarkable because in the intervening years Ashley's life and parliamentary activity had been dominated by the all-consuming question of the regulation of hours of work in factories. This entry reveals his heart. It shows his continued passion and concern for the unfortunate inmates of asylums. It illustrates his recognition of the complexity and importance of the judgments made and the need for independent people to be involved in the critical decisions. In the particular case under discussion the commission, voting for the first time since its foundation, divided by six to four that a particular individual should be released. Ashley sided with the majority. He stated: "It is an unpleasant and responsible office either to detain or discharge a patient: in the first case you hazard the commission of cruelty to the prisoner; in the second to his friends or the public."[9] Though the individual was clearly a rogue Ashley pointed out that, despite his manner and demeanour, not a single act of violence or other inappropriate behaviour or action could be proved. Tellingly, perhaps indicating the depth of his concern for the welfare of humanity, he went on to say:

In fact a decision on our part, that he was rightly detained, would have authorised the incarceration in a Bedlam of seven-tenths of the human race who have ever been excited to violence of speech and gesture.[10]

There is little doubt that had that been the case, Ashley would have been included. He had sat as the chairman of this hearing for three days, each of five hours, and unpaid!

The difficulties of encouraging the erection of county asylums for the poor and the effective regulation of the private asylums continued. In 1839 a select committee of the House of Commons was appointed to investigate conditions at the Hereford Lunatic Asylum. Ashley was appointed as one of the members. Hereford was a private asylum, run by Dr John Gilliland, to which the local authorities referred patients. The case illustrated the continuing complexity of mental health provision. The report pointed out that both in terms of regulation and visitation the legal provisions had not been complied with effectively. The committee also found neglect of duty in the supervision of patients. The county magistrates had eventually refused a licence, but Dr Gilliland then successfully applied to the Hereford city magistrates. The report was thus dealing with the matter of competing jurisdictions in the matter of licensing asylums. In essence, if the owners of a private asylum did not succeed in gaining a licence from one court, they might simply apply to another. The report's conclusion was that licence applications should be preceded by a public notice. All of this, though it may seem rather esoteric, illustrates the complex challenges facing Ashley in his campaign to regulate the treatment of mental health patients and the importance of the detailed routine of committee work. (The commission of inquiry held four meetings; Ashley was present at all of them.) It was one thing to pass legislation, but another for those provisions to be enforced effectively. Ashley's willingness to work at the detailed level of committee work is a testament to his own passionate determination to make a difference.

The issues of licensing, regulation and visitation continued, not least because the relevant legal provisions required renewal every three years. Ashley was caught somewhat off guard in 1841 when the Radical backbench member of Parliament for Finsbury, Thomas Wakley, opposed renewal. He was concerned by lack of progress in treatment, continued inhumanity in the system, the lack of reach of the Metropolitan Commissioners, and the existence of different systems in the London area and the rest of the country. He asserted that "he was convinced there were hundreds confined in the lunatic asylums of this country, who were as sane as any who sat in that House – indeed more so, in some instances".[11] Ashley was unprepared, but promised to bring forward proposals for amendments in the law and agreed on the deficiencies of the system outside the metropolis. It is noteworthy that at this point Sir Robert Inglis intervened to state "that his noble Friend had earned one title more honourable than all others – that of the friend to the friendless – the sympathizer with every sufferer".[12] Wakley bore testimony to Ashley's zeal and energy but found the powers of the commission to be lacking. The effect of all of this was to encourage the bringing forward of a series of bills in Parliament in 1842 which eventually emerged as the Lunacy Inquiry Act. Under this Act the Metropolitan Commission was effectively given powers for a national inquiry. They were to focus upon treatment, including diet, the extent of the use of coercion and restraints, the provision of employment, and the general condition of those arriving at the establishment. They were to visit all licensed houses and county asylums and others if authorized by the Lord Chancellor or Home Secretary. The Bethlehem Hospital was excluded.

Again Ashley's time was being absorbed by "the factory question" yet he was also closely involved as the Metropolitan Commission's spokesman in the Commons on guiding and promoting these developing provisions on mental health. Ashley was undoubtedly being pulled in numerous directions, his mind filled with conflicting demands, yet he was determined to continue this work of visitation of the asylums in the interests of humanity. He often despaired of himself. Referring to one speech, he commented that he had found it difficult, with half of what he wanted to say remaining unsaid. On 17 May 1842 he recorded his visit to Hanwell, the Middlesex County Asylum, built under the provisions of the 1828 Act. He was clearly impressed by what he saw, "sufferings mitigated, what degradation spared, what vices restrained, what affections called forth".[13] It convinced him to change his position on the issue of the use of restraint. It also demonstrates how his practical gathering of information quickly translated into parliamentary action. Speaking to the House of Commons on the Inquiry Bill on 16 July 1842 Ashley noted his previous doubts about the practicality of the principle of non-restraint, but that he had been convinced of its merits by his visit to Hanwell, something of a model asylum. His visits to asylums continued over the years to come. The ability for a commissioner to arrive to inspect an asylum at any time of day or night was something he took extremely seriously. In a remarkable response to visiting the asylum in Peckham in 1844, he commented, "we too readily get him in, and too sluggishly get him out, and yet what a destiny".[14] Ashley was passionate about conditions and treatment. He believed that the system of visitation was an essential safeguard. He was concerned also for the spiritual welfare and destiny of these unfortunate individuals, no more to be excluded from God's purposes than anyone else. He lamented that the words of a lunatic were generally disbelieved and words, looks, gestures, and mannerisms given interpretations they could not bear in other parts of life. Showing just how seriously he took matters his own visit to the Hoxton Asylum in May 1849 was conducted at night and, apart from the ventilation, he reported himself satisfied.

Indeed the outcome was better than expected, there having been suspicions of misconduct – to Ashley proof of the value of the system of visitation.[15]

Ashley summarized his feelings and motivation in his diary for 9 November 1842:

Have been to London to transact business in Lunacy. This is a mighty subject, and one on which authority and power could be extensively and beneficially exercised. How often do I exclaim, for this and many other purposes –

"O Thou, my thoughts inspire,
Who touched Isaiah's hallowed lips with fire."
But God's strength is "made perfect" in man's weakness.[16]

The 1845 Lunacy Act

The 1844 report and subsequent Lunacy Act of 1845 were landmarks in the history of mental health provision. In essence the impact was to make national rather than local provision for the mental health system. The report built on its predecessors. Horrific conditions were revealed as well as the continuing inadequacies of the existing system of regulation, despite earlier legislation. The report was published in 1844. Ashley recorded its completion in his diary on 2 July – "Finished, at last, Report of the Commission in Lunacy… it contains much for the alleviation of physical and moral suffering."[17] The report, its compilation, the visiting and overseeing of the drafting and editing must have been a significant burden for Ashley as the commission's chairman. He reported to Parliament that the commission had held seventy meetings in the period 1842–44, each meeting averaging four hours' duration. He noted that he had been on one visit which had commenced at 11 p.m. and not been completed until 7 a.m.[18]

Members of the commission had visited 166 asylums, 99 of which were private premises licensed by the magistrates. A little under half of these admitted both private patients and paupers. It was here that most defects were observed. The investigation was comprehensive and went beyond the formal provisions of the Inquiry Act. They paid particular attention to "the lunatic poor". The commissioners noted that the "Asylums thus brought before our view, exhibit instances of almost every degree of merit and defect".[19] In excess of 20,000 people were in asylums, over two-thirds of them at public expense. The report surveyed conditions in each private house. In some instances there was much to commend and in others much left to be desired. After reviewing general conditions the report made recommendations concerning personal appearances for licence applications and public notices of application. Other recommendations concerned size and the usual areas of visitation, certification, a resident medical officer, and licensing.

The report was a masterpiece and Ashley moved quickly. On 23 July he moved a motion for an Address to the Crown, praying Her Majesty to take into consideration the report of the Metropolitan Commissioners in Lunacy. He used this device because the term of office for the commissioners would expire in the next session and he wanted to begin the process which would lead to major new legislative provision. The speech showed his command of the subject, the depth of his knowledge, and his passionate commitment to ensure that proper provision was made. He emphasized that it was the duty of the House to make suitable arrangements for the detention, treatment, and release of those suffering from insanity. He deplored the fact that current legislation precluded the commissioners from exercising any control over patients housed in single homes where there were many horrible abuses. In such an unregulated environment there was always the temptation to keep a patient confined since any return to health would result in the end of the allowance provided for their upkeep.

It was the concession of absolute secret and irresponsible power to the relatives of lunatics and the keepers of the asylums, and exposing them to temptations which he believed human nature was too weak to resist.[20]

Some of the county asylums were well run, but others were deficient, in particular failing to provide employment for inmates. Some asylums were too large. Ashley thought that there should be an absolute maximum of 250 people. There were particular problems with paupers in private asylums because of the low level of financial provision. Ashley then reported to the House a long list of abuses and poor conditions which the commissioners had uncovered in their visits. Describing conditions at Plympton in Devon he reported three women confined in a windowless day room eight feet by four. The whole scene was one of filth with the floor wet with urine and, in the neighbouring cell used for sleeping, excrement on the walls. Ashley went on: "The persons of these three unfortunate women were extremely dirty, and the condition in which we found them and their cells was truly sickening and shocking." He praised the movement toward more humane treatment. Dealing with the granting of certificates, licensing and issues of release Ashley maintained it was essential "to establish the necessity of instituting and maintaining the most vigilant system of frequent visitation".[21] Visitation was effective in London (naturally) and tolerable for the county asylums, but this duty had been shamefully neglected in the borough and rural asylums. He finished with an impassioned plea on behalf of the insane:

The House possesses the means of applying a real and a speedy remedy. These unhappy persons are outcasts from all the social and domestic affections of private life – nay more, from all its cares and duties; and have no refuge but in the laws. You can prevent, by the agency you shall appoint, as you have in many instances prevented, the recurrence of frightful cruelties; you

*can soothe the days of the incurable, and restore many sufferers
to health and usefulness. For we must not run away with the
notion, that even the hopelessly mad are dead to all capacity
of intellectual or moral exertion – quite the reverse; their
feelings too are painfully alive – I have seen them writhe under
supposed contempt, while a word of kindness and respect would
kindle their whole countenance into an expression of joy. Their
condition appeals to our highest sympathies, Majestic, though in
ruin.*[22]

To Ashley the cause was not simply one of public policy. He had an
intense personal interest, under God, in the welfare of humanity.
The Home Secretary, Sir James Graham, declared Ashley to be
entitled to the grateful thanks of his countrymen for his indefatigable
efforts. In return for the promise of cooperation over a bill, Ashley,
after some further debate, withdrew his motion.

Lord Ashley introduced two bills on 6 June 1845 which were
enacted in August of that year as the Lunacy Act and the County
Asylums Act. It was another long, detailed and powerful speech
from Ashley. The Lunacy Bill would consolidate the existing
provisions. Ashley proposed a permanent commission to enable
a more effective regime of visitation and a uniform system for
county and private asylums and hospitals where the mentally ill
were detained. Detailed provisions for the certification of the
insane were provided for including a personal examination of
the patient and being seen by the medical officer not less than
seven days before confinement. This would provide protection
against the improper detention of pauper patients. The powers
of the visitors would be increased. Provision would be made for
formal statistical returns of all single patients and provision for
visitation. The second bill concerned the provision of county
asylums. Twenty-four counties had no asylums and those that did
had asylums which were too big. In many of these there was such a
dominance of the chronically ill that it distorted the provision and

led to many lunatics being detained in workhouses. The proposal was that every county should provide an asylum and sufficient accommodation. Ashley also stated that chronic cases should be separated to enhance the possibility of cure for others. The commissioners would have a regulatory role, including a quarterly medical examination of all pauper lunatics with a return to the commission. Ashley reviewed the history of the treatment of the mentally incapacitated and praised medical advance. He moved his bills. Sir James Graham seconded, describing Ashley's speech at the close of the previous session as unforgettable. The first Lunacy Commissioners were named in the Act itself, including Ashley, who was elected chairman at the first meeting.

Ashley, occupied by so much legislation in this period, confessed his delight to his diary at the successful passage of the bills, alongside his other campaigns:

> *Most humbly and heartily do I thank God for my success. Such a thing almost before unknown, that a man, without a party, unsupported by anything private or public, but God and His Truth, should have overcome Mammon and Molech, and have carried in one Session, three such measures as the Print-works Regulation and the two Bills for the erection and government of Lunatic Asylums.*[23]

Shaftesbury's passion for the plight of the mentally ill was motivated by both his Christian compassion and his aristocratic sense of public duty. Diligence and hard work were the very practical consequences of his commitment. A number of themes begin to emerge. Shaftesbury was acutely aware of both the need for and the limitations of state intervention. It was a pattern that would continue to emerge in his thinking and practice even after his succession to the earldom. That part of the story will be told in chapter 11. Alongside his extraordinary campaign on behalf of the mentally ill Shaftesbury was also pursuing a campaign on behalf of those employed in factories and mines. All of this was intertwined with a determined struggle for the priority of Protestantism and his work with Evangelical missionary and social voluntary societies.

CHAPTER 6

MILLS AND MINES:
1832–1848

The second great theme of Shaftesbury's parliamentary campaigns of the 1830s and 1840s was factory and industrial reform. This chapter takes an overview of his work in this area from the early 1830s through to the final enactment of the "ten hours" principle in 1848. The industrialization of England had an enormous impact upon the face of society. Until the inventions of the late eighteenth century, manufacturing had been in essence a cottage industry.

The invention of the "flying shuttle" (developed by John Kay in 1733) and "spinning jenny" (invented by James Hargreaves in 1764), together with the development of the steam engine, effectively provided for the mechanization of the key processes of the textile industry. Increased production made possible a more rapid and profitable return on capital investment. These inventions led directly to the erection of large mills with the necessary equipment to ensure full-scale production. The one thing that was still needed was labour. This led to the large-scale movement of population away from the "cottage industries" in traditional villages to the new urban centres around the mills. Family relationships were thus replaced by employer relationships. The employment of children was both cheap and effective as their fingers were nimble and wages low. Overwork and ill-treatment were the order of the day in many places. As production increased so shift working was introduced. Many of the youngsters were housed in apprentice houses; there was often one set of beds for two shifts of children. The ill-health, poor conditions, and mistreatment of children working in these factories and mills gave rise to much concern. However, the issues also represented part of the cultural and intellectual debate about the move from an agrarian to an industrial economy.

The campaign for factory reform

Ashley was not the first campaigner on factory conditions. There were reports and commissions on the subject in the late eighteenth and early nineteenth centuries which culminated in Sir John Hobhouse's Cotton Mills and Factories Act of 1825 placing some modest restriction on the hours of labour for children. The Act covered only cotton factories (after lobbying) and was generally ineffective. A noted supporter of factory reform was an Evangelical Tory member of Parliament, Michael Thomas Sadler. In 1832 he moved the second reading in the House of Commons of a bill to regulate the employment of children and young people in mills and factories. The basic proposal was to limit employment to ten hours a day – hence the "Ten Hours Bill". Sadler was neutralized by the matter being referred to a select committee, albeit under his own chairmanship. Ashley later claimed that Sadler's bill "was stifled in its birth by a vote of the House, which sent it to a committee-room, the hopeless subject of a coroner's inquest".[1] The techniques have not changed. Sadler had originally sat for Newark then switched to the safe Tory seat of Aldborough in Yorkshire for the 1831 election. Following the passage of the Reform Act of 1832 Aldborough lost its representation in Parliament. Sadler stood for Leeds and was defeated. Robert Southey wrote to him, lamenting the loss of Sadler and others from the House. He asked, "Who is there that will take up the question of our white slave trade with equal feeling?"[2] The factory operatives who were the main campaigners for reform, especially in the north of England, formed themselves into what were known as "Short-Time Committees". In February 1833 one of the leaders of the movement, the Reverend George Bull, wrote to the committees to explain what progress had been made. He explained that Ashley had given notice to the House that he would re-introduce Sadler's bill. He described Ashley as "noble, benevolent, and resolute in mind". He explained that he had met with Ashley on several occasions. Ashley had given the credit to Sadler and declared himself only to have "zeal and good intentions", but agreed to undertake the task as his duty to God and the poor. Interestingly, Ashley declared to Bull that the question was a matter of religion rather than policy.[3]

Why did Ashley take up the question and from whom did the initiative come? In his own memorandum, five years later, Ashley claimed that he had read extracts from the evidence presented to Sadler's committee in late 1832, but that he had not been aware of the issue being raised previously. This seems a little odd given Sadler's extensive speech on the matter earlier that same year. However, parliamentary proceedings were dominated by the subject of reform. Ashley claimed he had written to Sadler offering what assistance he could after his defeat but heard nothing. He traced the meetings with Bull to the Tory Evangelical Sabbatarian MP, Sir Andrew Agnew. Ashley had been a member of the Select Committee on the Observance of the Sabbath Day under Agnew's chairmanship in 1832. He notes that "they both proposed to me to take up the question that Sadler had necessarily dropped". He expressed "astonishment, and doubt, and terror, at the proposition".[4] He returned home to pray and consult the Word of God. It is difficult to untangle this web. Ashley was clearly someone identifiable to the "short-timers" as a potential parliamentary champion. Ashley was also undoubtedly well known among this group of Protestant, Ultra-Tory MPs. The influence of Southey should also not be overlooked. "I know not where the love of gain appears in more undisguised deformity than in a cotton-mill", he wrote to Ashley in January 1833. He added, full of his Tory paternalistic romanticism: "I know not how a cotton-mill can be otherwise than an abomination to God and man."[5] So it would seem that a combination of Christian belief, the religious influence of others, a sense of duty and righteousness together with classic paternalism combined to cause Ashley to take up this particular mantle.

Ashley moved quickly to introduce a bill that would prevent the employment of children below the age of nine years in the cotton and woollen industries. In addition it would restrict children under eighteen to ten hours a day and eight on Saturdays. No one under the age of twenty-one was to be employed to work at night. Opponents sought to delay progress in the matter by seeking a royal commission. The government acquiesced. On 3 April 1833 a debate and vote took place in the Commons on a motion for a commission. Sadler's select committee was accused of bias in not taking evidence from the manufacturers. In addition it was claimed that the impact of the bill would be to reduce profits. Ashley opposed the motion. He rehearsed the history of regulation (the same strategy that he adopted in his speeches on lunacy) and objected that a motion for a commission was simply a delaying tactic. It was time, he said, to challenge the whole system and "he would push the Bill as long as he breathed". Ashley made clear that the reason for promoting a Ten Hours Bill was that one for nine hours would not succeed. Ashley, as usual, had done his homework, quoting the evidence from previous committees. As far back as 1818 evidence was presented of children being stunted in growth and distorted in their limbs by the excessive labour and unhealthy atmosphere of the cotton mills. Ashley quoted extensively from the medical evidence on the health of children in cotton, woollen and silk mills, especially girls. He claimed that victims had been hidden away from inspectors when they visited to make enquiries. He went on, "The manufacturers who were now asking for a commission to take evidence, had already had full opportunities of presenting their evidence."[6] On a vote the House approved a commission by one vote, 74 to 73. The opponents included the usual Tory-Protestants, Ashley, Agnew, J. P. Plumptre, and Sir Robert Inglis. On 17 June Ashley's bill was formally read a second time – with the government minister Lord Althorp indicating that the commission's report would be available the following week.

The commission had moved fast. The report was not the whitewash that had been feared, but Ashley's political instincts were correct. The government was seeking to head off any formal adoption of the Ten Hours position and would do so by a combination of delay and compromise. The select committee report adopted a skilful political position. It argued that younger children needed more protection than was offered by Ashley's bill. The recommendation was eight hours maximum to the age of thirteen, but no protection at all after that. The commission also sought to legislate for some educational provisions and the appointment of inspectors. Given Ashley's advocacy of the inspection regime in his work on mental health it is perhaps slightly surprising that he included no such proposals in his initial bill on factory hours. However, unlike the lunacy reforms, Ashley had taken over from others a set of existing proposals, indeed rather hastily, and this may explain the omission.

Ashley was astute in his response to the government's position on the report. He agreed with the proposed provisions on greater protection for the younger children and for the appointment of inspectors. The latter he claimed not to have included in order to make the bill more palatable to its opponents. He held his position on the protection of young people aged from thirteen to eighteen – especially as it related to girls – and also on provisions relating to accidents. He also supported the educational provisions. The somewhat different approaches of Lord Ashley and the commission are revealed here in the discussion over the education clauses. For Ashley the concern was to provide moral and spiritual education. The commissioners had a much more utilitarian approach, concerned for the general progress of humanity and the best harnessing of resources available. A common goal but very different ideological approaches was a characteristic of Ashley's encounters with many other reformers of his time. The basic difference was Christianity.

When the House went into committee on Ashley's bill, Lord Althorp argued that limiting children and young people to ten hours' labour a day would seriously damage the country's manufacturing interest. Ashley claimed that the eight-hour day for children would lead to the employment of the same children in two different sets of factories. What really grated for the aristocratic Ashley was that the new urban landscape offended against his vision of rural paternalism, of local relationships and responsibilities, of *noblesse oblige*. Large-scale manufacturing with waged workers contradicted his idealistic agrarian vision as well as his Christian faith. Ashley was defeated and the government introduced its own bill, which became the Factory Act of 1833. No children under the age of nine were to be employed. Children between nine and thirteen could work for nine hours a day and not more than forty-eight hours in a week. Young people between thirteen and eighteen were to work no more than twelve hours a day or sixty-nine hours a week. There was to be no night work under eighteen, education was to be provided and inspectors were appointed. Silk and lace factories were excluded. Ashley was disappointed, although he maintained that the Act did contain some useful protections and that, most importantly, the principle had been conceded.

The Factory Act provided for different clauses to come into operation on different dates, the legislation not being fully operative until 1836. In the intervening time there had been two changes in the administration. Peel came into office at the end of 1834, appointed Ashley a Lord of the Admiralty, and then fell from office in April 1835, to be replaced again by Melbourne. Just nine days after the clause restricting the labour of all under the age of thirteen came into operation, notice was given in the Commons by the government of an attempt to reduce the age limit to twelve years. Ashley entered immediately into the fray, moving that the bill be read again in six months' time – one of the classic parliamentary devices to defeat a proposition. He was furious. He quoted extensively from the commissioners' report on the principle of the need for legislative intervention. He poured scorn on the claim that 35,000 children would be thrown out of work. He accused the government of hypocrisy and saw the bill as a first step toward the repeal of all protection for children. The government scraped home in the division with a majority of two, and gracefully withdrew the bill. It was an impressive performance by Ashley, still only thirty-five years of age.

The episode illustrates the numerous vested interests that conspired against the campaign for an improvement in the conditions in factories. There was a great deal of lobbying of the government. It was to take more than another ten years before the essential principle of the Ten Hours Movement was enshrined in legislation. Without Ashley's terrier-like passion and resilience it might have been much longer.

In 1836 Ashley was the author of an article in a Tory periodical, *The Quarterly Review*, on "the factory question". On paper Ashley was able to set out the arguments at length. He referred to the impact of excess labour on the physique of children, "stunted forms, sallow complexions, sickly and mis-shapen children, and youth bowed down by the infirmities of age". He went on, not mincing his words:

> … *thousands and tens of thousands of these unhappy beings ensure a daily torture; many deprived of their parents, at least of any parental affection and tutelage, by this corrupting system… thousands perish in early childhood.*[7]

There were few workers in the factories over the age of forty. They had either been broken in health or simply could no longer keep up with the demands. Numerous committees had been established and Ashley rehearsed the familiar history that had formed the basis of his parliamentary speeches. He went into great detail, quoting from medical evidence presented to previous inquiries. In respect of the 1836 commission Ashley maintained that "it recommended one thing and proved another".[8] What he meant by that was that although the commission had argued against the Ten Hours provision it had conceded the principle of intervention. Indeed much of its evidence supported many of the contentions of the campaigners for reform. The report contained evidence of extreme overwork and tiredness as well as swellings, deformity and illness. He denounced the move to reduce the age of full protection to twelve years old as faithless and amounting to legalizing slavery. He summarized his opposition to a system "which from childhood to death treats man as a machine, estimates his value by the amount of his work, and regards him as useless, but when he is 'a-going'."[9] He went on to dismiss the manufacturers' claims concerning child unemployment, reduced wages if labour were to be so restricted, and advantages to foreign competition.

In 1838 Ashley was again on his feet in Parliament seeking to introduce a Factories Regulation Bill – one clause of which would be a "Ten Hours" provision. Once more he accused the government of hypocrisy. The government won the vote by eight. *The Times* described Ashley's speech as "impressive and striking". The paper joined in the condemnation of the Whig government for its broken faith and promises, describing their conduct as "scandalous" and attacking their "treacherous promises and frivolous postponements".[10] His speech on 20 July ran to seventeen columns in Hansard. He particularly attacked the lack of implementation of the penalties provided for in the 1833 Act. He also criticized the practice of granting certificates of age for working in factories solely on the basis of height – this led to much abuse of the system.

He compared the granting of a 45-hour week to newly freed West Indian slaves on plantations with the less favourable sixty-nine-hour week faced by children in factories. The outcome would be the judgment of God. Ashley was a master of rhetoric but his speeches were full of evidence and facts. They were extraordinary feats which increasingly attracted the admiration, if not support, of opponents. In 1839 he also spoke at length on the report of the Factory Commissioners. In 1840 the House of Commons agreed to a motion from Ashley asking for a select committee to inquire into the operation of the "Act for the Regulation of Mills and Factories", the 1833 legislation. Ashley was appointed chairman of the committee. This was an amazing piece of work. In the midst of his work on lunacy, chimney sweeps, factories, and in the same year also mines, Ashley presided over six reports from this commission on child labour over a period of five months, chairing numerous meetings with a final report published in 1841. The first witness was the veteran factory inspector Leonard Horner, and the committee took evidence from a wide range of witnesses. Conditions had certainly improved. This comprehensive report was a testament to Ashley's untiring commitment and prestigious hard work. It provided him with much evidence for his parliamentary speeches as the factory question proceeded as well as for another article in *The Quarterly Review* in December 1840. In the midst of all of this a letter from Mr Horner to *The Times* revealed the extent of Ashley's personal involvement with individuals. Horner reported on Ashley's intervention in two particular instances. In one, the case of a sixteen-year-old girl mutilated in an accident with unfenced machinery in a mill in Rossendale, Ashley had instituted a legal action for damages as the girl's "next friend", given this would be beyond her father's means. He had undertaken this at his own expense and risk. The mill owner travelled to visit Ashley who was in Cowes, on the Isle of Wight, a lengthy journey from Lancashire. Eventually he agreed to pay damages and the surgeon's bill, to fence his machinery, and to issue a public letter of apology. The paper added that Ashley deserved the title "the Infant's friend" and praised his eloquence, far-sightedness, and humanity.[11]

Strange alliances and bedfellows

Ashley made a strange bedfellow with radicals, such as John Fielden and Richard Cobden among others. To some extent Ashley was ill at ease with the Short-Time Committees. He was no radical. He had no truck with the fledgling trade union movement and considered both socialism and Chartism as enemies of the state. At one meeting in 1833 he found himself sharing a platform with the trade union pioneer Robert Owen and the radical Irish nationalist Daniel O'Connell. Ironically, perhaps, the leadership of much of the movement for the protection of the factory and other workers lay in the hands of aristocratic Tory paternalists. Frequently these individuals were also Evangelical Protestants. This group included leaders outside Parliament, Oastler and Bull, as well as the legislators. The opponents were usually the mainstream liberal Whig establishment, often closely connected to the manufacturing interest, though there were mill owners who supported Ashley. The Tory paternalists were, of course, more attached to the rural, landed, and agrarian view of England: a country where everyone in a community knew each other and knew their place, but because of the personal relationships there was genuine community, care, and provision for those in need. Here industry was cottage-based, the parents exercising a watchful eye over the children. In addition most benevolent landowners provided some land to enable a modest amount of agricultural production to supplement the cottage industry – the principle of "cow and cottage", mentioned earlier. An economy based upon waged labour, huge factories, and mills with near-constant production turned this vision upside down. The move to an industrial economy and society was unlikely ever to be able to accommodate this perhaps utopian view of rural England. Indeed it is doubtful how many of the workers will have shared it, certainly not in its fully worked-out version. Indeed, one of Ashley's objections to the employment of females in mines and factories was that it drew them away from their domestic duties.

The relay system

One, perhaps unintended, consequence of the amendments to the law which were enacted in 1833 was that manufacturers began to introduce "relays" of child workers. The opponents of reform argued that to restrict the hours of children to ten hours would have the inevitable effect of restricting the hours of the adult operatives in the same way. Indeed, although Ashley and the factory campaigners would have been unable to carry such a vote, it was a fact not lost on them either. The adult workers needed the children alongside them in order to operate the looms. However, by restricting the hours of the younger children to eight hours, the operatives were able to run two eight-hour shifts with one sixteen-hour day for the adult workers. This had a number of consequences upon child labour. For children who lived in apprentice houses, often orphans, living facilities were now often shared by two groups of children. In addition children were sometimes simply too tired to go home and remained on the factory premises between shifts. Education and refreshment provisions which were not enforced contributed to this pattern. Even when further limitations were imposed in 1844, the relay system provided ways out. Although the hours of labour were supposed to be either morning or afternoon again there was a lack of enforcement and indeed complicity from the adult operatives. Hence the pattern of shifts, together with the compulsory rest and refreshment and the educational provision, continued to leave children on factory premises for excessively long hours.

Mines and other industrial reforms

Ashley's campaigning was not neat and linear. Numerous causes vied for his attention. From the early 1840s he was actively involved in Parliament on behalf of climbing boys (see chapter 8), children in mines, and other causes for industrial reform. All of this was running alongside his work in Evangelical mission and social reform movements. No sooner had the ink dried on the six reports from the Factories Commission than Ashley turned his attention to children in mines. He had long been accused of only concerning himself with children in the factories. He set out many of the difficulties faced by child labour in a whole series of industries from needle-making to calico-printing and mines and collieries. Children, he said, were taken into employment in the mines from eight or nine years of age to supplement the family income. He quoted one inspector from 1833 referring to some children under six years of age working twelve or thirteen hours a day. He mentioned the dust, the damp and the heat, girls as well as boys working in the pit, and the terrible accidents to which they were exposed. The House agreed a commission of inquiry into the employment and conditions of children employed in mines and collieries and in other manufacturing industries not covered by the existing legislation.

The Children's Employment Commission concluded in May 1842 with over 2,100 pages of report, minutes, and evidence. The report dealt with the age of employment, women and girls in the mines, ventilation, drainage, temperature, hours of work, meals and holidays, physical treatment, accidents, wages, disease, illness, deformity, and early death. The report was both extraordinary and devastating. It would be impossible for either the country at large or the government to remain inactive in the light of its findings. Indeed, Ashley would make sure that they did not. The commissioners found evidence of children employed as young as five years old, many areas where children of six years old were employed, and even some instances of children aged four in the pit. Many, though not all, collieries employed women and girls who frequently worked stripped to the waist, while the men often worked completely naked because of the temperatures. This led to both the problem of immorality in the mines and, of course, the neglect of domestic duties. However, it was not just traditional paternalism that dictated the outlook on women and girls in the mines. The work itself was very hard, heavy, and physically destroying. Some mining districts stood out against the employment of females in the collieries. Conditions, however, were, quite simply, appalling. If the coal seams were thin, then the roadways would be small and cramped. The height of many of these roads were only twenty-four or thirty inches high – making the employment of children indispensable – but even then often only on hands and knees. There was also evidence of the failure to ventilate mines properly which led to loss of life through the gases which remained in the mine. In some instances drainage was so poor, that miners had to work all day long in drenched clothes. One commissioner reported:

> I have met with pits where it rained so as to wet the Children to the skin in a few minutes, and at the same time so hot that they could scarcely bear their clothes on to work in, and in this wet state they had to continue fourteen hours, and perhaps had to walk a mile or two at night without changing or drying their clothes.[12]

The nature of the occupation of children in the mines included air-door boys, fillers, slack-boys, pitchers, pushers, and drivers. Air-door boys or trappers, often the youngest in the mines, operated the doors on roadways necessary for ventilation. The slack-boys crawled under the seam of coal behind the colliers and the older boys who removed the coal (the fillers), in order to remove the smaller pieces, the slack. Pitchers assisted in loading the skips. Pushers, often ten or eleven years old, sometimes older, pushed the wagons along the roadways, especially when there was not enough room for donkeys. Drivers were those who drove the horses which were often used. Hurrying consisted of loading small wagons and pushing them along narrow roadways often on hands and knees.

On other occasions the trucks were pulled by young children with chains. Men and women, boys and girls, all worked naked at least down to the waist.

The mines were violent and dangerous places, not least for children and women. In one year, 1838, the commissioners noted 349 deaths from accidents in a sample of districts. The fatalities among those under the age of eighteen amounted to 120. The nature of the accidents ranged from falling down shafts and suffocation to crushing. Other problems included low wages and the infamous "truck" system whereby wages were paid in kind (often at inflated prices in factory shops or in taverns) rather than in money. The physical state of the children in the mines was appalling. The effects ranged from extreme fatigue, poor muscle development that sometimes amounted to deformity, stunted growth, a crippled gait that worsened with age, and irritation of the head, back and feet. Disease was rampant and premature old age and death common. Perhaps the overall position is best summed up by one of the commission's investigators:

When the nature of this horrible labour is taken into consideration, its extreme severity, its regular duration of from 12 to 14 hours daily, which, once a-week at least, is extended through the whole of the night; the damp, heated, and unwholesome atmosphere in which the work is carried on; the tender age and sex of the workers… a picture is presented of deadly physical oppression and systematic slavery, of which I conscientiously believe no one unacquainted with such facts would credit the existence in the British dominions. [13]

Ashley wrote in his diary on 7 May 1842: "Perhaps even 'Civilization' itself never exhibited such a mass of sin and cruelty. The disgust felt is very great, thank God; but will it be reduced to action when I call for a remedy?" He swung into action. The report of the commission was so devastating and comprehensive that when Ashley moved the first reading of a bill on 7 June 1842 it was to an unusually receptive House. The classic paternalism and *noblesse oblige* mixed up with his Christian convictions emerged. Ashley argued that "if those who have the power will be as ready to abate oppression as those who have suffered will be to forgive the sense of it, we may hope to see the revival of such a good understanding between master and man, between wealth and poverty, between ruler and ruled, as will, under God's good providence, conduce to the restoration of social comfort, and to the permanent security of the empire". He went through the commissioners' report on the age of employment and the employment of women district by district. He reported similarly on the general conditions in the mines and described the nature of the employment:

> *The child, it appears a girdle bound round its waist, to which is attached a chain, which passes under the legs, and is attached to the cart. The child is obliged to pass on all fours, and the chain passes under what, therefore, in that posture, might be called the hind legs; and thus they have to pass through avenues not so good as a common sewer, quite as wet, and oftentimes more contracted. This kind of labour they have to continue during several hours, in a temperature described as perfectly intolerable.*

He went on to describe the degrading and harsh nature of the employment of girls and the impact on women more generally.

> *... some of the evils of so hideous a nature, that they will not admit of delay – they must be instantly removed – evils that are both disgusting and intolerable – disgusting they would be in a heathen country, and perfectly intolerable they are in one that professes to call itself Christian.* [14]

The speech lasted two hours. He noted his success in his diary and asked God to keep him humble. Spiritually he remained dependent upon God: "…without Thee I am nothing worth, and that from Thee alone cometh all counsel, wisdom, and understanding for the sake of our most dear and only Saviour, God manifest in the flesh, our Lord Jesus Christ!"[15]

Ashley's bill prohibited all female labour in mines. In addition it outlawed the employment of boys under ten years of age. The bill also made it illegal for shaft lifts to be in the care of anybody under fifteen years of age, provided for a system of inspection, and outlawed the truck system of paying wages in kind, not just within the mining industry. The progress of the bill through committee on 22 June 1842 (a committee of the whole House) was very different to the contests over factory hours. The evidence was so overwhelming, so appalling, that it was very difficult for members to oppose Ashley's bill. Ashley received helpful support in the House from Lord Palmerston, the future prime minister. On 24 June Ashley sought to make further progress with report and third reading stage. The Whig MP for Bolton, Peter Ainsworth, sought to delay progress by seeking a reference to a select committee, on the grounds that the bill would lead to unemployment. The House disagreed and sent the bill to be read a third time. Among the letters of congratulation received by Ashley included one from Prince Albert, assuring him of the support of Queen Victoria. The third reading was successfully achieved on 6 July despite the opposition of Ainsworth and with another worthy intervention from Palmerston. The next problem was for the bill to negotiate the House of Lords. The government's ministers in the Lords were more lukewarm to Ashley's bill, seeking to restrict it only to its clauses on female employment. Ashley noted wryly, as he sought a peer to sponsor the bill, that everyone admired it, but none would choose to take it on. He finally gained Lord Devon to promote the bill. In his diary Ashley bemoaned how many supported him in private but not in public – including the Duke of Wellington. However, "God will overrule, and turn all things to His glory at last."[16] The bill passed – though Ashley noted with some incredulity that only three bishops turned up for the key vote on the bill's clauses in the Lords – and received the Royal Assent on 10 August 1842.

Ashley recorded in his diary:

> *Took the Sacrament on Sunday in joyful and humble thankfulness to Almighty God for the undeserved measure of success with which He has blessed my effort for the glory of His name, and the welfare of his creatures… Whatever has been done, is but the millionth part of what there is to do; and even then, should such an end be accomplished, which man never yet saw, we should still be "unprofitable servants". The more I labour, the more I see of labour to be performed, and vain at the last will be the labour of us all. Our prayer must be for the Second Advent, our toil, "that we be found watching".*[17]

The diary entry reveals much about Shaftesbury's motivation in the midst of several parallel campaigns on industrial reform. To the impact of his faith we will return in a later chapter. Shaftesbury continued to work on behalf of those working in industry. Needlewomen, workers in calico-print works and lace factories, and milliners and dressmakers were groups that attracted his attention. During a tour of the factory districts in September 1842 he visited various workers, including colliers and weavers, at Manchester. He also went down a coal mine, "easier to talk after you have seen".[18]

Final enactment of Ten Hours principle
Sir James Graham introduced a bill to the House of Commons on 6 February 1844 to restrict the hours of labour in factories to six and a half hours for children aged nine to thirteen, and to twelve hours for women and children over thirteen years of age. The Ten

Hours principle was not conceded. Silk mills, however, were to be regulated for the first time. There were also provisions for fencing off dangerous machinery. As the bill headed for Committee on 15 March, Ashley moved an amendment that would define "night" – the period when no work was permitted – to run from 6 p.m. to 6 a.m. The impact of this would be to restrict the effective working day, after rest and meals, to ten hours for young people aged under eighteen years. Ashley's speech occupied twenty-nine columns in *Hansard* and took two and a quarter hours to deliver. He adopted his usual techniques of speech-making, although there was probably an overemphasis on the issues of female labour and domesticity. Ashley felt things had gone well but with the debate adjourned he noted that "official whips will produce official votes".[19] Although the struggle with the government was continuing and undoubtedly frustrating to the operatives themselves progress was being made step by step. When the debate resumed, on 18 March, Ashley's amendment succeeded by 179 to 170 votes. He could not believe the outcome and filled his diary with thanks to God, "oh, gracious God, keep me from unseemly exultation", for "the recovery of the people from Egyptian bondage".[20] On 22 March the government was defeated again, this time by 186 to 183 votes on its clause for a twelve-hour working day for those aged from thirteen to eighteen. However, Ashley's proposal for ten hours also fell, by 187 to 181. Graham announced an adjournment until 25 March. Yet as Ashley noted, "the cause is mightily advanced".[21]

The government withdrew the bill and then inexplicably decided against any compromise and brought in a replacement bill which held the age limit at eight but also the working day for young people at twelve hours. The government's continued hostility provoked much discontent within the Ten Hours movement. On 10 May Ashley moved a Ten Hours amendment to this new bill. The government threatened to resign if defeated and the amendment was lost overwhelmingly when the vote was taken on 13 May: so close and yet so far. Other matters occupied Ashley's parliamentary time over the next two years, lunacy, mines, and chimney sweeps. In 1846 he reintroduced a Ten Hours Bill and then, in a somewhat bizarre twist, resigned from the Commons because he had changed his mind on the repeal of the Corn Laws. It was ironic that the government of Robert Peel and James Graham should defeat the original Ten Hours proposal under threat of resignation, yet when Ashley came to support Peel's other legislation he resigned out of conscience in deference to his electorate. However, the die was cast and the Ten Hours principle was now increasingly widely conceded. Ashley was re-elected to the Commons in 1847 to represent Bath. In the meantime John Fielden piloted the Ten Hours Bill to its successful conclusion as the Factory Act 1847. It limited the hours of labour for those under eighteen to sixty-three per week from 1 July 1847 and fifty-eight per week from 1 May 1848 which, with a maximum of eight hours on a Saturday, effectively limited the working day to ten hours. The problem was that the Act permitted work between 5.30 a.m. and 8.30 p.m. and the dreaded "relays" reappeared. In 1850 Ashley promoted a compromise which provided for a working day of 6 a.m. to 6 p.m. with one and a half hours for meals – actually a ten-and-a-half-hour working day. The impact, however, was that for the first time ever there was a comprehensive restriction on hours of labour for all workers, regardless of age or gender.

CHAPTER 7

THE EMERGING PROTESTANT: 1838–1845

Shaftesbury's faith was built and expressed on the basis of Protestantism. He looked to the Bible and to the sixteenth-century Reformers as models and inspiration for his life. This historic manifestation of the Christian faith informed his beliefs, his actions, and his commitments. It was this point of view which determined his passion and involvement in the various voluntary missionary societies at the centre of his life. He was also closely connected to the concept of "national Protestantism", that particular outlook which saw the state as Protestant with a responsibility to maintain that position. Although Shaftesbury did not line up with the Ultra-Tory Protestants in every respect he identified with their position very closely. This group were among his most consistent supporters both in his social campaigns and in the missionary societies.

Politics and life

Ashley had prevaricated over the principle of Catholic emancipation in the late 1820s. It is then perhaps not entirely clear why he formed such a close identification with Protestantism. The decision to support Roman Catholic relief was essentially a pragmatic one. It was also one which caused yet another rift with his father. Ashley's Evangelical Protestantism grew through the late 1820s and 1830s. He began to link his basic Evangelical convictions to his adoption of premillennialism and his latent Tory Protestantism. This increasingly brought to the fore the role of the Protestant faith in the life of the nation. He expressed this in various attitudes and positions throughout his life, not least in his virulent opposition to Tractarianism – the high church alternative to Evangelical convictions – its doctrines, and increasingly its practices.

We have already seen, as early as 1833, while touring Europe, Ashley's critical response to many Roman Catholic practices. This would continue to inform his opposition to such forms of worship at home, whether within or outside the Church of England. Shaftesbury demonstrated a campaigning side to his Protestantism, not all of which sits easily with modern notions of toleration. Whenever he viewed the Reformed faith under attack or the Bible threatened by revisionists he leapt into action, which may not have always been the best response.

The period 1835–45 saw Ashley engaged in his campaigns on children in factories, mines and other industries, the beginnings of the campaign for the sweeps (see chapter 8), and his increasing involvement with voluntary mission societies. This was together with his continuing "behind the scenes" work on mental health reform. Amazingly he still found time and capacity for his family and personal life. Three more children were born in the late 1830s: Evelyn (1836), Victoria (1837), and Lionel (1838). In addition it is in this period that the campaigning Protestant side of Shaftesbury begins to emerge.

Ashley's diaries are a marvellous work. They consist of

numerous volumes of closely written text recording thoughts, ideas, emotions, and, of course, a good deal of the minutiae of family life. He had maintained the diaries sporadically from around 1825, including volumes dedicated to travel and religious thought. In late September 1838 Ashley resolved to resume his record with more determination and focus. His second entry records his meeting with the new Vice-Consul for Jerusalem. Ashley waxed lyrical about "the ancient city of the people of God".[1] Ashley, romantic though he was, always tried to earth his vision and his plans – he sent a small donation to the Vice-Consul for the support of Jewish converts to Christianity. The demands upon Ashley's life and his commitment is shown by his activities in the first part of October 1838. On 3 October he was at the Lunacy Commission for the conclusion of a three-day hearing, on 4 October he chaired a meeting of the Church Pastoral Aid Society – "Under God's good providence, this Society has wrought wonders" – and the same day saw the baptism of his youngest son, Lionel, who had been born that year. He recorded in his diary his hopes for his son's faith that "he may never be ashamed to confess, and to fight for, a crucified Saviour!" He noted also the "service abominably performed by the curate".[2] On 11 October he went to Windsor for a few days with the Queen. To Ashley this was a great honour and it shows the multiple relationships and links which he developed throughout his life. Some of these came from his upbringing and family connections, others from his faith commitments, yet others from his campaigning. He had great respect for both the monarchy and the Queen herself. He viewed her with the warmest affection and loyalty and praised her friendliness, hospitality, and good humour. He described the timetable of a typical day with the young Queen Victoria:

Let me see, the hours were ten o'clock for breakfast, unless it were preferred to breakfast in one's own room; two o'clock for luncheon; a ride, or a drive, at three o'clock for two hours or

so; dinner at half-past seven. A military band at dinner, and the
Queen's band after dinner, filled up, and very necessarily, the
pauses of conversation. We sat till half-past eleven at a round
table, and then went to bed.[3]

Ashley was, of course, ever watchful for any signs of deviation from the historic Protestant faith that he could detect among the bishops of the Church of England. When two bishops put their names to a volume of sermons associated with the denial of the divinity of Jesus, Ashley recalled the fourth-century originator of this particular heresy: "Were Arius alive now, he would be promoted to Canterbury."[4] Shaftesbury was always capable of polemic, especially of the Protestant variety.

Ashley was drawn into the ill-fated three-day administration of Sir Robert Peel in May 1839. The prime minister, Melbourne, resigned that month and on Wellington's advice the Queen turned to Peel. In the cauldron of court politics there was the particularly sensitive issue of the need to reconstruct the royal household to counteract the influence of Whig courtiers. Peel approached Ashley for help. He asked Ashley to take an office in the Queen's household because of the role he could play in Victoria's religious and moral development. Within three days Peel had resigned. Melbourne was back, seeking to persuade the Queen to include Tories in the government, or else too many concessions would be needed to the more radical elements of the Whigs.

In 1839 Ashley was clashing with the government over proposals that education grants should be distributed more widely – including to schools where Roman Catholic versions of the Bible were used (that is, versions which included the books known as the Apocrypha, not generally accepted as Scripture by Protestants). He tried to enlist Wellington, but the Duke, although supportive, was unwilling to campaign on the matter. Ashley attacked the measure in Parliament but the government's position prevailed.

Another travel diary was kept in 1839 as he travelled to and through Scotland with Minny and Antony. Upon reaching the shores of Lake Windermere Ashley noted his hopes for physical and mental refreshment for both himself and Minny. While away he read up on Thomas Fowell Buxton's account of the slave trade and he called on Robert Southey only to find that he was absent. Regretting that he might not see the Laureate in this world, Ashley recorded his gratitude and indebtedness to his writings and friendship. Southey was by now quite ill though he was not to die until 1843. Ashley praised the Presbyterian Church for its stance against popery and the importance it attached to the atonement. However, he lamented the domination of the minister in the conduct of worship. The party visited the castle in Edinburgh and enjoyed walks in the Scottish countryside. He noted that Minny reminisced of times and people past and of those who were growing old without, as he saw it, all the advantages of a pious faith. The journey continued and included more visits and suffering a robbery from their carriage. They saw the northern lights, enjoyed the wonderful scenery, visited churches and cathedrals, and were even entertained by Highland dance. By early September they had reached Inverness, with Ashley reflecting upon his encounter with Gaelic life and culture. At the end of September in Glasgow he visited a Blind School – describing blindness as the heaviest of God's visitations next to insanity. To the modern mind it remains odd to see such afflictions described in such a way, but to Shaftesbury, God was sovereign in all things – it stirred his sympathies but did not detract from his trust in God. The journey home took them via Northumberland, Durham, Ripon, York, and Chatsworth, then back to London on 9 October. The party had been absent for two months.

Shaftesbury was a people person. He was at ease with every level of society. He could visit, dine with and entertain monarchs and archbishops, yet never neglected to meet, encounter, and seek to understand the poorest sections of society.

Naturally, not all of Ashley's relationships were entirely positive. Most difficult was that with his own father. At the end of 1839 there seems to have been some reconciliation. For perhaps the first time Ashley noticed "sincere marks of kindness and affection!"[5] He praised God for the reconciliation with his father, since it would have been terribly sad had the latter died without making peace with his own son. In fact the sixth Earl would not die for more than a decade. Right at the end of the year, 16 December to be precise, Ashley's mother-in-law married Viscount Palmerston. This was another set of relationships which were to be of deep significance in Shaftesbury's life. On Christmas Day 1839 Ashley was at St Giles, in church, sharing holy communion and reconciled with his father. The estate, which he would in due time inherit, was a great love of Shaftesbury's. It would also be a great burden. On 31 December he was gardening.

In 1840 we see Lord Ashley sitting as a magistrate and, together with Minny, attending the wedding of Victoria and Albert. Ashley was also at this time lamenting his – in his own eyes – lack of achievement: "full of schemes and no accomplishments".[6] Even if it were true, which is doubtful, it was certainly premature. The details of Ashley's life work in parliamentary campaigning are told in other chapters. He mused, however, over the fullness of the agenda:

> My hands are too full, Jews, Chimney-sweeps, Factory Children, Education, Church Extension etc., etc. I shall succeed, I fear, partially in all, and completely in none. Yet we must persevere; there is hope... hope is displayed for the things of this world and the next.[7]

In 1841 he was invited to stand for election in Leeds (he declined), Melbourne's administration having lost a motion of confidence by one vote. He attended again upon the Queen – for Ascot. Ashley expressed his dislike of endorsing horse racing by his presence, but this was overridden by duty to and respect for the monarch. In June he received a honorary doctorate of letters from Oxford – surely a fitting tribute – but he recognized that his support and indeed his sympathies lay with the common people. On 6 July he was returned for the fourth time for the county of Dorset. Peel offered Ashley a place in the royal household – two years after a similar discussion. However, times had changed. Ashley always had a rather uneasy relationship with Peel. He was concerned about the factory question, that he was sought after simply because of his name, and that various other offers had been considered and rejected. Ashley was not immune from vanity concerning his appropriateness for high office, but was genuinely concerned to be allowed the freedom of his opinions and principles. He turned Peel down. Bickersteth wrote to him to commend his stand on principle rather than being seduced by the trappings of power and worldly honour. Bickersteth and Shaftesbury both represented a distinctively other-worldly spirituality and a practicality decidedly of this world.

The Jerusalem bishopric

The campaign for a bishopric in the holy city of Jerusalem was a symbolic objective of Protestantism in the 1830s and early 1840s. The campaign and establishment of the new see was a potent combination of national Protestantism and Evangelical revivalism. For the former, the bishopric was a symbol of Protestant pride, for the latter a sign of the return of Christ. Hence a religious aim became caught up with the established church, romanticism, prophecy, and the future of the Jewish people. Little wonder it attracted Shaftesbury's interest.

Lord Ashley mused over the question in his diary as early as 1838. He wrote, "Could we not erect a Protestant Bishopric at Jerusalem…?"[8] The notion of such a presence in the East had also been prominent in the aims of the London Society. This linked in with the expectation of Jewish conversion and the return of Christ. Such an idea received enthusiastic support from Frederick William IV of Prussia as part of his vision for united Protestant action. The Prussian envoy, Chevalier Bunsen, was quickly in touch with Ashley to try and formulate a plan for presentation to the British government. Ashley also referred to the objectives of the bishopric in an article he wrote for the *Quarterly Review* in 1838. In reflecting upon the prospects for the Jewish people, Ashley's rather romantic establishment Protestantism came again to the fore. He recalled the vision of a church on Mount Zion in Jerusalem, "where the order of our services and the prayers of our Liturgy shall daily be set before the faithful in the Hebrew language".[9] To an English Protestant of the established church, when Jesus returned, there was little doubt that he would want to do so to the accompaniment of the liturgy of the Church of England! Ashley reported in this article that a church was already established in Jerusalem and money collected to fund a building. The foundation stone was laid in February 1840.

The plan was for there to be a joint bishopric, partly funded by Prussia and partly by Britain with each power nominating alternating bishops. In 1841 Bunsen was in close touch with Ashley as the plans progressed and a bill was introduced to Parliament to establish the bishopric. Ashley was the intermediary, arranging a meeting between Bunsen and Peel, the prime minister. He described Bunsen's mission as "a wonder". Britain was to nominate the first holder of this historic post. The position was offered to Alexander McCaul, a prominent member of the London Society, but he declined. Rather, he suggested, the post should be held by a converted Jew. Bunsen later attributed to Ashley himself the suggestion of Michael Solomon Alexander. He was a former rabbi, a convert, a missionary with the London Society, and a Hebrew scholar. Ashley wrote to Frederick William praising the Prussian king's role. He also played a key part in settling the arrangements with the Archbishop of Canterbury, meeting Archbishop Howley with Bunsen. The bill passed on 22 September with Ashley filling his diary with praise the next day – and regretting that he had not recorded the details of the events.

The progress of events was not completely straightforward. The government in reality was lukewarm. The church hierarchy had been outmanoeuvred. The Puseyites, the high church Tractarians, were most unenthusiastic and now put pressure on the Bishop of London. Ashley complained of "the monstrosities of Puseyism",[10] and thought Dr Pusey's complaint that the Church of England would become protector of all Protestant communions to be an epitaph worth having. The essential complaint of the Tractarians was that the Church of England was cooperating with German Protestants rather than being reconciled to Rome. Ashley was also pressing Peel for government assistance in transporting Alexander out to Jerusalem. The prime minister was not enthusiastic. Alexander's consecration as bishop was postponed on more than one occasion. On 25 October Ashley reported in his diary that he had received a note from Peel that a naval ship would be provided. On 26 October Ashley noted with gratitude that some high churchmen, notably Archdeacons Samuel Wilberforce and Henry Manning, were supporting the bishopric. After all, it was a bishopric that was being established!

On 7 November Ashley attended the consecration of Michael Solomon Alexander. Services of celebration followed before Alexander (after refusing the first ship offered by the Admiralty) set sail for Jerusalem on 29 November. A Protestant project had been successfully completed. Two days after the consecration of Alexander, Ashley sent the new bishop's portrait and a book of prayers to Bunsen, inscribed as follows:

To my dear friend, Bunsen, the worthy minister of the best and greatest of the kings of this world, as a memorial of our solemn anxious, and by God's goodness, successful labours, which, under His grace, we have sustained for the consolidation of Protestant truth, the welfare of Israel, and the extension of the Kingdom of our blessed Lord. – Ashley.[11]

The Oxford Movement and Tractarianism

The Oxford Movement had its origins in the thinking, writing and spiritual practices of a group of prominent Oxford clerics. The key individuals were John Henry Newman, Edward Bouverie Pusey, and John Keble. The beginnings lay in John Keble's "Assize Sermon" in 1833 in which he objected to the state's interference in the life of the church. The occasion of the sermon was the Irish Church Temporalities Bill, a seemingly rather unusual vehicle upon which to launch a spiritual renewal movement. However, the bill concerned the suppression by the state of Irish bishoprics (because of the small size of the Protestant population). As well as the issue of what should happen to the endowments, it raised the whole question of the nature of the church and the role of the state. The group were also known as the Tractarians on account of the ninety tracts produced between 1833 and 1841 dealing with various matters of doctrine and belief – the "Tracts for the Times". More disparagingly they were often referred to as "Puseyites". The essence of the movement lay in the doctrinal and spiritual claims of a unified church, a spiritual church, a catholic church. Hence the movement sought to emphasize a more catholic understanding of the Church of England's foundation documents. That quest was like trying to square a circle. They placed more emphasis upon apostolic succession (continuity of bishops), catholic spiritual practices, the sacraments, and the place of tradition. As a consequence less weight was given to conversion, the Bible, the atonement, and the Reformation. To begin with the movement was largely concerned with thought, only later did the issues come to be played out more explicitly in matters of ritual and ceremony. Shaftesbury was in the forefront of the Evangelical response and resistance in both aspects.

Lord Ashley first joined the battle in 1841 as the tussle over the Tracts came to a head. A leading Tractarian, the Reverend Isaac Williams, was nominated for the vacant chair of the Professor of Poetry at Oxford. It is not entirely clear why anybody would think it appropriate to canvass Ashley for his vote in favour of Isaac Williams. However, he was approached by Roundell Palmer (Lord Selborne) and Ashley responded with some vigour. Ashley disputed that Williams could lay claim to be a moral teacher in a Christian university. The position sought would convey authority. Ashley pointed out that the candidate was the acknowledged author of Tract 80, entitled "Reserve in Preaching the Doctrine of the Atonement". The argument, though nuanced and complex, was given away in the title. Interpreting the doctrine of reserve positively, the idea being propounded by the Tractarians was that the atonement was a deep and mysterious matter that should be held back or reserved for the teaching of the baptized. Even if Evangelicals accepted the more charitable interpretations of the doctrine, for them, the atonement was a central and a converting ordinance. Ashley, after the courtesies, did not hold back.

There is no power on earth that shall induce me to assist in elevating the writer of that paper to the station of a public teacher. I see very little difference between a man who promulgates false doctrine and him who suppresses the true. I cannot concur in the approval of a candidate whose writings are in contravention of the inspired Apostle... I will not consent to give my support, however humble, towards the existence of exoteric and esoteric doctrines in the Church of England, to obscure the perspicuity of the Gospel by the philosophy of Paganism... [12]

Ashley was not going to vote for Williams. The matter may have rested there if the protagonist had not been Anthony Ashley Cooper. He was now approached to support the opposing candidate, the Reverend James Garbett. Not only did Ashley offer his support but he became the chairman of the committee established to secure his election. Ashley, perhaps not entirely helpfully, made clear that the issue of poetry was of secondary importance to religion in the

election. Ashley's letter to Roundell Palmer had been published
and battle lines on both sides were drawn up. Attempts were
made to avoid a contest, but to no avail. In late 1841 and early
1842 there was a friendly exchange of letters between Pusey and
Ashley. Ironically the two men were in fact, as noted previously,
cousins. Pusey pleaded with Ashley for a softening of language
and for greater understanding. Ashley's lengthy reply held nothing
back. He referred to the content of the Tracts and to Froude's
"Remains", and denounced the Church of Rome. Richard Hurrell
Froude had been one of the first Tractarians and after his death
in 1836 his journals and letters were published as his "Remains".
These revealed spiritual practices and a depth of austerity that
shocked Evangelicals and went far beyond the doctrinal debates
in the Tracts.

The outcome of the election in 1842 was that Williams withdrew
when he realized how far behind he was on pledges. Ashley and
the Protestant cause had been victorious in what was essentially a
doctrinal contest with the Oxford Movement. Other, even more
acrimonious battles, were yet to come.

The Tractarian struggle continued in various guises. In May
1843 Pusey was investigated after preaching a sermon at Oxford
and suspended from preaching for two years. Then in 1844–45
Keble demanded the revival of auricular confession (that is, to a
priest) as part of the discipline of the church. The Tractarians were
reaching crisis point. Pusey announced that he could not subscribe
to the Thirty-Nine Articles in their "natural sense". Back at Oxford,
Convocation (the University's parliament) was summoned to
condemn a book written by the Tractarian W. G. Ward. The point
was that Ward was in infringement of the requirements for his degree
by writing contrary to the Articles. Ashley attended the vote and
heard Ward indicate that he did not renounce one single doctrine
of the Roman Catholic Church. Ashley voted with the majority of
391 for censure and of 58 for deprivation of his degrees. Several
prominent high church advocates were now moving to Rome. This

was the ferment in which the debates about the grant to the Roman Catholic seminary at Maynooth took place to which we will turn shortly. In October 1845 Newman's forlorn attempt to reconcile the Church of England's plainly Protestant Articles with Roman doctrine finally unravelled. The inevitable decision was made and Newman converted to Rome. Others followed over the course of the next several years. They included Archdeacon Manning in the aftermath of the "Papal Aggression" (see chapter 8) and of the Gorham case – in which an Evangelical cleric was acquitted by the Judicial Committee of the Privy Council on matters related to baptism. However, not all went and those who remained included Pusey. The Oxford Movement itself now moved into its second phase. This was the adoption of ritual ceremonial and practice in churches of the Church of England. To that we will return.

Private life

A second daughter, Mary, was born in 1842. In 1843 Ashley was again travelling in Europe. Amid other demands on him he became involved in matters concerning education and also the odious opium trade. He described his own life along the lines of: late to bed and early to rise! In early 1844 Ashley and Minny decided that Antony should enter a school on the Isle of Wight. He noted in his diary, the anxiety of every parent, "Dear Antony is about to start school. I cannot bear to part with him; he is a joy to me."[13] Antony wrote to his parents while he was away; collecting him at the end of June, Ashley was delighted to find him well. He lamented the expense of taking Minny and three of the children with him, but noted that such occasions meant a great deal to children and praised the school. In August Ashley was back on the Isle of Wight for rest and recuperation with all the family – although there was a trip to London and also a visit to Parkhurst Prison on the island. He was troubled by what he saw. A few days later he was taking a relaxing walk by the seashore. He left the island to visit St Giles near the end of August taking just Antony with him. Referring to Mary he noted in his diary, "My heart misgave me as I saw baby straining her darling little face through the bars of the pier to get a last sight of us".[14] He committed them into the Lord's care. Throughout his life Shaftesbury demonstrated a deep and personal love for his family and children. For him there was no disconnection between his public and private lives. After the holidays he toured the factory districts and later in the same year visited Rugby to assess its suitability for his eldest child, Antony. He concluded favourably on the school, indeed in preference to Eton. The latter he feared was more concerned with refinement than truth. By the end of 1844 Ashley noted that relationships with his father had again broken down following a speech in Sturminster the previous year in which he emphasized the responsibilities of landowners – and criticized conditions in Dorset. His father was not amused.

Maynooth

Ireland and Roman Catholicism were two subjects which caused considerable angst for British governments in the nineteenth century. When the two controversial subjects were combined tension was heightened considerably. There is no surprise that the Earl of Shaftesbury was prominent in these matters.

The College of Maynooth was founded in 1795 in County Kildare in Ireland. Central to its purpose was the training of candidates for the Roman Catholic priesthood to serve Ireland's Catholic population. Previously ordination candidates had been trained on the continent. The British government had a vested interest in peace and good order in Ireland. Providing the Catholic population with priests from the seminary at Maynooth would contribute to good order – since they would be less under the influence of revolutionary France. A modest and uncontroversial grant was made to the College. In 1809 the level of the grant was fixed at £9,000 per annum and it remained at this level until 1845.

The Irish policy of Queen Victoria's governments was a combination of pragmatism and principle, though mainly the former. There was growing political unrest in Ireland in 1845, at least in part because of the failure of the 1844 potato crop. Peel wished to be conciliatory. The College of Maynooth was on a perilous financial footing. The building was in decay, the library was inadequate, and staff poorly provided for. In the Maynooth Bill the proposal was to increase the annual grant from £9,000 per annum to £26,000 per annum. An annual vote on the grant would no longer be needed. In addition a one-off sum of £30,000 was granted for repairs.

Protestantism protested. Ashley was in the vanguard of the opposition when the bill came for second reading in the House of Commons on 16 April 1845. He did not, however, go so far as one of the Ultras, Colonel Sibthorpe, who stated he would rather shave his head than forget he was a Protestant!

Ashley made clear he respected Roman Catholics as individuals and went out of his way to be moderate and conciliatory in his views toward his fellow members and citizens. He drew a distinction between Catholic emancipation (which gave Roman Catholic citizens freedom of action) and the Maynooth Bill (which gave state support to Roman Catholic principles). It was a coherent argument in many ways, except that the state had been supporting Maynooth since its inception, but not at the levels now proposed. The bill, he claimed, threatened the Protestant establishment. His main objection was that the Protestant Parliament of a Protestant state was endowing a Roman Catholic seminary. He had no objection to the Roman Catholics voluntarily supporting a college. He supported their right to do so, but not with government money in perpetuity. He claimed, not entirely justifiably, that the result was that the state was taking on the whole expense of educating the Roman Catholic clergy. He added, again with a degree of hyperbole, that the bill would mean that the principle was being conceded that "the Roman Catholic religion shall never cease to be the religion of Ireland".[15]

This was probably an exaggeration, but when it came to the defence of Protestantism, Ashley, like the Ultra-Tory national Protestants, was more than willing to exaggerate. It was not the role of the state to fill gaps in the funding of Catholicism. The same principle did not, of course, apply to Protestantism. Ashley also argued this was the thin end of the wedge. A grant to Maynooth would soon be followed, indeed inevitably so, by the endowment of the Roman Catholic priesthood. The link may not be entirely obvious to the modern mind. This would threaten the Protestant establishment in Ireland. It would mean that the Roman Catholic religion would be viewed as no longer dangerous, either spiritually or politically. The essence of the matter, of course, was that Ashley would continue to view Catholicism as a threat in both respects, even if he were the only person left on earth advocating that viewpoint. He described the impact as that of removing from the Church of Ireland its missionary character. He viewed Catholicism with such disfavour that the only possible response was evangelistic. He concluded his speech to Parliament as follows:

> Nor can I… assent to a measure conducing, in any degree, to suppress or even retard the advancement of the Protestant faith, which we believe, and may be allowed to assert without offence, to be a well-spring of civilization and happiness, of social and religious freedom.[16]

Ashley probably knew his spirited defence of Protestantism would fail. He said as much in his diary entry of 7 April. Here he also referred to the government's "haughty contempt of the deep, solemn Protestant feeling in the hearts of the British people! Can a statesman, ought a statesman, to force a measure, by dint of a legislative majority, utterly hateful to the great mass of the nation?"[17] Perhaps not quite as deep, nor quite as hateful as Ashley would have liked. The government won the vote by 323 votes to 176, carrying with it a small majority of the Tories voting on the night (158 to 145), but sixty-four Tories abstained. This led to a further round of agitation with the Evangelical constituency. Petitions poured in, sermons were preached, and the government was denounced. The bill progressed to the statute book. On 3 May Ashley, reflecting on his own independence of mind, noted that it was his "duty to resist the national and permanent teaching of that religion which was declared and established by the Council of Trent".[18] The Act remained in place until the disestablishment of the Irish church in 1868. Shaftesbury was not willing to wait idly for such a future event.

To finish the story, in 1853, knowing that Parliament would not repeal the grant, Shaftesbury was on his feet again, in the Lords, campaigning for an inquiry into the teaching at Maynooth. He was riding on the coat tails of the Ultra-Tory national Protestant the Earl of Winchilsea who presented petitions against the grant but then demanded an inquiry into the social and moral teaching at Maynooth and its implications. The aim was barely disguised. Winchilsea's speech was not conciliatory. Neither was Shaftesbury's but it may have been somewhat more moderate than that of Winchilsea. Or perhaps not: "thousands of persons in this country believed that a national endowment of Maynooth was a great and heinous national sin, and they wished to exonerate themselves from all participation in that public crime, and to be uncontaminated by yielding support to a system contrary to the Gospel and the Word of God".[19] This would appear on the face of it to go beyond the request for an investigation of the social and moral curriculum. In essence the charge was one of the college exceeding its remit and of providing a setting for sedition. In reality the national Protestants and their supporters wished to defend the Reformed faith against Rome in any way that they could. A commission was duly appointed, but the effect had been to sideline the anti-Catholic position, although that did not stop Richard Spooner MP sponsoring, and losing, a regular division on Maynooth in the Commons. Shaftesbury's attention turned to the challenges of Anglo-Catholicism within the Church of England.

CHAPTER 8

SWEEPS, SANITATION AND THE SABBATH: 1840–1851

The 1840s were a period of enormous activism for Ashley with numerous interests and campaigns competing for his time. Legislative campaigns for children in factories and mines, the Maynooth controversies, and continued work on mental health occupied his attention. Displaying an extraordinary capacity he also embraced new areas of concern in this period.

The sweeps

In the early decades of the nineteenth century the emotive issue of "climbing boys" was a symptom of the changing nature of society. The wealthier parts of society, including the new moneyed classes created by the Industrial Revolution, demanded that chimney flues be cleaned. So did the insurance companies. However, the process of industrialization had not yet proceeded to such a point that mechanization was fully possible. How were these narrow flues to be cleaned? The answer lay in young children. Although from 1788 master sweeps were not supposed to take apprentices under the age of eight, the narrowness of the chimneys meant the younger the better. Lord Shaftesbury commented nearly one hundred years later that the rich preferred not to ask how their chimneys were cleaned. Parents, culpable in selling their children to the sweeps, simply gave the employers the assurance they needed on the age of the child. Children as young as four, five, and six years of age were engaged in this terrible and miserable existence. Some children were stolen from parents or extracted from the workhouse. The incentives which were provided to combat the reluctance of the youngsters to climb the chimneys were cruel. As well as physical blows, pins were sometimes forced into the feet of a boy by the lad following behind, or straw was set alight in the hearth. The impact on physical health included deformities of the spine and of the knee and ankle joints. These conditions arose not only from having to climb the narrow flue but also from these young children having to carry heavy bags of soot, perhaps weighing twenty to thirty pounds, over long distances. Burns, sores, stunted growth, and disease were prevalent. Poor diet and lodging, harsh treatment, and the absence of any educational, religious or moral provision were other factors affecting the trade. Once a boy had become too big to climb the chimney he was discarded on to the street to be replaced by another. Girls were also sometimes employed.

Around 1817 the total number of master sweeps was in the region of 200 and the number of apprentices about 500. Some were reputable, at least in the context of the times. They employed boys within the law, aged from eight to fourteen. However, many were scurrilous and all seemed to have employed younger children for the narrower flues. Some of the narrowest flues were as small as seven inches square. The select committee which investigated in 1817 referred to one sweep spending six hours in a narrow flue at Goldsmiths' Hall in the City of London. The committee also noted the culpability of many sweeps in accidental deaths. One sweep was jailed after six-year-old John Hewley (or Hasely) was forced up a chimney on the shoulders of a larger boy and then pulled down violently by the leg on to the marble hearth, breaking his leg and dying a few hours later. There were numerous other cases of deaths by burning and suffocation. In addition many children got wedged or stuck in the flues and were injured, even if rescued alive.[1]

The campaign for regulation

Shaftesbury, as with his other campaigns, was not the first to take up the cause. As with the factory question there had been earlier, albeit ineffective, legislation. Unlike the employment of children in factories the question of the sweeps had benefited from a raised consciousness among the religious community. Early moral improvement societies included the Society for Bettering the Condition of the Poor and, more specifically, the Society for Superseding the Necessity of Climbing Boys. Both of these societies gained support from the Clapham Sect, including William Wilberforce.

An Act of 1785 restricted master sweeps to six apprentices with a minimum age of eight years old. It was widely evaded and attempts to strengthen the legislation all failed. Following the select committee report of 1817 a further amending bill failed at third reading in the House of Lords. In 1834 the minimum age of apprentices was fixed at ten years old and there were some restrictions introduced on the size of flues and ill treatment. However, there were no effective enforcement provisions.

In 1840 Ashley, in the midst of the Ten Hours campaign, was one of four speakers on a resolution introduced to the House of Commons by Fox Maule, the Under-Secretary for the Home Department. The aim was to prevent the employment of children as sweeps. Ashley's great friend and supporter, Sir Robert Inglis, noted that the principle of interference proposed was the same as had been the case with the slave trade. Ashley's contribution, his first on the subject matter, was short, though the longest of the speakers. He thanked the government. Ashley suggested that the condition of children employed in the factories was ten times better than those of the chimney sweeps. The fire insurance companies were adopting machines and he "trusted that the system of sweeping chimneys by children would shortly pass away, for it had led to more misery and more degradation than prevailed in any other Christian country".[2] Ashley's interest in the subject was clearly being kindled. At the committee stage, on 26 June, he commented that "he had no notion cruelties so barbarous could be perpetrated in any civilized country".[3] He added that he had personal knowledge of the employment of one child of four and a half and another of six as chimney sweeps. He added the characteristic moral tone by noting that twenty-three climbing boys were in Newgate prison for various offences. Child sweeps received very low wages and chimneys were often swept in the early morning, perhaps four or five a day, leaving plenty of time for the child sweeps to be roaming the streets. Ashley did not disclose where this personal knowledge came from. It may have come, as was so often the case, from the City Missionaries – whom we will consider in a later chapter – or from his own initiative. In his diaries he certainly recorded his anxiety about the progress of the bill, which encountered some opposition in the Lords, including criticism from Wellington and, unusually, Ashley's fellow Evangelicals. He was clearly involved in one explicit move to "buy out" a boy apprenticed to a sweep near to his house. The master sweep stood his ground but Ashley records both the ultimate success and, of course, his ultimate motive:

> ... the child will this day be conveyed from his soot-hole to the Union School on Norwood Hill, where, under God's blessing and especial, merciful grace, he will be trained in the

knowledge, and love, and faith of our common Lord and only Saviour Jesus Christ.[4]

The legislation of 1840 had been ineffectual in a number of ways and the practice of using child sweeps continued, generally unregulated. The continuation of the practice was highlighted by a famous case in 1847. John Gordon, a master sweep, was convicted of manslaughter in the case of seven-year-old Thomas Price. The sweep was responsible for cleaning the flues of the furnaces of a chemical works. The flue in question was just under four feet in depth and just nineteen inches wide. Two sweeps were in the flue, including Thomas Price, whose job was to collect the soot swept down to him by the other sweep and then empty it out of the flue. The soot caught fire and the sweeps came out of the flue. Gordon ordered Price back into the flue and hit him. The boy had difficulty breathing and was brought out again, this time having inhaled the soot. Gordon then beat the boy with a stick. He died soon afterwards. The boy's body was covered in burns and bruises, but the cause of death was suffocation.[5] The case illustrated the continued problems of the enforcement of the legislation. Following these revelations Ashley became the chairman of the Climbing Boys Society in order to campaign for further protection. The remainder of this campaign belongs to the period after his succession to the earldom. We will return to it later.

A clean city and a grateful people

The modern view of Victorian England is essentially romantic. Victorian Christmas traditions are celebrated as though they were instituted by Jesus Christ himself. Romanticism as an intellectual movement played a significant part in shaping Victorian life and thought. Shaftesbury is, in this respect, something of an enigma. In one sense he was an incurable romantic, looking back to the perceived perfection of rural and aristocratic England. On the other hand he was a realist. He did not shy away from difficult, practical, and perhaps even embarrassing issues that mattered a great deal to ordinary people. Sanitation and public health became a major focus for Ashley in his parliamentary career, especially from the late 1840s onwards. Water supplies and sewage disposal became the unlikely locus for philosophical debate as well as practical action. Ashley, the Evangelical Christian social reformer, met with Edwin Chadwick, the utilitarian bureaucrat and social reformer. Motivations were different, solutions were often shared. Ashley extended his concerns beyond the narrow matters of sanitation into a much wider concern for the provision of burial grounds, the state of housing, and the protection of dwellings from unscrupulous railway companies. The five years 1839–44 feel like the era of the report. Even within the confines of Ashley's own concerns, there were reports on the Hereford Asylum, the Children's Employment Commission, and the Lunacy Commission (which he chaired), as well as Chadwick's 1842 report on the Sanitary Condition of the Labouring Population. In addition to all of that Ashley was sponsoring legislation on factory reforms, chimney sweeps, and the issues of mental health.

Sanitary conditions

Edwin Chadwick was a prominent social reformer of the mid-nineteenth century. He had worked for and been influenced by the utilitarian philosophy of Jeremy Bentham. This concept was based around the idea of "the greatest happiness of the greatest number". Although attractive at first sight it was open to the tyranny of the majority. Nevertheless, Chadwick became a very prominent social reformer, though shorn of any Christian motivation. In 1834 he was appointed an assistant commissioner for the Commission of Enquiry on the Poor Laws, writing a large part of the report. This led directly to the reform of the Poor Laws. He became secretary to the Poor Law Commission. He was then asked to produce a report on the Sanitary Condition of the Labouring Population. This was published in 1842. The report, although not entirely at this stage understanding the mechanism and science of disease (believing much to be "airborne" rather than "waterborne") set out the appalling state of public health and sanitary conditions. The report appears to have passed Lord Ashley by (he was occupied with other things). However, the effect of the Chadwick report was not really felt until 1848 when a Public Health Bill was introduced. At this point Ashley began to take an interest that ran through the remainder of his parliamentary career.

London stank. The huge movement of population had brought with it large amounts of waste, human and animal, into a concentrated area. The census of 1841 showed there to be, officially, 1,945,000 people in London. Unofficially, of course, there were many more. In just fifty years the population had doubled. There were some sewers, ancient, rarely cleaned, and in disrepair. Few could cope with the increased demands. Animal dung contributed to the stench. Horses, cattle, pigs, and sheep were adding around 40,000 tons of dung to the streets every year. Some houses were connected to the old sewers; but at least 200,000 cesspits lurked beneath dwellings, full and overflowing, emptied for a shilling – for those who could afford it or even be bothered – by the night-soil men of the shadowy underworld of London. In the poorer homes the contents of the cesspit oozed and seeped through the floors. Chadwick's report of 1842 contained evidence from one London surveyor of finding night-soil (a suitably Victorian euphemism for human faeces) from overflowing cesspits three feet deep in two houses. Even the arrival of the water closet did not prevent the "great stink" of 1858 – the closets simply discharged into sewers which in turn emptied straight into the Thames. Poor ventilation in workshops, high death rates, piles and mounds of rubbish all contributed to the smell, as well as to the fear of disease. The report also drew attention to the common lodging houses – to which the Earl of Shaftesbury would subsequently turn his attention. These were lodging houses in London and other towns and cities which housed many of the poorest workers or sometimes vagrants in the community. Conditions were appalling. They also raised inevitable religious and moral questions with the sexes often sharing accommodation. One problem in sanitary reform in early- and mid-Victorian London and other cities was that authority and responsibility for various functions was so diffuse that it could only be described as chaotic. Chadwick made the point in his report that the key issues of drainage, sewage, and cleansing were matters that required the intervention of the legislature. The principle was the same as that which led Parliament to intervene to protect factory children and chimney sweeps.[6] Ashley's interest was being kindled; as early as 1841 he accompanied Dr Thomas Southwood Smith, a prominent utilitarian campaigner on public health, on a tour.

What a perambulation have I taken today in company with Dr. Southwood Smith! What scenes of filth, discomfort, disease! What scenes of moral and mental ill! Perambulated many parts of Whitechapel and Bethnal Green, to see, with my own eyes, the suffering and degradation which unwholesome residences inflict on the poorer classes. No pen nor paint-brush could describe the thing as it is.[7]

The Corn Laws

Before turning to Ashley's role in public health legislation the wider context of his life in the mid-1840s should be set. The question of the Corn Laws was illustrative of the changing nature of politics in the 1840s. The existing legislation was essentially protectionist, seeking to control the price of grain for the benefit of the landed interest. Ashley's position in Dorset depended upon the defence of this interest. Peel too, as a good Tory, had come into power in 1841 intending to maintain the tariff system of the Corn Laws. Peel switched his views first and so began the process of the Tory party's transformation into a party of free trade. Ashley, as with Catholic emancipation in the 1820s, followed, but rather reluctantly. In October 1845 Ashley acknowledged in a letter to his electorate that the Corn Laws were doomed. His prescription was to accept the inevitable but to advocate a gradual change. Ashley's position satisfied nobody. He acknowledged in his diary that he had offended both sides of the debate. His entry on 24 November 1845 reflected his self-pity. All groups he bemoaned were against him, politically and religiously. He saw only the future desertion of the working people and then, he lamented, "farewell any hopes of future usefulness".[8] Both Peel and the Whig leader, Lord John Russell, were now open converts to abolition – the impact of the Irish potato famine acting as an impulse to swift action. With the Tories divided, Peel resigned, but Russell failed to form a government and Peel returned. Peel's proposal was now for total abolition. Ashley was in a dilemma. As he noted, "if I were to vote for abolition, I should vote in a sense diametrically opposite to the sense of their hopes and views when they chose me as their representative".[9] He resolved that he had no option but to resign his seat on principle, notwithstanding the impact upon the factory legislation he was currently sponsoring. As he noted, "Nearly my whole means of doing any good will cease with my membership of Parliament".[10] A few days later he resigned. Freed from parliamentary responsibilities he set off on another tour of the factory districts. In March he received a unanimous address of grateful thanks for his services from the Free Church of Scotland. By June the Whigs under Lord John Russell were back in power.

Ashley was not someone to waste time while out of Parliament and turned his attention to two of the voluntary societies which were to play a particular role in his life over the next forty years – the Ragged School Union and the London City Mission. The story of these societies and Shaftesbury's involvement will be told as distinct episodes in his story in chapters 9 and 10. In 1843, attracted by an advertisement, Ashley was drawn into the orbit of the Field Lane Ragged School and subsequently, from 1844, of the wider Union. In late 1845 and early 1846 Ashley was a regular visitor to ragged schools. It was similarly near the end of 1845 that we see Ashley more explicitly involved with the work of the City Mission. After a further summer tour in Europe, Ashley returned in autumn 1846 to letters from Bath urging that he contest the next election for that constituency. The same year he was to be found supporting the new Evangelical Alliance although he did not have too many hopes for its practical success. Early 1847 saw Ashley involved in relief efforts for Ireland. He then responded positively to delegations from Bath and contested the 1847 general election. On 31 July he was returned at the head of the poll.

The Public Health Act and the Board of Health

In 1848 Ashley was back in Parliament representing Bath and Lord John Russell had become prime minister. The Ten Hours Bill had passed the previous year under the new Whig administration and the government was now much more sympathetic to Chadwick's proposals for public health. The proposed Public Health Act enacted Chadwick's Benthamite vision. The key proposal was the establishment of a central Board of Health together with formal responsibility for water supplies and drainage being given to local authorities. Ashley spoke in the Commons debate. Indeed, his rather different approach came out in his speech. His essential concern was the impact upon the working class, not least their ability to have a home in a clean sanitary condition, in which to bring up their families. This had two other direct impacts, one upon political order and the other upon moral character. Nothing could be further from Chadwick's utilitarian outlook. It was, at least in some respects, classic conservatism. Treat the workers well and good order will be preserved. The middle classes benefit from this through not only the lack of political discontent but also through lower levels of taxation. Law was not just to be negative but also positive and there was no existing provision which "could furnish to the working classes a pure, ample, and constant supply of water".[11] He quoted from both evidence presented to Chadwick's inquiry of 1842 and the subsequent Report of the Health of Towns Commission in 1844. Ashley had now presumably had time to read and digest this material. There was, as ever, also Ashley's concern for the moral and religious character of the working class. Poor living conditions quite simply led to immorality and vice. This was especially so where male and female shared the same room, sometimes even the same bed. This, he argued, was the common testimony of those on the ground – City Missionaries, Scripture Readers, and District Visitors.

The Public Health Act 1848 was the first piece of legislation with public health in its title. A General Board of Health was established and Ashley was appointed one of the three commissioners (unpaid, as was often the case for his appointments). The other two commissioners were Edwin Chadwick and Thomas Southwood Smith. Thus Evangelical Christianity met Benthamite utilitarianism. Southwood Smith had even carried out a controversial dissection of Bentham's body in 1832 (the dead must be put to good use for the benefit of everyone else). Ashley was the spokesman in Parliament and, not unexpectedly, was an active participant in the board. Upon acceptance, Ashley noted in his diary that it would "involve trouble, anxiety, reproach, abuse, unpopularity", yet in his own mind the sanitary question was, as he put it, "second only to the religious".[12]

The Act and the board had their problems, one of which was Chadwick and his rather obsessive centralizing tendencies. There was also a constant struggle with funding from the Treasury. A further issue with the Act was that it excluded London. Responsibility for London lay with the Metropolitan Board of

Works and the Metropolitan Commission of Sewers: though equally chaotic, in 1852 Joseph Bazalgette became the Chief Engineer. He was responsible over the next fifteen years for the incredible reconstruction of the London sewer system.

The 1848 Act had set up the board for five years. It had struggled to be effective, not least over burials and water supply. The former question was one of importance to Ashley but, as we shall see shortly, the board overreached itself.

Domestic life

1848 was the year of revolution, notably in France. On the domestic front the challenge was from the Chartists. Ashley displayed all his usual traits with his comment, "A Sanitary Bill would, in five years, confer more blessing and obliterate more Chartism than universal suffrage in half a century."[13] In April of the same year he was with the Queen at Osborne House, on the Isle of Wight, to discuss the condition of the working people. There and subsequently he negotiated the attendance of Prince Albert, the Queen's husband, at a meeting of the Labourers' Friends Society.

An eighth child, Constance, had been born in 1845. Two more, Hilda and Cecil, followed in 1847 and 1849 respectively. Ashley and Minny had ten children, six sons and four daughters. In 1848 he visited his second son, Francis, at Harrow, where he was doing very well. Then, in 1849, tragedy struck. In May 1849 Ashley received word that Francis was seriously ill. Visiting him at Harrow on 21 May Ashley found him no better. Francis asked his father to read from Scripture and they prayed together. The next day Ashley recorded in his diary that they read and talked much of the free and full mercy of God in Jesus Christ. Ashley and Minny shared the visiting and caring. On 1 June Francis died at the tender age of sixteen. This was particularly hard to bear: Ashley described the loss as irreparable and a calamity. He took solace only in the knowledge that Francis was in the hands of his saviour Jesus. Ashley poured out entry after entry into his diary over the coming days. "No pen, no tongue, can set forth the charms and perfections of that blessed boy", he wrote. He was "received into the embrace of his precious Saviour,"[14] "the record of his name will long be fragrant".[15] Francis was buried at Harrow on 7 June 1849. The impact of the events also sent Ashley himself into a downward spiral – "Two objects are constantly by day and night before my eyes: I see him dying, and I see his coffin at the bottom of the grave... the pain ceases, and then, begins anew." The effect, he noted, "was far deeper than was then felt".[16]

The following year, Ashley's great friend Edward Bickersteth died. He had been foundational in Ashley's religious and social development and his loss was deeply felt. A few months later Sir Robert Peel died after a riding accident.

Sunday Observance and the Post Office

Among the many pillars of Protestantism stood respect for the sabbath. Once again if the strictures of the Bible concerning sabbath observation came to be violated by national institutions the Protestant standard would be raised usually with Shaftesbury at the head. In late 1849 it became known that Sunday working was to be introduced to the Post Office. At present there was no Sunday working in London, although there was in the provinces, where Monday was the "rest day". Ashley wrote in his diary on 6 October 1849.

> This movement for increase of Sunday labour at the Post Office is terrible; it is the fruit of a self-seeking Mammon-serving spirit, and the more difficult to encounter as it is hypocritically based on a pretence of reducing the labour of the provincial offices. Have written earnestly to Russell, Grey and Clanricarde; answers very unsatisfactory; the answers of men, who, whatever they may believe of Scripture, have _no zeal_ for God's service.[17]

The new scheme of labour began on 20 November with Ashley praying the Lord would bring confusion to the exercise. The Protestant machinery, such as it was, moved into action. Meetings were held, petitions raised, and sermons preached. On 30 May 1850 Ashley presented a petition to the House containing 31,000 signatures from Manchester seeking the abolition of Sunday labour in the Post Office. He claimed that over 3,800 petitions had been drawn up and that it was reasonable to suppose that these contained or represented over 1,000,000 individuals. Ashley then moved a humble address to the Queen. This was a technique he had used before which enabled the petitioner to set out their case in Parliament by asking the Queen to take action. In accordance with the traditions of Parliament it would then fall to Her Majesty's government to respond. Ashley's overall strategy was to suggest that it was not necessary to introduce such provisions into London and that the provincial offices should also cease working on a Sunday.

Ashley claimed that no other subject had ever generated more excitement or intensity in the public mind. This seems rather unlikely, and he was prone to making such claims whatever the matter under debate. He claimed that the issue went across normal political, class, and religious divides. He suggested that the case could be argued on grounds of religion, justice, and impact upon the community. This shows how Ashley, narrow as he was when it came to the interpretation of Protestantism, was able to recognize important arguments which affected wider society irrespective of the religious agenda. The crux of the petitions of the business community was that Sunday labour in the London Post Office was not necessary. A day of rest from labour it was argued was of inestimable benefit for the labouring classes and the religious obligations of the sabbath applied to all sections of the community. The objective was the prohibition of the collection, delivery, and transmission of letters on a Sunday. The benefit was not just to the relatively small numbers employed in the Post Office but to a much wider constituency of those forced to undertake business against their will on a Sunday. Ashley argued that the sabbath was God's wonderful provision for humanity. Worship and rest were divine mandates. He also appealed to justice: the House was seeking to impose on others what it did not expect of itself. He was also concerned about overwork and its effects, even premature death. Many workers also gave themselves to divine charity on the sabbath by working in Sunday schools. He concluded by saying:

> ... he could not repress the expression of his strong feeling of the immense goodness and wisdom of God in the institution of this period of returning rest, and of the immense injustice of those who would refuse the participation of it to their fellow-creatures... No new law was asked for, no restriction upon the freedom of the enjoyment of others, nothing that could in the least interfere with any privileges, rights, liberties, immunities; but simply that the power be given to these sons of toil to enjoy, if so disposed, the opportunity of observing the law of their God, and of "remembering the Sabbath-day that they might keep it holy."[18]

Ashley's address was approved by 93 votes to 68.

Ashley had little hope that action would be taken. Then, most unexpectedly, Russell, the prime minister, announced that Ashley's proposal would be adopted and for three weeks the London Post Office was closed and the Sunday post stopped throughout the kingdom. This time there was a torrent of letters and petitions complaining of the inconvenience, all because, as Ashley wrote, "certain aristocratic people will not have their gossip in the country every Sunday morning".[19]

On 9 July he rose again in the Commons to protest against the proposed rescinding of the closure order. The main objection seemed to be "inconvenience", and Ashley wanted to know precisely what inconvenience it was that resulted from the closure of the Post Office. He repeated his claim that, although a religious issue for some, the main thrust was justice for those employed. The government instituted an inquiry. The inevitable result was the re-establishment of Sunday labour in the Post Office.

So Shaftesbury the campaigning Protestant needs to be set alongside Shaftesbury the social reformer. Perhaps ironically to modern sensibilities it was the combination of these two elements which gave Shaftesbury's ideas about mission, social reform, and national responsibility some of their fire-power. He was not beyond compromise but he was also utterly consistent in the application of his beliefs to all aspects of national and personal life. He did this beyond personal ambition and popularity. Even if not all his judgments were ideal, he showed a complete disregard for his own position and career in advancing the cause of Protestant Christianity.

The Papal Aggression

A further matter of concern to the Protestant constitutionalists running in the immediate aftermath of the controversy over Sunday labour was the so-called "Papal Aggression". These events together amounted to perhaps the last coherent campaign of anti-Catholicism in England. Shaftesbury actively campaigned for the Protestant position.

In the autumn of 1850 Pope Pius IX issued a papal bull. In this declaration the Pope transferred the administration of the Roman Catholic Church in England and Wales from vicars apostolic to a new episcopal hierarchy. There were to be two archbishops and twelve bishops, each with clearly demarcated territorial districts. Significantly the new prelates were to carry territorial titles to match their jurisdictions. Lord Ashley's initial response was moderate, describing the decision as audacious, irritating, and proof of Rome's ambitions, but probably not worth a fight. However, matters soon took a turn for the worse. The Pope appointed Nicholas Wiseman as the Archbishop of Westminster and made him a cardinal. Wiseman issued a pastoral letter which talked about Catholic England being restored to its orbit in the ecclesiastical firmament. Russell saw this as a chance to strike against the Tractarians – the pro-Catholic party in the Church of England. He wrote to the Bishop of Durham denouncing the Pope's decision as amounting to a claim of sovereignty over church and state inconsistent with the supremacy of the Queen, never mind the rights of bishops and clergy. Linking the Pope's actions to the threat of Tractarianism aroused Ashley from his slumber. Less than two weeks after his initial measured response Ashley was up in arms. On 5 November 1850 Ashley referred to the deep and extensive feeling in the country against the Papal Aggression. He praised Russell's rather unexpectedly stringent letter to the Bishop of Durham. Protest meetings were held and petitions drawn up. The mood was darkening. Ashley returned from Edinburgh to London to chair a conference of clergy and laity on the matter. He was reporting in his diary on 25 November that the national anthem was being demanded three times in theatres. A large public meeting was held on 5 December, Ashley in the chair, to protest against what was described as the insolent and insidious attempt of the Bishop of Rome to advance the cause of Catholicism.

Two currents flowed together which prompted this reaction. First, the use of territorial titles (such as Archbishop of Westminster) was seen by the national Protestants as a claim to sovereignty. Second, the actions of the Pope were seen as an aggressive reassertion of Roman Catholicism. On both political and religious grounds Ashley joined the cause. Ashley's speech to the December public meeting was hair-raising. He had moved a long way from that initial diary entry. He described the Pope as a "foreign priest and potentate", usurping the Queen's sovereignty. If the matter of titles were of such little importance, why were the Roman Catholics insisting upon their adoption? He went on to say, "Mark the true reason: the Romish Church claims sovereignty and jurisdiction over every baptized soul." Indeed, in respect of territorial titles he added, "to call himself Archbishop of Westminster is to assert the whole spiritual sovereignty of the district and demand its subjection to the See of Rome". He went on, "We wage no war with the Roman Catholics of these realms, but we wage interminable war against the Pope and his Cardinals." Then, in a warning of the campaigns to come within the Church of England:

Let us turn our eyes to that within, from Popery in flower to Popery in the bud; from the open enemy to the concealed traitor; from the menace that is hurled at our Church, to the doctrine that is preached from our pulpit; from the foreign assailant, to the foes of our own household.[20]

Tractarianism, according to Ashley, had encouraged the aggressive actions of Rome. Leading lay Roman Catholics made public assertions of loyalty to the crown. The Queen's Speech gave notice of a government bill to prevent the assumption of ecclesiastical titles in respect of places in the United Kingdom.

In the Commons on 10 February 1851 Ashley was able to give his set piece speech on the issue. The essence of the argument was the jurisdictional claims implied by ecclesiastical titles. It was a matter of civil and religious liberty which affected all citizens, even Roman Catholics. The move, he claimed, was not necessary for the protection and development of Roman Catholicism – their rights were fully protected under the 1829 Emancipation Act. It was perfectly possible for the new episcopate to exercise spiritual functions without the territorial title. It would be better for Cardinal Wiseman to call himself Archbishop of the Roman Catholics of Westminster. The title Archbishop of Westminster implied a jurisdictional claim over all of the citizens of the area. Indeed Wiseman had claimed in his Appeal that Rome would not countenance any restriction on its jurisdictional claims. Ashley also argued that the move was not consistent with the civil and religious liberties of the people. We could not have, he claimed, a bishop undertaking synodical action, issuing decrees and canon law from the heart of the metropolis, effectively establishing an ecclesiastical empire. He argued that the Pope's measure was ill-advised because it placed English Roman Catholics in the unenviable position of choosing between Rome and allegiance to the constitution. He claimed that there would have been uproar across Europe if the Queen had divided Rome into districts each under a Protestant bishop to serve her subjects in those lands. He then, as he had done before, linked the external threat to the internal.

A revised version of the bill, before the House in March 1851, gave Ashley another opportunity. Again he drew a distinction between the Roman hierarchy and Catholic citizens. He was clear, however, that the Pope's recent actions were a violation of both law and sovereignty. It was his duty to protest against it. The bill tottered on toward the statute book, whereupon it was entirely ignored and repealed twenty years later.

The dead

London generated around 52,000 corpses a year. Their disposal was an issue for both decency and health, particularly in the case of the poor. The churchyards attached to parish churches were simply unable to cope with the vast increase in demand. There were some stories, which may have been apocryphal, of the mass burial of the dead in open graves. The burial industry was generally controlled by private burial companies. These companies set the fees, encouraged elaborate monuments, and generally failed adequately to respond to the needs of the less well off. Nothing was to prevent the interment of the dead from turning a profit. The Metropolitan Interments Bill 1850 was designed to empower the Board of Health to buy out the cemetery companies, close graveyards, regulate fees, and to establish the principle of extramural interment. This literally meant "outside the walls", and in practice was the catalyst for the move to large new burial grounds outside the main populated areas of London. Ashley pressured for these to be no more than a mile or two outside the city so as to reduce the costs of travel to the poor. The proposals generated some heat because of pent-up resentment against Chadwick's centralizing policies at the Board of Health. Ashley praised Chadwick's work and maintained that the chaotic nature of London parishes meant that they would be unable to achieve either economically or efficiently the necessary work under the Act. The matter, including that of ensuring that excessive costs did not fall on working people, could only be achieved by working on a larger scale. A strong and independent central authority was needed that was accountable to Parliament. The problem was that not all agreed that the Board of Health could or should be this responsible body. Shaftesbury denied later in the Lords that the Board of Health had wanted this particular responsibility.

The bill contained provisions for the cemetery companies to be bought out. Indeed after the Interment Bill had passed into law the board served compulsory purchase orders on the Brompton and Nunhead cemeteries. Two insurance companies refused to loan the board money, uncertain of its future existence, and the Treasury was unaccommodating. Its monopoly on the Metropolitan area was then challenged by the London Necropolis Company which sought to open a new cemetery just outside the boundary of the Metropolitan burial district. Competition was uncomfortable. The board had gone too far, committing to purchase without the funds. There was a good deal of haggling over the price with the two cemetery companies, but arbitration produced rather a good deal for the board. The funds for these, but no other cemeteries, were authorised in new legislation in 1851. In order to achieve its purposes the London Necropolis Company had to sponsor a private bill through Parliament. Shaftesbury unsuccessfully opposed the bill on second reading on the grounds of the poor financial prospects, the arrangements for transport of corpses, and the use of a common grave for pauper funerals. He objected to what he described as private speculation in the burial of the dead.[21] Shaftesbury also complained about the distance of this cemetery – Brookwood, near Woking – from the metropolis itself.

Throughout the 1840s Ashley was closely connected with two voluntary mission agencies through which he exercised much influence and involvement with both Christian evangelism and social reform. To these two organizations, the London City Mission and the Ragged School Union, we will now turn.

WALKING THE METROPOLIS: SHAFTESBURY AND THE LONDON CITY MISSION FROM THE 1830s TO THE 1880s

The idea of a City Mission was one that accompanied industrialization. As large populations gathered in urban centres, Evangelical Christians sought new ways to bring the message of Christianity to the populace. This chapter reviews the history of the London City Mission, Shaftesbury's links to it over a period of some forty years, and the challenge of social welfare.

Origins and aims

The London City Mission was formed on 16 May 1835. The

founders set out the objectives:

> *The object of this Society shall be to extend the knowledge*
> *of the Gospel, irrespective of peculiar tenets in regard to*
> *church government, among the inhabitants of London and its*
> *vicinity (especially the poor) by domiciliary visits for religious*
> *conversations and reading the Scriptures, by meetings for prayer*
> *and Christian instruction; by promoting the circulation of*
> *the Scriptures and religious tracts; by stimulating to a regular*
> *attendance on the preaching of the Gospel; by increasing*
> *Scriptural education; by the formation of loan libraries; and by*
> *the adoption of such other measures as the managers may judge*
> *important, in order to attain the designs of the Society.*[1]

It was also laid out that the society would employ paid personnel, who had to be Evangelicals who showed evidence of personal piety. The metropolis was to be divided up into districts with the purpose of bringing the inhabitants to "an acquaintance with salvation through our Lord Jesus Christ and of doing them good by every means in your power".[2] A journal was to be kept and six hours a day spent in visiting.

The objects have been fully laid out as they illustrate the issues which the society would face and indeed Shaftesbury's engagement with the LCM over some four decades. The motivation was essentially spiritual. The second annual report, in 1837, declared that the "one great object is, to win souls for Christ".[3] Education also appeared but only in subservience to the religious principle. The question that dogged the Mission throughout its existence, was the place, if any, which was to be accorded to the social welfare of inhabitants – the question of "temporal relief" as it was known. The means were to be divine rather than human. What this meant in practice was that the activities and organization of the society was to be based upon faith and prayer rather than patronage and wealth.

A key feature of the City Mission was home visiting ("domiciliary visitation"). In its second year the society's agents made nearly 210,000 visits. Although the explicit aim was conversion the visits of the missionaries "brought to light some horrible instances of human depravity".[4] It was inevitable that some tension would emerge between the spiritual objectives of the society and the experience of the missionaries on the ground as they encountered London's poverty. The sanitary, housing, and social conditions of the poor were constantly before the eyes of the missionaries. Reports on common lodging houses included: "I have seen beds so extremely dirty that they would hardly be fit accommodation for pigs; and the stench of the room is perfectly intolerable."[5]

One missionary commented somewhat poignantly on the sanitary state of housing by noting in respect of one landlord: "Although he receives enormous rents, he will not be at the expense of having water in any of his houses."[6] Another missionary probably overstepped his brief by commenting on the low wages, long hours of work, and poor housing conditions of the silk weavers in the Spitalfields district. It is easy to see how the experience of the missionaries on the ground was able to feed the evidence gathered by the Earl of Shaftesbury for his speeches and campaigns.

The City Mission operated on three basic principles. The first of these was that of "catholicity". This meant that the Mission focused on its universal mission across denominations. Its aim was to unite Evangelicals whether or not they belonged to the Church of England. An early magazine put it rather well. The London City Mission was not a denominational institution on the grounds that "the Redeemer never meant that a perishing world should wait for its salvation, until the Church has reached that general unanimity which, it is generally admitted, cannot be found on this side of eternity".[7] Wise words then as well as today, these sentiments would prove deeply attractive to Shaftesbury. The principle was well summed up in 1843 by Edward Bickersteth, the Anglican clergyman who had so deeply influenced Shaftesbury's own theological development:

And it ought to be a joy of heart to real Christians, that
Christians of different denominations should unite together,
and spend their strength, not in fighting with each other…but in
united works of brotherly love for the salvation of the souls of our
fellow-men.[8]

In practice this meant that differences over doctrine, church government, and the sacraments were treated as secondary in the light of the united mission.

The second guiding principle adopted by the City Mission was that of "lay agency". What was meant by this was that the society would employ paid lay people to carry out its work. This again was to prove highly appealing to Shaftesbury. The aim was to employ agents who lived among and identified with the very people whom they visited, taught the Scriptures and prayed with. The task of making Jesus known to the poor was beyond the capability of the clergy not least because of the size of the parishes and their populations. The Bishop of London's response to the size of population was to build more churches – Baptist Noel, a prominent Evangelical, commented in 1837 that "the erection of those churches was no security that they would be filled".[9] The missionaries of the society were to go to those very places where no one else went.

The third principle for the society was that its aims were purely spiritual and no social welfare relief was to be offered by the missionaries. This led to considerable tension and soul-searching. The committee of the London City Mission proved themselves to be unprepared for, and largely unable to deal with, the response to the social needs of the populace by many individual missionaries on the ground. From the beginning the City Mission considered it appropriate for the missionaries to direct those in need to other agencies, but not to intervene themselves. As early as 1839 the question of the relationship of the missionaries to the provision of temporal relief had gained the attention of the General Committee. The position adopted was to warn against confusing the spiritual and social relief messages, as the former could be compromised. In other words individuals might accept the Christian gospel message only because it opened the door to relief of poverty. The committee reiterated that those in need could be pointed in the direction of others. The practical problem was pointed to by the Bethnal Green missionary, in respect of a woman he was visiting: "He dared not to direct her to the Saviour as the bread of life, until he had first saved her from starving, by furnishing her with the bread that perisheth."[10]

This was a clear breach of the rules, yet openly reported in the society's *Magazine*. That was in 1845. In 1851 the committee rejected cooperation with the Leicester Square soup kitchen. In 1861 one missionary, J. M. Catling, was summoned before the General Committee when he wrote to *The Times* to thank a philanthropic society for a supply of bread and coal tickets (that is, vouchers) for the relief of the poor on his district. Catling argued that the extraordinary temporal distress at the time in the district required an extraordinary response. The committee temporarily suspended the ban on temporal relief only to reimpose it fifteen days later. The tension was unbearable. The issue arose again in 1867 and 1868 – the committee acknowledging that the rules had come to be generally flouted. The basic principle was, however, repeated. Missionaries were not to engage in temporal relief. Some missionaries queried whether their wives might administer such relief. In 1870 the South-East London Committee asked for a relaxation of the rules, breaches of the which in Bermondsey were noted, including helping with a soup kitchen.

Shaftesbury and the City Mission

Shaftesbury's relationship with the London City Mission shows how he was able to link his voluntary evangelistic work, his passion for social welfare and his campaigns in Parliament. Unlike many of the other societies with which Shaftesbury was connected, the City

Mission, in accordance with its faith principles, had no patronage from the great and the good as Presidents and Vice-Presidents, and so he never occupied a formal position within the society. His connection grew from the 1840s onwards. He was an occasional speaker at the annual meeting but he developed particularly strong relationships with a number of individual missionaries.

Shaftesbury was an advocate of the two major principles upon which the London City Mission was founded – Evangelical catholicity and lay agency. The former would bring great benefit to the masses of the metropolis. Shaftesbury told the LCM that he wished for "more union between the Church of England and Dissenters".[11] It was a theme that marked out his beliefs. His overriding concern for the welfare of the ordinary working people led Shaftesbury to demand united action on their behalf beyond any denominational differences. There was, in short, a greater purpose of mission.

The City Mission's mode of operation also appealed to Shaftesbury. "I love the aggressive principle," he said in 1879. What he meant by that was the way in which the missionaries sought out the poor and despised, so often passed over by others. He pointed out that the City Mission was no armchair society, but actively hunted out those in need of the message. He thus endorsed systematic district visiting, what he described as "your perpetual activity", at all times, night and day, domiciliary visiting, and allocating missionaries to special interest groups such as the cabmen.[12] The force of home visiting was that it was an individual encounter, "carrying the Gospel to men's hearts from house to house, from heart to heart, from man to man, from soul to soul, from individual to individual".[13]

Shaftesbury was equally committed to the Mission's use of lay agents in its work. To the June 1848 annual meeting he said: "I do value this Society, because it affirms one great and indispensable principle in these days; it affirms the principle, the invaluable principle, of lay agency.[14]

To Shaftesbury this principle was a key tool for engaging the gospel with contemporary culture and society. The practice, he indicated, was essential to gain access to the dens and alleys of London. Not only were these representatives of the mission, "living agents", but many of them were drawn from the very ranks of those they were enlisted to serve – essentially the principle of incarnation.

Shaftesbury acknowledged none of the tensions that the City Mission committee saw between evangelistic mission and social welfare. He unashamedly stated that the operations of the London City Mission had social, religious, and political aspects. The social features concerned the Mission's work in education and moral improvement. The political element of the work was that the Mission touched people beyond the pale of civilized society. Shaftesbury told the 1879 annual meeting that the City Mission penetrated the deepest and darkest holes in London, against whose overcrowding, lack of clean air and water, and degeneration he had protested all his life:

> ... you will fail altogether so long as the domiciliary condition of the people of London and in our great cities is allowed to remain what it is. What hope can you have of religion and decency when you have, as I have seen, three or four families in a single room? In such circumstances you have everything destructive to the body and soul of man coming with redoubled force upon these unhappy people. [15]

As early as 1848 Shaftesbury had made this point about the dual concern for the temporal as well as eternal welfare of the people. Shaftesbury saw then "that great associations such as this send forth these men, day by day, and hour by hour, for no purpose whatever but their temporal and eternal good".[16] But not so according to the Committee.

It was the compelling evidence of the circumstances of the poor of London that led to Shaftesbury's emphasis on the social as well as the spiritual. The Evangelical based their relationship with God on the idea of the experience of a personal relationship; so also it was the experience of the conditions of the metropolis that generated Christian concern for others created in the image of God. So Shaftesbury was able to call for "prayers to the advancement of God's honour and the welfare of their fellow-creatures". He was able to see the missionaries as a great body of men, "well instructed, well armed, and well determined to promote the physical and the religious welfare of this vast and seething people".[17] He had earlier described the City Mission "as a manifest and undeniable proof of the practical spirit of Christianity".[18] The City Missionary was in a unique position to watch for and counteract the rise and progress of evil, be it physical or spiritual.

So we have seen how the Earl interpreted the objectives of the London City Mission in a somewhat different way from that of the General Committee. How was Shaftesbury able to maintain his own commitment to the Mission in the light of these different emphases? The crux of the answer lies in the fact that Shaftesbury's principal relationships were with the individual City Missionaries rather than a formal relationship with the General Committee. Indeed, John Weylland, a friend of Shaftesbury and supporter of the City Mission, noted that it was through several of the early missionaries that Shaftesbury was drawn into the organization's orbit. Many of the missionaries shared Shaftesbury's view on temporal relief but the absence of formal patronage structures seems to have insulated Shaftesbury from some of the tension. Indeed, when he did hold a formal position in a society, Shaftesbury felt bound by its policies. At different times he offered to resign as President of both the Church Pastoral Aid Society and the Bible Society over policy differences. Both offers were refused.

A significant amount of the evidence gathered by Lord Shaftesbury for use in his campaigns for social reform was gathered in cooperation with the missionaries of the London City Mission. At the opening of the LCM's new mission house in 1874, Shaftesbury recalled that the first intimation of the scandal of the lodging houses was given to him by a City Missionary. The evidence which he presented to the House of Commons, "came entirely from the labours of the London City Mission".[19] As Lord Ashley, he told the 1848 annual meeting that:

> *I ought to stand forward at this emergency, and declare what I have seen and heard in my many peregrinations through the dens and recesses of this metropolis in company with your admirable and devoted missionaries.*[20]

He expresses it more personally, and very powerfully in an introduction he wrote in 1881 for a book by Weylland.

> *My experience of their value dates back over half a century. In all the operations in which I have been engaged, these men were my companions and fellow-labourers, and I derived unbounded assistance from them in the matter of Ragged Schools, Common Lodging-Houses, Special Services, and in every effort for the improvement of Society… In all difficulties of research, our first resource was to the City Missionaries, because we knew that their inquiry would be zealous and immediate, and their report ample and trustworthy.*[21]

These are moving and humble words. They build further upon the link of the legislative campaigns and the voluntary societies. They also illustrate and expand the connection of evangelism and social reform. They show the debt which Shaftesbury owed to the missionaries, his own skilful use of the material, but also the long-term impact of the Christian urban missionary upon the improvement of society.

Two names featured regularly in Shaftesbury's connections with the missionaries, Thomas Lupton Jackson and Roger Miller. Speaking at the Mansion House in 1881 Shaftesbury referred to his long association with Jackson and his work among thieves. He noted that Jackson had been concerned for both their eternal destiny and also their present condition. In 1848 as Ashley he had sponsored a bill in the House of Commons to facilitate emigration, the aim being to assist felons and others who sought a reformed life to start afresh. Modern critics, of course, would dismiss such efforts as shifting the problems out of sight and out of mind. However, in the context of the time, nothing could be further from the truth. Thomas Jackson arranged a meeting for London's thieves at which Lord Ashley addressed them on the issue of emigration. Over three meetings some 394 individuals were present, all of whom had been in prison for theft. Shaftesbury may indeed have been a paternalist but he was no armchair politician. His heart was genuine in its desires for both the eternal and social welfare of those in need. The idea of an English aristocratic member of Parliament being led to a secret meeting with felons in the heart of the London slums by a City Missionary may seem romantic, but in reality was a courageous, practical, and tough response to need. Jackson was quite explicit at these meetings that he too was concerned with both their eternal and temporal welfare. Ashley and Jackson cooperated closely over the emigration scheme, but it remained outside the official sanction of the City Mission. After Jackson's death the obituary notice in the London City Mission *Magazine* noted that Jackson "was regarded with especial favour by Lord Shaftesbury".[22] The Earl frequently visited Jackson and his work, sometimes even unannounced.

Roger Miller died in a railway accident in 1848 and at the City Mission's annual meeting of that year Ashley stated the he had "lived with him on terms of intimacy and friendship; I may say, that day by day, and night by night, we have perambulated the places of which you have been hearing".[23] Weylland noted also that Ashley, "even visited with him upon the district, and made use of the information he gained in the House of Commons".[24] After Miller's untimely death, Ashley appealed through the letters column of *The Times* for adequate provision for his wife and family. Miller had been instrumental in inaugurating a ragged school. Ashley had presided at the meeting and later entertained the missionary and school teachers at his own house. Miller, like Shaftesbury, was closely associated with the ragged school movement and responsible for one of Ashley's first formal connections with the City Mission. This was in 1845 when Ashley presided at the fourth annual meeting of the Broadwall Ragged School in South London. Ashley had heard of Miller's achievement's in gathering together 130 in a ragged school – and a lifelong friendship ensued.

The ragged school movement originated with the City Mission around 1840, though the Mission subsequently declined to adopt the venture as part of its official work. This may have been because of the explicit dual aims of the ragged schools, both spiritual and social. Nevertheless, the City Mission always indicated its general support and many of its missionaries remained closely involved. Ashley, at the 1848 annual meeting of the City Mission, said "whenever you enter a Ragged School, remember this – we are indebted for nine-tenths of them to the humble, the pious, the earnest City Missionary".[25]

These personal links with the missionaries were very influential on Shaftesbury. Cooperation with the City Mission was an important mechanism for Shaftesbury to expound and practise his understanding of mission. This is the case notwithstanding that in some aspects of this concept of mission the General Committee stood against one of their most prominent advocates. The City Mission's Evangelical catholicity and principle of lay agency appealed deeply to Shaftesbury's own position. The role of the missionaries in supplying evidence for his parliamentary work as well as active cooperation on the ground in the range of missionary activities is a key factor in understanding the seventh Earl of Shaftesbury

EDUCATING THE POOR: SHAFTESBURY AND THE RAGGED SCHOOLS FROM THE 1840s TO THE 1880s

The name seems rather quaint and old fashioned. The title "ragged" would be an unlikely choice today. However, this should not distract us from the impact of this movement in Victorian England. Shaftesbury was associated with the ragged school movement for over forty years. In practice it represented the principal way in which he expressed his commitment to Christian social welfare on the ground. His passion and compassion for those neglected by society shines through. The work was not without its difficulties and disappointments. Shaftesbury's rather romantic outlook undoubtedly overestimated the impact that these schools could have in an increasingly secular as well as industrial society. The rapid decline, even collapse, of ragged schools following the Education Act of 1870 (which introduced compulsory state education) was a real blow to Shaftesbury. Indeed that particular piece of legislation is a significant milestone in seeking to understand the loss of Evangelical vision for society after that date.

Origins and aims

In the period up to 1870 there was spasmodic provision of schooling by various charitable societies. The particular problem which the ragged schools sought to address was the education and welfare of children from the lowest echelons of society. Very often, because of their appearance, general condition, and clothing these children were excluded from the charity schools. Many of the early ragged schools came into existence through the offices and efforts of individual City Missionaries. The question which arose was how to give some framework, coherence, purpose, and meaning to the ragged schools as a whole. On 11 April 1844 forty people gathered in order to give "permanence, regularity and vigour to existing Ragged Schools and to promote the formation of new ones throughout the metropolis".[1] The finalization of the matter was postponed pending consultation with the LCM. The City Mission confirmed that it did not wish to take the ragged schools formally under its wing. The reconvened meeting passed various resolutions. One of these was a simple statement of purpose. Ragged schools were aimed at providing free education to the children of the poor. The Ragged School Union formally came into being on 5 July 1844. A further gathering of teachers on 1 November 1844 elected a Managing Committee which then proceeded to invite Lord Ashley to become the President. His acceptance of the position was conveyed to the committee on 6 December 1844 as was the agreement of W. W. Champneys and Baptist Noel, two prominent Evangelicals with a heart for evangelism and social welfare, to become Vice-Presidents.

The basic aim was the education of the poor so as to enable them to read the Bible. For any Evangelical reading the Bible was essential to life because it opened the door to salvation. This was likely over time to attract criticism from utilitarian or more liberal reformers as well as perhaps some modern critics looking back. Although this might imply that for the RSU the educational objectives were secondary to the evangelistic, it was, in fact, not so clear cut. At the formal institution of the rules of the RSU at the Special Meeting on 4 November, 1844 the policy established was that of assisting both young and old "in the study of the Word of God", and "the Instruction of the Children of the poor in general".[2] The same meeting also established the principle that the RSU would be interdenominational and begin and end all meetings with prayer. So the RSU stands in the tradition of many of the societies with which Shaftesbury was associated of unity around a single purpose with various opinions permitted on matters of church order and government.

At the second annual meeting the RSU Secretary, William Locke, drew the social needs of the city to the attention of those gathered. The RSU certainly had moral and religious objectives but he also drew attention to the wider responsibility of society toward the least fortunate. The *Ragged School Union Magazine* commenced publication in January 1849. On its first page it referred to the RSU as "a *recognized social movement*".[3] From the beginning the RSU advocated its concern for both the soul and the body. The combination of these factors came out in an early magazine: "The principles of this Society are benevolent, philanthropic, scriptural; they are, moreover, missionary and aggressive."[4]

This is another statement that seems somewhat odd to the modern mind. We are not used to seeing the combination of charitable and evangelistic concerns so explicitly stated. This particular permutation grates against the contemporary presumption of state involvement. It also sits a little ill at ease with the presumption of some that Evangelical Christians were only concerned with the next world, rather than this one.

Crucial to the purposes of the RSU was the idea of reaching those excluded from the other educational provisions of society. The second annual report referred to the aim of "removing every ragged, destitute child from our streets, and to placing of that child in the path of industry and virtue".[5] Again whereas commentators today might simply see traces of moral reformation and the Protestant work ethic this overshadows the noble ideals, both social and religious. These aims found their outworking in the establishment of schools of industry attached to ragged schools. Similarly the ragged school movement led directly to the founding of the Shoeblacks Brigade to provide direct employment. At Old Pye Street School in Westminster a Juvenile Refuge and School of Industry was established with the RSU financing a tailor and a shoemaker as teachers of their trades.

The extent and influence of the movement upon the poor grew rapidly. The first annual report noted 20 schools, 2,000 children, and 200 teachers. The twenty-fourth report, in 1868, reported 257 schools with 31,357 scholars. The tenth report in 1854 reported on RSU activities covering industrial classes, Shoeblack Brigades, Refuges, placing scholars in employment, emigration, mothers' meetings, libraries, Penny Banks, and Clothing Funds. By 1870 the list had expanded to cover meals societies, sanitary associations, flower shows, rag collecting, Shoe Clubs, Coal Clubs, Provident Clubs, and Barrow Clubs. The last of these was to enable loans to be made for barrows (or perhaps a potato oven) from which a living could be gained from selling vegetables. The impact of the RSU on the poor and as part of the Evangelical Christian response to the city should not be underestimated. This is also shown by the role of RSU teachers during the cholera outbreak.

Ragged School teachers have been found equal to this crisis. Bible in hand, they have not been afraid to enter into the most wretched hovels, where parents and children, dying or dead, demanded their Christian sympathy. Caring, however, like their

*Divine Master, for bodies as well as souls, by the medicines
provided by the Ragged School Union, they were the means
of arresting in very many cases the terrible disease which was
rampant in the infected districts. By these means they reached
many hearts which, if inaccessible to Christian doctrine, can at
least understand Christian action.*[6]

Shaftesbury and the RSU

Shaftesbury occupied the chair for the first annual meeting of the
RSU in 1845 (as Lord Ashley) and did so every year up to 1884. In
February 1843 an advertisement appeared in *The Times* on behalf
of the Field Lane Ragged School. The school, at that time run under
the auspices of the district City Missionary, was seeking help and
assistance. Ashley had been among those to respond and so began
a lifetime of involvement with the ragged school movement.

Shaftesbury's links and connections with the myriad organizations
which arose out of the activities of the RSU were extensive. He had
a particular concern for the well-being of the costermongers. These
were a proud, close-knit group of barrow holders and flower girls
who were always struggling to make ends meet. He was committed
to giving every possible aid and assistance in his power to helping
the poorest in London. Throughout his life Shaftesbury was to be
found not just occupying the chair in the Exeter Hall meetings, but
also frequently at the gatherings of individual ragged schools. His
diary records his activity. In November 1845 he was at Broadwall
Infant Ragged School followed in December by a tea-meeting at
Jurston Street Sunday School, followed again by a similar event
the following year. The *RSU Magazine* for July 1849 showed Lord
Ashley occupying the chair at the annual meetings of Lomas
Buildings Ragged School, Stepney, Thrawl Street Ragged School,
Spitalfields, Camden Town Ragged School, and Field Lane Ragged
School. The August and September editions of the magazine added
Brook Street Ragged School and Clare Market Ragged School. Many

others could be added. Ragged schools were not glamorous. They often met in crowded and inadequate conditions, perhaps a room fifteen feet square accommodating fifty to sixty children and eight to ten teachers. Ashley's own description of one particular ragged school revealed the extent of the problems. There was an average Sunday evening attendance of 260, aged from five to twenty. This number included forty-two who had no parents, seven children of convicts, twenty-seven who had been imprisoned, thirty-six who had run away from home, nineteen who slept in lodging houses, forty-one who lived by begging, twenty-nine who never slept on beds, and seventeen who had no shoes or stockings.[7] In 1866 he became the President of the Golden Lane Mission which was aimed particularly at the costermonger community. His love for these groups was so deep he even said, "I should not regret if my last words were words of prayer for such a work as this."[8] The Earl of Shaftesbury, after his admission to the Order of the Garter in 1861, even referred to himself as KG and C – Knight of the Garter and of the Costermongers. He subscribed for his own barrow in a Barrow Club and his own donkey in a Donkey Club.[9] He was also closely involved with the refuge movement, often associated with ragged schools. This was interlinked with his parliamentary campaigns to reform the common lodging houses. He became President of the Reformatory and Refuge Union, involved as well in their connected work of "training ships".

Another area which grew out of the ragged school movement was that of the Shoeblack Brigades, founded in 1851 under Shaftesbury's patronage. The purpose was the combined aims of providing employment and encouraging disciplined lives. The boys' earnings were split three ways. A third was banked for the future, a third went to the mission to cover costs, and a third was retained by the boys themselves. One year after foundation there were thirty-six boys employed and 150,000 pairs of boots and shoes had been cleaned.[10] By 1856 the number of boys had increased to 108. The Shoeblack Brigades were criticized for providing no long-term employment but Shaftesbury was more concerned with personal formation rather than shoeblacking as such. He always linked such schemes to others, especially proposals for emigration (a new life elsewhere). Perhaps there was too much of the romantic in Shaftesbury but his aim was to enable those less fortunate than others to be lifted out of the social quagmire they found themselves in. Learning, discipline, and thrift would equip them for a better life; a life he always hoped would be dependent in a personal way upon God.

Shaftesbury's commitment was real and practical. He continued in all his activities to put into practice the principle he had established during the battle for the Ten Hours Bill. This involved visiting first hand those places where the RSU was active and involved, often, of course, alongside the City Missionary. So, the RSU *Quarterly Record* of April 1877 reports on a statement from 1845 of a Mr Tompkins, who seems to have been a City Missionary, that he had found seventeen wretched and homeless creatures under arches near a school: "Lord Ashley hearing of it, with his accustomed promptness and philanthropy, visited this scene of wretchedness at midnight…"[11] Nothing was beneath this indefatigable man.

The unity of body and soul was a key theme for the RSU. Shaftesbury was ever keen to hold these ideas together. In his diary he expressed his admiration of a worker at Golden Lane, "who gave all his spare time to advance the knowledge of Christ and the earthly and heavenly interests of man".[12] Similarly he paid tribute to the teachers who devoted so much to "the advancement of the temporal and eternal welfare of the neglected children".[13] Moreover, Shaftesbury was determined to labour "so long as there is a soul to be saved, misery to be relieved, and ignorance to be enlightened".[14]

The RSU, like so many of the Evangelical mission societies, adopted the principle of lay agency. As with the LCM this was combined with the principle of Evangelical catholicity. However, it is still difficult sometimes to distinguish Shaftesbury's Christian motivations from the expressions of English Tory romanticism: both of these attitudes ran deep. In 1871 he declared the parental system to be the grand principle upon which the RSU acted. In 1877 "the whole system proceeds from the parental principle which these children know nothing of at home".[15] The system had been invented by God – at least according to the Earl. Hence Shaftesbury was able to declare that one result of this concern for both temporal and eternal welfare was that many of the lowest classes became "as mild and amiable as any of the rest of the human race".[16] A few years earlier he had said that the ragged children "adorned the station of life to which they belonged".[17] Shaftesbury was not really a moderate in anything, including his rather extreme expressions of Tory paternalism.

Shaftesbury's understanding of the end of time influenced his views on the RSU in a number of ways. In essence he believed in an interventionist God. He described the ragged school movement as stamped by the finger of God. He praised the RSU's endeavours: "I think there is no work that can be so acceptable in the sight of our blessed Lord as this care that you manifest for the most destitute, forsaken, and oppressed of the infantile race."[18] In his speech at the Mansion House in 1884 accepting the freedom of the City of London he applied the principle of "light" and "dark" – the former represented, of course, by the Evangelical societies, the latter by the social and domestic conditions of London.

Christians were to look ahead to the end of time, the final consummation of all things, but this prospect of future glory should prompt them now in their desire to carry out their duty for God in the interim. In 1851 he had called upon the annual meeting to recollect their privileges, their means, and their responsibilities. Ten years later he gave thanks for the RSU as a precursor of Christ's return.

Come, then, forward, and with every energy that God has given you, pray and offer up your thanks for the great blessings he has conferred, and prepare for the advent of the kingdom of our blessed Redeemer.[19]

Shaftesbury's commitment to the work of the RSU was unswerving. As early as 1845, passionate churchman as he was, he nevertheless noted in his diary:

If the conduct I pursue be at variance with the doctrines and requirements of the Established Church, I shall prefer to renounce communion with the Church to abandoning those wretched infants of oppression, infidelity and crime.[20]

He told the RSU more than a quarter of a century later:

I will undertake to say that the history of the Ragged School system exhibits a record of benefits conferred on society, and of grace bestowed by God, such as is scarcely to be found anywhere else within the range of modern history.[21]

In a testimonial to Joseph Gent in 1866 for his long-standing work for ragged schools, Shaftesbury summarized his own commitment to the RSU reflecting some of the crucial distinctives of the Evangelical mission societies:

I believe the Ragged School movement, as it has been conceived and executed, is the finest movement that has ever taken place under the Christian dispensation; it is most catholic in its character, and in unison with the Gospel, and devoted to the honour and glory of God.[22]

The Education Act of 1870 was a watershed for the ragged school movement. The number of schools declined rapidly in its aftermath. To Shaftesbury his whole basis of understanding and approach was being undermined. His reaction to what was taking place also reveals the love he had for this work.

Prizes in Exeter Hall last night. Never was I more touched; never more sorrowful. It is, probably, the close of these Christian and heary-moving spectacles. The godless, non-Bible system is at hand; and the Ragged Schools, with all their divine polity, with all their burning and fruitful love for the poor, with all their prayers and harvests for the temporal and eternal welfare of forsaken, heathenish, destitute, sorrowful, and yet innocent children, must perish under this all-conquering march of intellectual power. Our nature is nothing, the heart is nothing, in the estimation of these zealots of secular knowledge. Everything for the flesh, and nothing for the soul; everything for time, and nothing for eternity. [23]

He noted with regret the inevitable fact of the sinking of the ragged schools, though his heart could still be lifted by the atmosphere at the annual ragged school prize-giving.

Shaftesbury was honoured and loved within the movement. The Ragged School Union formed an important part of nineteenth-century Evangelical missionary effort. The RSU was also central to Shaftesbury's life and concerns. That Tory paternalism was mixed up in his deeply Christian motivations, that an excessive romanticism clouded vision – neither of these is denied. However, that also should not serve to eclipse the main objectives and motives behind Lord Shaftesbury and his work for the ragged schools.

CHAPTER 11

THE EARL: CAMPAIGNER FOR THE POOR 1851–1854

Shaftesbury played a particular role in the affairs surrounding the Great Exhibition of 1851. This exhibition, the height of Victorian self-proclamation to the world, was intended to be a visible demonstration of the power of the human mind, intellect and progress. He noted in his diaries that there "was a great struggle to obtain a proper place for the great works achieved by the Bible Society".[1] Shaftesbury had an enormous capacity for holding firmly to the "big picture". To him it was impossible for a Christian nation to seek to celebrate its achievements without an honoured place for the Bible. This was the national Protestant outlook at its best and most outward-looking. He was, of course, just as firm that a Christian nation should not send young children up chimneys or down mines. His aim was to secure a place for the Bible Society "where we could show proofs of all that we had done to the praise of God".[2] Shaftesbury even met with Prince Albert on the matter and was, in the first instance, rejected. He then appealed to the intellectual advance and power represented by the process of biblical translation into 170 languages and 230 dialects. This was the argument that won the day. Shaftesbury remained critical of the elevation of human rationality which the exhibition represented. It was designed to represent human progress, but all the innovations and developments were, he claimed, subsisting alongside the hard and vile human heart.

Except the 148 translations of the Bible, exhibited by the Society (and these the Commissioners have thrust into a remote corner), there is not one thing to distinguish a moral from a material existence, a Christian from a heathen generation.[3]

Ashley had mixed views on the exhibition itself. He certainly joined in the general enthusiasm for the nation's opportunity to shine. He was irritated by the dispute over the stand for the Bible Society. He pointed out that there was no dispute over the display of weapons of destruction. He visited the exhibition on 17 May, enjoying the sun and the crowds. Then on 1 June Ashley received the news that his father was dangerously ill and he rushed, by train, to St Giles. The next day, at seven o'clock in the morning, his father died. This was not only to mean a new career in the House of Lords, but also as the master of the estates. For the latter he was not trained and was, by and large, ill-suited. In a simple ceremony on 10 June, the sixth Earl was buried. The year closed with the newly ennobled seventh Earl engaging in a lengthy piece of retrospect in his diary on Christmas Day. He reviewed his efforts and achievements, his sacrifices and his standing. He concluded with:

I have had one single object perpetually before me. It was God's grace that gave me the thought; God's grace that has sustained me hitherto, to have, in truth, but one end, the advancement of His ever-blessed name, and the temporal and eternal welfare of all mankind.[4]

Shaftesbury's first acts as "Lord of the Manor" were characteristic. He closed the estates tap-room at nine o'clock each evening (in order to control the effects of the consumption of alcohol) and he appointed a Scripture-reader. It was soon clear that the affairs of the estate had been mismanaged. On 22 August he inspected cottages on the estate and found them in a poor condition. There was little he could do – he had low income and high debt. Less than six months later he left the estates and he turned his attention again to national affairs and the ministries of his faith.

Lodging houses

One of the other aspects of public health which concerned Shaftesbury was the condition of common lodging houses, and the housing of the working class more especially. The expansion of the railways and the consequent need for demolition of housing, had a particular impact upon the dwellings of labourers and artisans.

In December 1847 Ashley had written for the *Quarterly Review* on the matter of lodging houses. These lodgings, aimed at labourers, single workers and those travelling into London for work were unregulated and notorious for their poor conditions. The typical house would consist of seven fairly small apartments. Sixty adults as well as children would be housed here. Many were occupied by both male and female and often by violent and degenerate characters. In another he pointed out the lack of air and ventilation. One room had six beds and thirty-two individuals. Shaftesbury's solution was to provide "model" lodging houses. He moved for a bill in 1851. He again linked sanitation and morality. Nothing, he said, "produced so evil an effect upon the sanitary condition of the population as overcrowding within limited spaces". He went on, "if people were in a low sanitary condition, it was absolutely impossible to raise them to a just moral elevation".[5] He used evidence gathered by the City Missionaries to support his case in describing the conditions experienced by what Ashley referred to as the migratory population – those that moved from one lodging house to another. The missionary described one room eighteen feet by ten feet in which twenty-seven male and female adults, thirty-one children and two or three dogs had slept the previous night. These houses were never cleaned or ventilated and literally swarmed with vermin. He contrasted these conditions with the example of the "model" lodging houses. These had open spaces for the children and individual rooms with bed and chair. The issue was rent and return on capital. Ashley was convinced that the better conditions of the model houses would mean less time off work and hence the higher rents could be afforded. Two acts resulted, one regulating lodging houses generally (those with permanent residents) and the other the common lodging houses (for transitory occupation). These provisions empowered local authorities to establish lodging houses, to make by-laws (for example, separating men and women at night) together with provisions for inspection, registration, controlling admissions, and cleanliness. In his speech on the second reading of the Lodging-Houses Bill on 8 July Shaftesbury dealt with multiple occupancy, poor drainage and ventilation, and general neglect. The issues did not just affect London but provincial towns and cities as well. There was widespread neglect when it came to the dwellings of the labouring classes. In 1853 Shaftesbury reported back to the Lords that the Common Lodging Houses Act was working well, citing testimony from the Police Commissioner and also a City Missionary. Admissions were regulated, walls and ceilings whitewashed, and ventilation improved. He proposed a new bill to cover more stringent penalties and further provision on inspection and registration.

More sanitation

Ashley had been trying to resign from his post on the Board of Health, but to no avail. He was irritated by the appointment of Lord Seymour as President, which Ashley viewed as reducing his role to that of a clerk.[6] Perhaps there was also some pique at being passed over. He had made the sponsoring of a bill to deal with London's water supply a condition of remaining as a commissioner, but it became clear that the government would not proceed with a measure. Ashley complained about the strictures of both the Home Office and the Treasury on the effective functioning of the Board of Health. He was not a centralizer of the Chadwick variety. The toil was also having its effect on his health. In January 1851 he complained about his "disorders", and that he was harassed and overwhelmed. He went on: "I want neither honour, nor praise, nor payment; but I want some little fruit of protracted toil and expended health."[7] Ashley poured himself out for his campaigns, but his own mental and physical health was fragile.

In 1852 the Earl of Shaftesbury, in the aftermath of another cholera epidemic, moved in the Lords that the sanitary state of the metropolis required government intervention. Succeeding to the earldom had not reduced Shaftesbury's capacity for long speeches – this one occupied over sixteen columns in *Hansard*. In his usual meticulous way Shaftesbury set out the facts. He did so first of all by comparing the mortality rate in healthy districts (at 1.4 per cent) with various districts of London (ranging from 2.1 per cent to 2.95 per cent). Death by preventable disease was on the rise. This was, he suggested, in no small part the consequence of deficiencies in sanitary conditions for the capital's population:

They crowded together in the overpopulated lanes and alleys, living in miserable domiciles, where they found no pure air to breathe, no clean water to drink, and no drainage to carry off the filth. They were surrounded by every cause of disease and death; and when they came to die, there were no means for interring them with propriety and safety.[8]

The burial of the dead, poor drainage, inadequate sewers, the insufficient supply of water, and its quality were all significant features. He gave a vivid account of evidence of the conditions inside the common lodging houses. He had himself personally inspected parts of the city. Certainly he had done this many times.

Many dwellings were simply unfit for human habitation. These conditions affected several thousand houses and several hundreds of thousands of the population. To all of this had to be added the effects of manufacturing, bone boiling and fat boiling, manure heaps, knackers yards and piggeries. Then there was the smoke nuisance, "that everlasting source of the thickness, darkness, and filth of the London atmosphere".[9] The consequences of all of this were physical, moral, and social. The impact ranged from drunkenness, with the pernicious influence of the gin-shops, to resistance to education and religion. Disease and weakness of constitution were prevalent.

Personal life and other matters

In this period it was the years 1852–53 which brought the most pressure upon Shaftesbury. This is understandable given his succession to the earldom and the claims upon his time of defending the Protestant state, social legislation, and continued work for voluntary mission societies. Lord John Russell's government had fallen on 20 February 1852 to be replaced by Lord Derby and the Tories. Shaftesbury described himself as harassed and worn out by the constant demands – almost every night given to business and meetings as well as all day. He had sold his house in Brook Street and moved into the old family residence where he had been born in Grosvenor Square. The family, perhaps not surprisingly, had outgrown the Brook Street house. He had many happy memories – not least of the toil, study, and preparation which he had undertaken there. The move was, though, an added burden.

In September 1852 the Duke of Wellington died. This was more painful news for the Earl who held the Duke and his convictions in high esteem. Unlike Peel, in Shaftesbury's eyes Wellington embodied what it meant to be a principled Tory. Peel, though, had been the more successful politically. Wellington's death left the Chancellorship of Oxford vacant. There were rumours that Shaftesbury was a candidate. He denied it and it was probably both unlikely and unrealistic. He added, with his usual hyperbole:

> *I had rather, by God's blessing and guidance, retain those places for which there are no candidates – the chairs of the Ragged Union, the Colonial Dormitory, the Field Lane Refuge... This is clearly my province. I am called to this, and not to any political or social honours.*[10]

After the campaigns on Sunday observance and Papal Aggression it is not at all surprising that Shaftesbury led the protests at the sentencing of two Florentine shopkeepers to five years' hard labour in 1852 for abandoning the Church of Rome. Shaftesbury enlisted Prince Albert's help who appealed personally to the Grand Duke of Tuscany. Shaftesbury worked closely with the Protestant Alliance in the matter and saw the persecution of the two shopkeepers as a sign of the last days. Shaftesbury determined to set out for Florence. It was an idea which was unlikely to help. The incident illustrates the Earl's impulsiveness. Despite the burden of the range of his concerns and activities any threat to Protestantism would enrage the seventh Earl. Wise counsel won the day. In due time the usual diplomatic channels won the day and Francesco and Rosa Madiai were liberated in March 1853.

In 1852 Shaftesbury was also protesting against the revival of Convocation – the gatherings of elected clergy from the Provinces of Canterbury and York. Protestants were suspicious of these purely clerical gatherings which had been in abeyance since 1717. They were concerned that they would provide cover for the revival of Roman Catholic practices such as private auricular confession to priests.

All of this, alongside his parliamentary work, took its toll. In April 1853 he complained of having many bills in hand and was sneered at for his activity. The next day he commented, "engaged more than ever".[11] His work with ragged schools and lodging houses might be small work, as he put it, but it was his career to which he was called by God. Despite the "vexations, disappointments, rebuffs, insults, toil, self-denial, expense, weariness, sickness, all loss of political position, and considerable loss of personal estimation",[12] Shaftesbury made clear he would do so again. In June he was still saying he was "harassed by public and private business… Chimney-sweeps, juvenile mendicants… Speeches and Chairs without end".[13] He was kept going by the assurance that it was God's work.

Financially Shaftesbury continued to struggle. He had significant demands upon his resources, from his estates, his family needs, and his own work. Like so many of the aristocracy Shaftesbury was asset-rich but income-poor. He carried significant debt and mortgages. He was concerned for the proper provision for his children. He wanted to improve the workers' cottages on his estates – it was an embarrassment for the great reformer to be responsible for sub-standard provision for his own workers, as his opponents lost no opportunity to point out. There were also repairs to be made to the main house. Shaftesbury was determined not to divert monies from either religious or other philanthropy, or cottage improvement. The solution was to sell paintings. As he put it, "it is far better to have a well-cottaged property, people in decency and comfort, than well-hung walls which persons seldom see, and almost never admire unless pressed to do so".[14] He added that he must, "surrender more heirlooms, dismantle my walls, check ancestral feeling, and thank God it is no worse…" Shaftesbury then launched into a polemic against lawyers' fees that is almost timeless!

These lawyers multiply business, and charge prodigiously for
every step of it; they send in their accounts very seldom, so that
the client has no notion of the expense he is incurring by a series
of apparently small items, little suspecting that every question
gives rise, perhaps, to a dozen letters, and each letter costing as
many pounds; and then, when the account does come in, no man
that has lived, does live, or will live, can check it.[15]

The same year Shaftesbury sought to settle Lionel at Harrow.
He committed him to the Lord, praying that he and another son,
Evelyn, would embrace their father's faith. While there, he visited
the grave of Francis. Lionel shone.

Sweeps again

Following the earlier attempt at legislation on child sweeps, Lord
Shaftesbury continued to present the evidence to Parliament of
the nature of the continuing problem of evasion. The existing
legislation prevented master sweeps taking on apprentices under
the age of sixteen. However, as he explained to the House, the
master sweeps got round this provision by employing children
instead to carry the brushes, bag and tools. Once inside a house, the
master sweep would lock the doors and the children were forced
up the chimneys. Shaftesbury's proposal was that no one employed
to carry the equipment should carry the bags further than the door
of the house. Again his religious motives emerged but Shaftesbury
was at pains to point out that the sweeps were entitled to "those
rights, physical and spiritual, to which, by the laws of God, and he
wished by the laws of men, they were fully entitled".[16] Opposition
in the Lords led to the classic delay device, practised many times
before and since, of reference to a select committee. Despite
Shaftesbury's membership of the committee it recommended that
no further action be taken. The following year, 1854, he tried again.
Shaftesbury introduced a bill to the Lords which proposed penalties

for the use of a child under sixteen years old in assisting the trade of a sweep. Here the numbers claimed to be involved were put by Shaftesbury at 4,000. He described the trade as a "disgusting and unnecessary" employment. This time he referred to another recent case in the public domain – the ill-treatment of a five-year-old child in Nottingham, James Hart. The sweep forced the boy up the chimney using his sweeper's brush and then pulled him down by the legs and beat him. The doctor who examined him reported burns, ulcers and swellings. Shaftesbury used this as an example of the atrocities (as he described them) occurring daily around the country.[17] Very few climbing boys were employed in London, where mostly machines were used; the problem lay more in the provincial towns and cities. An attempt to derail the bill by Lord Clancarty failed and the legislation moved to the House of Commons. Here it ran into further and sustained criticism over its lack of precision. The arguments made were that a blanket ban on a child assisting a sweep would lead to unintended convictions for those genuinely employed to carry the bags or ride the sweep's donkey. Similarly since most sweeping was done in the early hours there would be problems of enforcement. Shaftesbury expressed his doubts in his diary:

> *Great anxiety about Bill for relief of Chimney Sweeps. Have suffered actual tortures through solicitude for prevention of these horrid cruelties. What a mystery that our efforts have been so long unavailing. The accursed system is, I fear, returning to London.*[18]

Later that month he was suffering from "giddiness", most likely induced by his anxiety and depression over the fate of the bill. The proposals were lost on 19 May. He lamented the lack of government support, "not a word of sympathy for the wretched children", and, "again I must bow to this mysterious Providence that leaves these outcasts to their horrible destiny, and nullifies, apparently at least, all our efforts to rescue them in body and soul".[19] His depression and gloom came through in his diary on 21 May:

> *Sunday. Very sad and low about the loss of the Sweeps Bill –*
> *the prolonged sufferings, the terrible degradation, the licensed*
> *tyranny, the helpless subjection, the enormous mass of cruelty and*
> *crime on the part of parents and employers, are overwhelming.*
> *The prospect is gloomy…*[20]

All of this shows his own passion and personal feelings at the progress of his parliamentary campaigns in this period. His faith again shines through – especially the unity of body and soul. Shaftesbury was passionate about the destiny of both. Earlier that very month Shaftesbury had been offered the Order of the Garter, as Lord Aberdeen had said in his invitation, "to mark my admiration of your unwearied exertions in the cause of humanity and social improvement".[21] Minny wanted him to accept. One factor was the fees of £1,000, which Shaftesbury did not have. The next day he declined on the grounds of his need for complete independence in pursuing his objectives. It was a completely unselfish act. He noted in his diary that he was not "indifferent to the honour" but also that "I am sure I have done wisely".[22] Now, less than a month later, the Sweepers Bill in tatters, he commented that "The Collar of the Garter might have choked me". His resolve, however, was undiminished.

> *I must persevere, and by God's help so I will; for however dark*
> *the view, however contrary to all argument the attempt, however*
> *painful and revolting the labour, I see no Scripture reason*
> *for desisting; and the issue of every toil is in the hands of the*
> *Almighty.*[23]

We will return to the story of Shaftesbury's campaign on behalf of the sweeps, which continued for the next twenty years.

The end of the Board of Health

The Board of Health was in good hands but not in good shape. To continue in existence the Board would need its terms renewed by Parliament. The debate raged about whether the Board should be a separate department, or should be subsumed within another or whether there should be a completely new department – Chadwick here being one of the critics' targets. In March 1854 Shaftesbury had defended with some vigour – and justification – the role of the Board of Health in the cholera outbreaks, most recently in 1848– 49 and 1853. He also had to defend the Board and its character in July of the same year. The writing, however, was on the wall. In the Commons the Board, and Chadwick, were under attack. Proposals to extend the Board's life, albeit with a different composition, were defeated. New arrangements were the order of the day. Chadwick had been persuaded to retire. The Earl offered his resignation, resisted by Palmerston, now at the Home Office. The Commons vote on 31 July made the decision for them. A new Department of Health was established. He lamented:

> No choice of resigning or remaining; the House of Commons threw out the Bill this day... thus after five years of intense and unrewarded labour I am turned off like a piece of lumber! Such is the public service. Lord Seymour has had his own way.[24]

A final dinner was held for all those connected with the Board's work on 5 August.

Shaftesbury continued to campaign upon general issues of public health, not least the abiding question of London's water supply, for the rest of his parliamentary career. In 1871 he told the Lords that "there was scarcely a pint of water in London which was not distinctly unhealthy, and that a great deal was positively unsafe".[25] He warned against the power of the water companies. In 1879 he reminded the House that the matter had been before the public for thirty years and recalled the efforts of the Board of Health. The Metropolitan Water

Board was not created until the Metropolis Water Act of 1902, some seventeen years after Shaftesbury's death.

Housing and the railway companies

The expansion of the railways was one of the key elements of the Industrial Revolution and a significant characteristic of Victorian England. In 1842 Queen Victoria, who had been whisked from Slough to Windsor at the average speed of forty-four miles per hour, sent a message to the railway company to say she had not enjoyed it and to ask that the next time the train should proceed more slowly.[26] London termini were built, mostly in the period 1840–60, and new lines constructed. The railways were run by private companies. In order to construct a rail track a company needed to promote a private bill in Parliament. This was in order to give the companies the powers necessary to buy land and for the compulsory purchase of dwellings and clearance. The railways provided transport into London, not only for those coming from a distance, but also for those who were now able to afford to live further out from the centre. The dwellings that needed to be purchased and removed in order to make this possible often belonged to labourers and poor inhabitants of London. The dwellings of the poor were not to stand in the way of the comforts of the rich. Enter, once again, on to the scene as the champion of the poor the Earl of Shaftesbury. The Earl intervened several times from the 1850s onwards in order to oppose the private bills sponsored by the railway companies. He presented petitions and spoke in Parliament in defence of those whose homes were affected. He first brought the matter before Parliament in 1853. He did so again in 1861, 1863, 1865, 1866, 1868, 1874, 1875, 1876, and 1884 either directly in respect of a railway proposal or other improvement scheme or to promote better housing conditions for the working class. His basic premise was that the railway companies should be responsible for the persons displaced by their works. A labourer losing his house would probably also lose his job. The railway companies should provide at their own expense lodgings equivalent to the number destroyed. He claimed to have discovered that a mere seven private bills had led to 1,145 houses being demolished and 5,422 people displaced. It was the tip of an iceberg. Shaftesbury estimated that 200 improvement bills were due to come before the House in this particular session. He went on, "your Lordships will see that the ravages they will cause will be as great as if a foreign army had invaded the country, plundered the inhabitants, and dispersed them in all directions". He emphasized again that he had personally visited threatened districts and described the inhabitants as living in "ignorant security".[27] He referred to the unacceptable pressure that was exerted with three to four weeks' notice of demolition and the consternation and distress which were caused. The consequence was often further overcrowding of already inadequate dwellings. He mentioned an earlier instance of 1,000 houses demolished and 12,000 inhabitants dispersed. He added:

My Lords, I will not now repeat my proposition, however just I may think it, and although I believe it will be the principle eventually laid down by Parliament – namely, that those who gain the whole profit should bear some measure of the loss inflicted by these displacements of the working population. But I must protest against any further sanction being given to those wild schemes by which large numbers of these poor people are turned out of their abodes, and sent into the overcrowded tenements in all directions.[28]

He argued that the poverty was neither necessary nor inevitable. He blamed it mainly upon intoxication and ruinous living conditions. In March 1861 he complained that a planned railway through St Giles Cripplegate would bring grievous wrong and injury to decent people who had long resided there. The proprietors of houses might have received notice to quit, but not those who lived there, some of them for the past twenty-five years. He was critical about the suggestion of the poor moving to the suburbs.

> *The houses are not built, the land is not purchased, the site is not yet fixed upon; and even when these villages are forthcoming it will be very difficult indeed to persuade the people to leave the neighbourhood of their work, where they now live, and go to so great a distance.* [29]

In 1863 he protested against the loss of over 1,000 homes proposed by one of the railway companies and with no notice given to the inhabitants. Just nine days later he was on his feet again to object to the Great Eastern Railway Company's proposed new line which would lead to the destruction of dwellings around Finsbury Circus. Again no notice had been given and the House needed to remember that they were dealing with people's lives. Many were tailors and shoemakers who needed to live near to their place of work.

> *He would oppose every Bill that proposed to take, open spaces of the character to which he had just referred, or which, without due notice – for that was the point – proposed a devastation of the dwellings of the working classes.* [30]

He told the Lords in 1865 that the proposals and schemes in progress indicated that over 3,500 dwellings were to be destroyed, displacing 20,000 people. In 1876 he was telling the House that in the previous twenty-four years, over a million people had been displaced in various improvement schemes – not all of course connected to railways. One of his final speeches to Parliament, in 1884, at the age of eighty-two, was to support a proposal to appoint a Royal Commission into the housing of the working class. London was much improved but there were many vested interests in delay and inaction.

Shaftesbury was both consistent and persistent. He had a remarkable ability to integrate his thinking and actions in various areas. Even within the realm of public health, in its widest sense, he understood the interaction of water, sanitation, lodging houses, housing, and the implications of powerful vested interests on the ordinary people. He also showed a tenacity matched by few. In many of his legislative campaigns he made use of his other work and links with the Evangelical voluntary societies with which he was so closely connected.

CHAPTER 12

BISHOP-MAKER:
1855–1866

The middle years of the nineteenth century were times of both trial and influence for Shaftesbury. He continued his many interests and campaigns with vigour and zeal. His personal life suffered much tragedy. During Palmerston's premiership he enjoyed a significant level of influence upon ecclesiastical policy. His stock remained high. He remained passionate about Christianity, the gospel, and the welfare of those who, as he saw it, were created by God and for whom Christ died.

The tragic death of Francis in 1849 was followed six years later by the loss of the third son, Maurice, who had been born in 1835. He was not a healthy boy and from 1848 was suffering from epilepsy. Shaftesbury and Minny knew that they would need to provide for him for life – no mean burden for the cash-strapped aristocrat. He was more worried, with all his experience of mental health, about what would happen if Maurice's parents were to predecease him. From 1853 to 1855 Maurice resided in Switzerland and Shaftesbury had only been able to see him twice. Maurice died in 1855 as Shaftesbury was travelling to Lausanne to visit, the Earl much saddened that he could not be with his son at his death. Shaftesbury, writing to another son, Evelyn, took solace in reports of Maurice's trust in Christ on his deathbed. Evangelicals needed conversions and they looked for them, especially among their nearest and dearest, right to the very end. Nevertheless, Shaftesbury went on to lament that he had lost two precious sons in their youth. Maurice was buried in the local cemetery, his father arranging for the erection of an appropriate tombstone.

A few months earlier Shaftesbury's great friend and supporter, Sir Robert Inglis, also died – "a man so single, so peculiar, has seldom existed in public life".[1]

The offer of office

When Palmerston assumed office in 1855 Shaftesbury's star again seemed to be rising. So it did, albeit in ways not at first anticipated. In February 1855 Shaftesbury was offered a seat in the Cabinet as Chancellor of the Duchy of Lancaster. However, political manoeuvring meant the offer was withdrawn. Following a reshuffle of ministers just a month later he was offered the place again. Writing to Palmerston in February in response to the first offer he was concerned about "so large a surrender of many important occupations".[2] He remained concerned about further support for Maynooth, the question of sabbath observance and extensions of papal power, as he saw it, in the appointment of Roman Catholic chaplains to gaols. Surely he would be an uncomfortable member for any Cabinet? Minny wanted him to accept. For the moment, in order to satisfy the Whigs, the offer was suspended. When the offer was renewed Palmerston told Shaftesbury he could have a free vote on his key matters of conscience. This was really quite a remarkable compromise to be offered to entice Shaftesbury into government. It showed the esteem in which he was held and the weight attached to his opinions. Shaftesbury, however, was not right for Cabinet government. He valued his independence of thought, speech, and action too highly. It might even be said his principles were too high for government. *The Globe* newspaper went so far as to announce Shaftesbury's appointment. The Editor of *The Times* and Lady Shaftesbury pressed him to accept. Minny urged, "I do *beseech* you not to refuse. Reflect how *much more* weight everything has, coming from a Cabinet Minister."[3] Lady Palmerston also joined the advocates. Shaftesbury's biographer, Edwin Hodder, reports that Shaftesbury said to him that he had never faced such perplexity in his life and was at his wit's end. Shaftesbury concluded that office was not a divine call and that God had called him to labour among the poor. Lady Palmerston wrote to Shaftesbury urging him to attend the Palace to be sworn in. Palmerston himself was in a dilemma. He knew Shaftesbury to be feeling the pressure and wanted to find an alternative to relieve him. Shaftesbury even dressed and was awaiting a carriage. He prayed for counsel, wisdom, and understanding. A note arrived from Palmerston. The pressure was over, the prayer answered. The Earl of Harrowby was sworn in as Chancellor of the Duchy of Lancaster on 31 March 1855. In the autumn of the same year Palmerston offered office again to Shaftesbury – this time it was firmly refused by the Earl. He saw himself, probably rightly, as more effective outside the government than inside it.

Religious Worship Bill

In 1855 Shaftesbury promoted the Religious Worship Bill. This was designed to repeal ancient and disused legislation, though still on the statute book, which made illegal a gathering of more than twenty persons additional to the household for worship in a house. To the Earl of Shaftesbury it was a missionary matter. Every possible facility and every possible opportunity should be provided for the gospel to reach the people. It was of particular relevance to the working class who were often excluded from churches. In mission houses, Sunday and Ragged Schools, a gathering which ended with prayer and singing could be declared illegal. To the establishment it was a loosening of authority and order. Bishops and Puseyite peers ganged up together against the bill. Shaftesbury carried the day by just 31 to 30 on 12 June 1855. He described the high church, Lord Derby and his friends as "insolent, interruptive, discouraging". The opposing bishops, led by Oxford, "exhibited… great ignorance, bigotry, and opposition to evangelical life and action".[4] In committee the bill was emasculated and Lord Derby introduced a substitute bill on behalf of the select committee. In essence this granted exemption for activities conducted by or with the consent of the incumbent. This was not dealing with the matter of concern to Shaftesbury. He saw this as an attack upon the laity, upon Dissent, and upon missionary work and innovation. The bill granted permission for prayers to be said in opening or closing religious meetings. Shaftesbury was incandescent at any suggestion of needing permission to pray. Shaftesbury was supported by Lord Brougham and forced the withdrawal of the Derby Bill. He wrote in his diary about his "great success in exposing its follies, its falsity, its impudent ambition for the bishop to gain new powers over the clergy and the laity".[5] Less than two weeks later, fortified by an Evangelical meeting, Shaftesbury introduced another bill. Modestly revised in order to gain support from the Archbishop of Canterbury the new bill provided for the conduct of public worship anywhere in a district by incumbent, curate, or persons authorized by them without being fettered in any way and for the freedom of householders to use their houses for worship without restriction of number, and legalized all mission and mission-related meetings of which worship was a part.

Bishop-maker

Lord Palmerston is another name which towers over nineteenth-century politics. He was in the public service, in one capacity or another, for over fifty years. Born an aristocrat and displaying many of the same characteristics as Shaftesbury, he was, at the outset, an archetypal conservative. However, from that position Palmerston moved first of all to a position of "liberal conservative", and ultimately to be a leading liberal politician of the century. He had entered the Commons some thirty years before Victoria mounted the throne. As foreign minister his policy was characterized by diplomacy backed up by the threat of military intervention. Palmerston was prime minister for two terms between 1855 and his death in office in 1865. His life was also closely intertwined with that of Lord Shaftesbury, an unusual alliance in some respects, but which had significant implications in the area of church appointments. Palmerston, as noted earlier, was related to Shaftesbury through the Earl's wife, Minny Cowper. Officially he was Shaftesbury's step-father-in-law. Whatever the complexities of the family relationships, it brought Shaftesbury into close contact with Palmerston. Despite their differences the two men held each other in great respect. Palmerston supported most of Shaftesbury's social reforms, sometimes explicitly and helpfully with interventions in the House. Palmerston was in fact an Irish peer who did not have the right to sit in the Lords and so remained in the Commons for all of his political career. His religious views were moderate, even modest. He was certainly no Evangelical. Shaftesbury claimed that on his deathbed Pam (as he was known) had expressed his firm trust in Christ. He died on 18 October 1865. Shaftesbury had been present to watch and pray by the bedside, although he was not in the room at the actual death, and he recorded many of the details of these last hours in his diary. Palmerston was afforded a state funeral in Westminster Abbey. The deathbed scenes showed the great affection Palmerston had for Minny. Shaftesbury records that Pam tenderly loved and admired her, describing her as a sunbeam. Shaftesbury also acknowledged his own personal relationship with Palmerston. He recognized the esteem in which he was held by Palmerston and returned the admiration fulsomely. Palmerston, he said, had always been open, generous, attentive, and respectful toward him.

Allowing for the selectiveness of the eulogy, during the ten years for which Palmerston had been prime minister, he had leaned more heavily on Shaftesbury for advice about the church appointments, notably bishoprics, for which he was responsible than any other person. Shaftesbury perhaps exercised here more direct influence upon government policy than at any other time. Ten years earlier the Earl had been scathing about Palmerston's ability when it came to ecclesiastical appointments. He told his son, Evelyn, that his nominations would be "detestable". He added that Palmerston "does not know, in theology, Moses from Sydney Smith. The vicar of Romsey, where he goes to church, is the only clergyman he ever spoke to…"[6] Shaftesbury "the bishop-maker" displayed and exercised considerable skill in offering advice. He did not seek to press home any unfair advantage which might provoke a reaction. He compromised on some appointments. However, also, he did not hold back in ensuring that faithful, Evangelical candidates were appointed to bishoprics through his influence on the Prime Minister. The tenor of these appointments were a dismay to the high church party. Samuel Wilberforce of Oxford described Palmerston's appointments as wicked.

To Palmerston nominations to bishoprics were not mere political patronage, but a chance to promote the best candidate. The issue was that he did not have either the insight or the expertise when it came to church appointments. He needed advice. To whom was he to turn? There was one obvious candidate for advice within the family, the Earl of Shaftesbury.

Shaftesbury did not deny his own influence on appointments. He was keen however to make it clear that Palmerston was a man of honour who acted with disinterested integrity in making his ecclesiastical decisions. His natural inclination was not in the direction of the high church party and he was keen, good liberal that he was, to ensure good cooperation with nonconformists. During the course of his time as premier Palmerston was responsible for the appointment in England and Ireland of five archbishops, twenty bishops and ten deans. In addition there were appointments to be made to a variety of Regius Professorships. Shaftesbury gave his own account of his role as "bishop-maker" in his diary after Palmerston had died. He acknowledged that Palmerston had been mainly driven by justice and to act with propriety and political impartiality. Shaftesbury claimed to look at every appointment from Palmerston's point of view and that he had passed over many good candidates whom he himself would have preferred. His maxim was: "I must propose what you and I can defend, not that which could be defended by myself alone."[7]

Shaftesbury's diffidence may have been masking a more concerted strategy: a plan, though, borne from personal and familial knowledge of the prime minister, appreciating Palmerston's aversion to high churchmanship, but also understanding the need for moderation and care. Palmerston shared with Shaftesbury an aversion to the high church tendency to be dismissive, rude, and even contemptuous toward nonconformists. It gave Shaftesbury another opening to shape the character of the senior church appointments. It may also have been part of the reason for the opposition and criticism from the high church party and its supporters toward Palmerston's nominations. In 1855 Shaftesbury had demurred at any suggestion that he would influence Palmerston. In fact he told his diary:

> *He has never in his life, and never will, so long as he has breath, consult me on anything. It is not very likely that he will consult anybody; but, if he do, it will not be one connected with the Evangelical party.*[8]

In this Shaftesbury was manifestly wrong. Although Shaftesbury claimed, with justification, that the list of nominees was widely drawn, he also noted that no senior appointment was made without him being consulted. Shaftesbury was concerned to rule out both liberal "neologists" (as they were known) with their rationalistic views on the bible and Tractarian sympathizers. Looking back in 1865, he said:

The first bishops were decidedly of the Evangelical School; and my recommendations were made with that intention. I could not foresee the duration of his power, and I was resolved to put forward men who would preach the truth, be active in their dioceses, be acceptable to the working people, and not offensive to the Nonconformists. He accepted my suggestions on these grounds, and heartily approved them.[9]

The Earl successfully obtained the appointments of Baring to the see of Gloucester and Bristol, Villiers to Carlisle, Bickersteth to Ripon, and Pelham to Norwich – all Evangelicals. He also ensured the appointment of Francis Close to the deanery of Carlisle. Shaftesbury then reported that Palmerston had sought more of a balance in appointments in order, given the length of his time in power, that he could satisfy colleagues who were "higher". Pam did not want this to stand in the way of fit and suitable candidates, but wondered if the two principles could be combined. Shaftesbury, inevitably, was doubtful. More caution was clearly needed but Shaftesbury wished to maintain the basic principles. There was pressure, not least from the Tractarians, for more learned occupants of sees. Shaftesbury saw this as a cover for pushing their own candidates.

However, Shaftesbury also recognized the political realities. In his view Palmerston's position had not changed but practical politics also had to be dealt with. Shaftesbury was rather resistant to the automatic appointment of scholarly bishops.

Professors, tutors, and dons of colleges are by no means, on an average, men fitted for Episcopal duty. The knowledge of mankind, and experience of parochial life, are not acquired in musty libraries and easy-chairs. Practical divinity is one thing, speculative divinity another, and the accomplishments that make

an active and useful bishop, are purchased at the cost of that
learning which would make him a theological champion, armed
at all points, and ready on all occasions. [10]

Nevertheless, as time went on he resolved to seek broader appointments as best he could. It was Shaftesbury who was behind Archibald Tait's appointment as Bishop of London. He was recommended explicitly as a broad churchman and Shaftesbury concluded that, despite some reservations, there was much in him to be commended. Palmerston did also on occasion exercise his own judgment and Shaftesbury was keen not to alienate him. He did regret agreeing to the nomination of Jacobson to Chester, at Gladstone's behest no less: the bishop then refused his sanction to the Bible Society. On this and some other occasions Shaftesbury's advice and wishes were set aside by Palmerston. The reality is that there were both Evangelical and non-Evangelical appointments in both of Palmerston's stints as prime minister (1855–58 and 1859–65). Shaftesbury was extensively consulted and had considerable, but not exclusive influence.

This was all a complex and time-consuming matter for Shaftesbury. It required skill and care. Shaftesbury himself often sought advice from his close friend Alexander Haldane, a leading Evangelical. Shaftesbury told Haldane that his "wide experience, sound judgement, and Christian heart, were of signal, nay, indispensable importance".[11] Shaftesbury fell again into romantic language about Palmerston as he surveyed the prospects following the prime minister's death. Given the family connection, he might be forgiven.

Domestic life

The Earl practised what he preached. There was nowhere better than his own estates in Dorset to put the principles of high Tory paternalism to work. In 1856 Shaftesbury re-established the ancient custom of "harvest home" on his estates. This was paternalism in practice as it should be – the landowner dispensing his largesse. *The Times* described the scene. Some 350 labourers and servants gathered and proceeded to church led by a band. There followed a dinner, with beer made available, the park was open, the band was playing, and cricket and other games were provided. In good old-fashioned paternalistic British fashion, the Earl made a speech. The paper reported:

> *The noble EARL rose and said… He thought these celebrations were of great value in bringing together all classes of society… to show they were dependant one upon the other… he was sure that if landlord and tenant, employer and employed, those who had property and those who had none – except that honest property of their labour – would join in one great effort to advance each other's welfare and to maintain their Christian character, they would arrive at that condition of things which was the happiest and safest that could be attained in this fallen world.*[12]

Pressures of life often bore heavily on Shaftesbury. He dealt with all his own correspondence. On 27 March 1857 he wrote in his diary, "sit down and weep over the sad, wearisome, useless expenditure of time and strength on the letters I must read, and the letters I must write". He went on to complain further of the burden, the time consumed, the uselessness of many of the letters and how much more good he might undertake if the strain were less. He added, "I am worn out by this dull, monotonous, fruitless occupation."[13] He complained of nervous fatigue, a hundred letters unanswered and the lack of time for both recreation and public affairs. He was lifted, as usual, by the May meetings of the great societies, not least by his son, Antony, appearing on the platform at the RSU meeting. He was greeted with enthusiasm and cheering. The episode also made Shaftesbury melancholy as he recalled his two dear departed sons.

Exeter Hall and theatre services

During this same period Shaftesbury's opposition to Sunday bands in parks led to anxiety on his and Minny's part that their London house would be targeted. The threat, stirred up in the papers, passed without incident. All of this laid the groundwork for Shaftesbury to push further with provision for worship accessible to the working class and without undue power or influence in the hands of the bishops. In 1857 worship services commenced on Sunday evenings in Exeter Hall aimed at the working class. Some clergy attempted to use the 1855 Act to prevent services from happening in unconsecrated buildings.

Shaftesbury saw the progress of the gospel as paramount. He introduced an amendment to the Religious Worship Act – and found much opposition from clergy as well as bishops. Shaftesbury's bill provided for occasional worship services in any building. In the end he was forced to compromise and support a bill from the Archbishop of Canterbury that required the sanction of the bishop to be given – too much episcopal power for Shaftesbury's liking. Shaftesbury's prime commitment was to ensuring that as many as possible could hear the gospel message of salvation. Nothing should be allowed to stand in the way of that objective, especially the bench of bishops. The Sunday evening services at Exeter Hall had been very successful and thought was now given to how to extend them further. He commented in his diary on one particular service:

> An attendance of more than three thousand – order, decency, attention and even devotion. They sang well and lustily, and repeated the responses to the Litany (the only part of the Liturgy used…)… Another service this evening… Fuller than before; hundreds sent away.[14]

In January 1860 five theatres were opened for public worship. The average attendance was around 20,000, many of whom were listening to the Word of God for the first time. Shaftesbury assisted in many of these services, reading from the Bible, and it was mainly the poor – labourers and costermongers – who formed the congregation. On 24 February 1860 Lord Dungannon rose in the House of Lords to move a resolution declaring such services, led by clergy of the Church of England, to be irregular, inconsistent with order and injurious to the advance of religion.

Shaftesbury rose. The services, he said, were aimed at those who did not frequent regular places of worship. In addition many in London were nomadic: these circumstances required special means. Many of the Church of England and nonconformity had joined together in this enterprise. Shaftesbury praised this unity. He argued that these services strengthened the cause of the church. The talk was of inhibition. He doubted the legality but added:

> *I question whether any human being or any law has the power of preventing a clergyman in his capacity of a Christian citizen from performing that great duty, the salvation of souls, in season and out of season, at all times and in all places, to any who may be disposed to hearken.*

He quoted a letter from a clergyman of the Church of England. "I presume the right of Christian men to exhort an ungodly multitude, wherever found, ought not to he interfered with; and it was only as a Christian man that I addressed the multitude in the Garrick Theatre. I wore no ecclesiastical dress, and used no part of the Church service." He complained bitterly that the Church of England "despite the pressing and fearful necessity, is bound so tightly by rule and rubric, and law and custom, that she can do none of the work".[15] Some years later these services were still happening. He noted in his diary in 1867 that he had been to three special services in London theatres describing them as "a great work, a good work, a deeply needful work".[16]

The Garter

In 1859 the factory workers of the north of England presented Minny with a bust of the Earl at a meeting in Manchester's Free Trade Hall. The following year, at Christmas, Shaftesbury was reflecting upon his life and calling. He acknowledged disappointments, but this was not the time to retire. He noted, "I feel a singular reluctance to withdraw from the field, dark and dismal though it be". It was God's call and to God he must give account on the "day of final account". He added, "this is why I cannot resolve to retire, though I see clouds gathering around, and, within and without, am not what I was".[17] It was the usual pressures and internal conflicts within Shaftesbury raising their head once again.

His daughter Mary had suffered from a disease of the lungs for a long time and caring for her took a toll on Minny. Shaftesbury showed both his sense of the call of duty and also a deep personal love and care for his family. In February 1861 they were in Torquay. Minny was to remain there with Mary while the Earl returned to London. The solitude, he said, of the London house would be very great. He noted: "I must continue my work, so long as God gives me strength, while there is work to be done, not only while it can be done in circumstances pleasant to myself."[18] On 10 August Shaftesbury was full of praise for Minny's care of Mary which had lasted for eighteen months. He referred to her constant attention to Mary's every need until the doctor declared that there was no hope, and then she collapsed in exhaustion and weakness. He praised her devotion to her child: in the final days she rarely left Mary's side. Characteristically Shaftesbury sought prayer and prayed himself for a sign of Mary's acceptance of Christ into her life. She died on 23 September 1861 in the early hours. Shaftesbury, distraught, submitted himself to God's decree and confessed its wisdom and goodness.

In 1854 Shaftesbury had declined the offer of admission to the Order of the Garter. He wanted to be in hock to nobody and, as we have noted, the fees were rather high! On 10 December 1861 Palmerston wrote to Shaftesbury offering him the "Blue Ribbon" of the Knighthood of the Order of the Garter, a personal honour bestowed by the monarch. Palmerston rightly stated that its conferment on Shaftesbury would gratify the whole country. Shaftesbury recognized Palmerston's kindness, generosity, and openness. Shaftesbury prevaricated a little, not least on the matter of fees. He noted his limited income and that he would not be justified in incurring such a level of expense simply for a decoration. While the debate was going on, Albert, the Prince Consort, always a confidant, friend, and supporter of Shaftesbury, died. The same diary entry recorded the death also of his co-worker for the improvement of sanitary conditions, Southwood Smith. He noted also the Queen's kindness toward him and, characteristically, prayed for her salvation. A few days earlier he had, with some foresight, noted:

> *I shrink from contemplating the calamity. I see and feel the shock to the Queen. She has never known sorrow, and is unprepared for it. It will leave her melancholy, friendless, without a support, an adviser; no one to aid her in public affairs, no one in private.* [19]

In respect of the Garter, however, circumstances were now different and after some delay he accepted. The official costs appear to have amounted to a little over £600, including £130 for robes, helmet, sword, etc., over £37 to the Dean, £90 to the church, and nearly £103 in stamp duty on various documents. It is thought that Palmerston paid the fees himself. The Garter Principal King of Arms, Sir Charles George Young, wrote, probably to Palmerston, that, in response to "your Lordship's desire I beg to enclose to you the account of fees, charges and disbursements incurred by Lord Shaftesbury's admission into the Order of the Garter". He added: "all the documents connected with the matter have been forwarded to the Earl of Shaftesbury but no account has been sent nor has any application been made to his Lordship for payment".[20] Shaftesbury noted in his diary:

I have reason to believe that the arrangement he made was to pay the whole expenses himself, but to keep it secret from me. This is, indeed, truly generous and friendly.[21]

Estate management

We have noted several times Shaftesbury's struggle with financial matters, with his need for and ability to obtain an income, and with his own inadequacies or poor judgment on estate and financial affairs. Palmerston, of course, had some insight into the family's struggles from the inside. Palmerston, presumably aware of the problems through Minny, wrote to the Earl in November 1861 recommending that Shaftesbury ask his lawyers to investigate his land steward. The income of the estate had been overcommitted and Palmerston reported that the land steward, Waters, was reported to be closely linked to horse racing and betting. Some seven months later the Earl noted that Pam had sent £5,000 to Minny to support the children's education.

The estimate of the embezzlement from the estate amounted to at least £12,000 over the twelve years of the steward's employment. Shaftesbury feared that the real figure was much higher. Shaftesbury attached much blame to the auditors, Burnett, Newman, & Co., to whom he paid £100 per annum. He noted, with hindsight, how he had often had to wait three years for accounts. The auditors had described the accounts papers as arriving in "confusion and entanglement". The issues had only come to light following Shaftesbury's "severe remonstrance to them". He pointed out that they had failed to examine the estate bank account: "if they did examine the books, their neglect is greater than one would imagine, for they must have disregarded all those cheques which bear, on their very face, fraud and embezzlement". [22]

Shaftesbury noted that the auditors had never seemed to notice that there was no increase over many years in the rent roll, the rents simply covering the interest payable. He noted:

Have dismissed Waters, under pretence of allowing him to resign. Shall never discover my whole loss by mismanagement, peculation, trickery, and direct fraud. It has been a yearly and an occasional plunder. [23]

Litigation followed and a year later the Earl noted the annoyance of expensive lawsuits from both the former steward and a tenant. He lamented the cost, even if there were a victory at court. Extraordinary events followed the discovery of Shaftesbury's losses. In November 1863 the wealthy philanthropist Samuel Morley, together with a group of the Earl's friends, offered Shaftesbury £10,000. Many smaller donations also came in. In July 1864 this group of five friends, led by Morley, provided Shaftesbury not with the original £10,000 promised, but in fact with £12,500. The Earl wrote:

My dear Mr Morley,

Nothing can be more delicate, nothing more kind and generous than the conduct of my five friends – I deeply and sincerely feel it… I bless God for this happy interposition. [24]

Sweeps again

The Children's Employment Commission was appointed by Parliament as part of a continuing concern with the subject. The commissioners, acting on their own initiative in the light of evidence and submissions, decided to include climbing boys within their enquiries. The report was published in July 1863.

The Commissioners reported that, outside London and some other towns, the use of climbing boys was on the rise and the existing legislation largely inoperative. Even in the metropolis the illicit use of climbing boys was increasing. The current provisions were systematically violated and there was also much ignorance about the necessity of climbing boys across all classes in society. Moreover, evidence of violation was difficult to obtain and the magistrates reluctant to convict. The number of children still employed amounted to several thousand. The age of the boys was still very young, often six to eight years old. The hours were long and frequently concentrated in the early morning. Ill-treatment was still prevalent. Some of this was deliberate such as rubbing brine into the flesh even after the skin had been torn in order to harden the skin for the work. The commission also reported on the use by master sweeps of an ash-plant as a cane. The commissioners noted some recent convictions as evidence of the continued evasion and ineffectiveness of the Act, notwithstanding the cases coming to court. They revealed much more. At Ashton-under-Lyne a seven-year-old had been badly burnt. At Preston a boy was severely flogged for refusing to re-enter a hot flue. Two climbing boys had recently died in Nottingham and one in London. There was evidence of twenty-three boys killed in chimneys since 1840. In addition to all of this there was the incidence of "chimney sweepers' cancer". Occasionally, climbing boys were still being bought and sold. Education was widely neglected. The commissioners proceeded to expound the benefits and practicalities of the use of machines in the cleaning of flues and chimneys. They recommended a complete ban on the employment of children under sixteen within the trade in any capacity. Among other things the report recommended the licensing of master sweeps, a wider range of penalties, and the requirement upon the police to enforce.[25]

Shaftesbury needed no further invitation for action. He introduced to Parliament the Chimney-Sweepers and Chimneys

Regulation Bill. The Earl spoke on 3 June 1864, making another masterful, long, and detailed speech drawing much on the report of the Children's Employment Commission. These children, he said, suffered during all of their most vulnerable years of childhood. Since climbing boys were unnecessary this amounted to wanton cruelty. The blame, he opined, lay not primarily with the master sweeps but with the householders who were reluctant to have machines in their houses, and so permitted climbing boys to be sent up the chimneys. He went on: "Many householders refuse to alter their flues, or to incur the smallest expense for putting in soot doors, and persist in setting the law at defiance."[26]

The House, he argued, had a responsibility not to perpetrate this cruel and disgraceful system. The principle involved was that of alleviating toil and suffering. He reminded them of the predictions of calamity that had preceded the factory legislation: now there was only praise on all sides. Attempts to amend or remove certain clauses were all defeated.

Other matters

The 1860s were also the period of many developments in biblical criticism and related matters which raised Shaftesbury's ire. We will leave a more formal look at his theological position until a later chapter. However, the publication of more liberal theological works, including *Essays and Reviews*, *Ecce Homo*, and the writings of Bishop Colenso on the Pentateuch (the first five books of the Old Testament) caused Shaftesbury to fire off regular salvoes. The laity, too, he argued had signed the Thirty-Nine Articles and demanded their defence. In speeches before CPAS and the Bible Society he protested. He claimed that Colenso's book represented a puerile and ignorant attack on the sacred and unassailable Word of God. In his diary on 12 May 1866 he recalled his speech to CPAS denouncing *Ecce Homo* as a most pestilential book. News reports claimed the Earl had added: "ever vomited from the jaws of hell". He slightly regretted it, but did not deny the words or their truth. Even Pusey weighed in on the attack on liberal rationalism. Shaftesbury wrote to his cousin advocating united action in defence of the atonement itself, which received an equally gracious reply. However, as we shall see, Shaftesbury had not yet finished with his campaign to rid the Church of England of the high church ritualism that Pusey represented.

Palmerston was succeeded by Lord John Russell as prime minister with Gladstone at the Home Office. They quickly ran into difficulties with the proposed second Reform Bill. After the administration resigned in 1866 a Conservative government was formed under the Earl of Derby, together with Disraeli. Shaftesbury, having been offered office in Palmerston's liberal administration, was now offered office again by the Conservatives. Derby asked him to take the post of Chancellor of the Duchy of Lancaster – there would be space for his other pursuits. Shaftesbury's reply declining the offer was noted in the introduction. He also noted in his diary his concern at potential conflict with the Home Office. The only possible political office he could assume was surely the Home Office itself. Derby was loath to give up. He does seem to have offered the Home Office to Shaftesbury and, failing that, the post of Lord President of the Council. It was all to no avail. Shaftesbury really did value his independence and probably was all the more effective for doing so. This was the last time that the Earl was offered government office.

CHAPTER 13

REGULATING RITUAL: 1866–1884

Early 1866 saw Shaftesbury continuing his social work with a scheme for a training ship moored on the Thames. Other "refuges" followed designed to provide respite and skills-based training for the homeless and destitute. His campaigns on public health and climbing boys continued together with his ever-expanding voluntary activities. On the wider political scene 1867 saw another Reform Bill – it is of little surprise that Shaftesbury was hostile. He spoke on the second reading. His essential point against too wide an extension of the vote (while proclaiming himself in favour of moderate reform) was that the vote was a trust and not a right. It would lead to socialism. However, the next decade was to be occupied by increasingly desperate attempts to stem the influence of Tractarianism and Ritualism within the Church of England.

Ritualism

The doctrines of the Tractarian movement had practical implications. If the doctrine of the real presence (that is, the actual, bodily, and local presence of Jesus in the consecrated elements of bread and wine) was accepted then this had implications for worship. In other words, the bread and perhaps the altar (rather than the Reformed "table") should be reverenced. Similarly if the role of ministers was that of "priests", presiding over the consecration of the elements, hearing confessions, pronouncing blessings, then they should wear the apparel of priests. All of this was beginning to lead to a rich ceremonial in a number of churches. Genuflection (bowing on one knee) before the elements, incense, the reserved sacrament (consecrated elements kept back for use among the sick, but also as an object of devotion), candles on the communion table, intoning or singing the services – all these began to feature in at least some parts of English church life. The English Church Union was formally established in 1860 from a predecessor organization founded a year earlier. The Church Union provided a focal point for ritualist sympathizers as well as a defence for those under attack from the rival Evangelical Church Association founded in 1865. There were many individual tussles and in a number of cases (not least that of St George's-in-the-East in London) rioting. Many broad church bishops, such as Charles Blomfield of London, were equally suspicious of ritualism.

By the mid-1860s matters had reached boiling point. Shaftesbury concluded that he must, before initiating any action, acquaint himself with the reality of ritualism on the ground. Hence one Sunday in 1866 he attended divine service at one of the main centres of ritualist worship in London. He went to St Alban's Holborn, where the minister, Alexander Mackonochie, was on his way to becoming an Anglo-Catholic hero. Shaftesbury was unimpressed. "In outward form and ritual, it is the worship of Jupiter and Juno," he said. He described the presence of a high altar at the top of several steps, with a cross and pictures and the chancel separated by an iron grill from the main body of the church. His description continued at length:

Abundance of servitors, etc., in Romish apparel. Service intoned and sung, except the Lessons, by priests with white surplices and green stripes.

This being ended, a sudden clearance. All disappeared. In a few minutes, the organ, the choristers, abundant officials, and three priests in green silk robes, the middle priest having on his back a cross embroidered, as long as his body. This was the beginning of the Sacramental service (quarter-past eleven), the whole having begun at half-past ten. Then ensued such a scene of theatrical gymnastics, of singing, screaming, genuflections, such a series of strange movements of the priests, their backs almost always to the people, as I never saw before even in a Romish Temple. Clouds upon clouds of incense, the censer frequently refreshed by the High Priest, who kissed the spoon, as he dug out the sacred powder, and swung it about at the end of a silver chain. The priests in the chancel, and the priest when he mounted the pulpit, crossing themselves, each time, once on the forehead, and once on the right and left breast. A quarter of an hour, or thereabouts, sufficed to administer to about seventy Communicants, out of perhaps six hundred present. An hour and three-quarters were given to the histrionic part. The Communicants went up to the tune of soft music, as though it had been a melodrama, and one was astonished, at the close, that there was no fall of the curtain.

God is a Spirit; and they that worship Him must worship Him in spirit and in truth. Is our blessed Lord obeyed in such observances and ceremonials? Do we thus lead souls to Christ or to Baal?[1]

His views had not changed from his encounter with Roman Catholic worship in 1833. His Evangelical Protestantism had been honed in battles over Maynooth, the Jerusalem bishopric, and the Papal Aggression. He did not fight those battles in order to let his beloved Church of England slip from its moorings in the Reformed faith. Over the next ten years Lord Shaftesbury was at the forefront of legislative and other battles to resist the practices of the ritualists.

In doing so Shaftesbury perhaps lost sight of a number of strategic issues. National Protestantism was in long-term decline. To expect the state to effectively enforce the provisions of Protestantism against Anglo-Catholicism was probably ill-judged. It was also unlikely to succeed. Neither of these factors, even if they had been recognized at the time, would have prevented Shaftesbury from proceeding as he did.

The attack on clerical vestments

His first legal move on clerical vestments came in 1867. He sought the leave of the House of Lords to introduce a bill "for the correction of certain ritualistic abuses which have crept into the Church of England".[2] He went on to say that the purpose of the bill was to regulate the use of sacrificial vestments (in other words the coloured robes worn by Anglo-Catholic clergy). He advanced two reasons. First, that they were offensive to the eye and to the nation. Second, that the law was unclear. Shaftesbury argued that other offensive matters such as the use of incense and candles were matters on which the law was clear and redress could be obtained through prosecution. Shaftesbury's bill sought to enforce what was known as "the Ornaments Rubric". This was a provision of the Elizabethan Prayer Book of 1559. In stating that the appropriate dress of ministers was to be that of the second year of the reign of Edward VI the framers left room for doubt. Elizabeth I, through her Archbishop, Matthew Parker, made clear in 1566 that this had been intended to mean the wearing of a simple surplice (in other words, not Roman eucharistic vestments). In 1604 the Canons set it all out clearly. The minister of public prayer and sacramental worship should wear a white surplice, an academic hood, and a black tippet or scarf – not silk. Shaftesbury's point was to give legal force to this provision through the statute book. The bishops were uncomfortable. They tried to head Shaftesbury off, first with a promise of their own bill and then with a Royal Commission on

Ritual. Shaftesbury moved the second reading of his bill in the Lords on 14 May 1867. He argued that he should pursue the legislation, notwithstanding the Ritual Commission, because he was dealing with just one aspect of ritual which was of particular concern. His line was that the use of priestly vestments was an innovation and all he wished to do was enshrine in statute the unbroken practice of the Church of England since the Reformation. He rehearsed the history in detail including resolutions of Convocation and also of the American bishops against ritualism. He added, "the Ritualistic system adopted in many of our churches has altogether changed their Protestant character and given to them the appearance of Popish places of worship, so as scarcely, and oftentimes not at all, to be distinguishable from those of the Church of Rome". Shaftesbury pointed out to the House that the Anglo-Catholic position itself was that ritual expressed doctrine. He quoted at length from a manual of Anglo-Catholic devotion and ceremony. He stated, "strange and abhorrent as they may be to our Protestant feelings, there are many earnest, though deluded, minds that hold and teach them".[3] Thirty years earlier he had claimed, perhaps tongue in cheek, that more space was needed at Bedlam for the Puseyites.

> *Are we to be subjected to a system of Ritualism which, if*
> *merely for decoration, is childish and irreverent; but which,*
> *if symbolical of the deepest mysteries of our faith, amounts to*
> *blasphemy? Will your Lordships take the trouble to look at the*
> *Preface of the Book of Common Prayer, and read that part of it*
> *which explains why certain ceremonies were retained and certain*
> *others were rejected?*[4]

Shaftesbury argued that he was acting in defence of the laity. The preface to the Book of Common Prayer referred to the abolition of ceremonies which had led to superstition and abuse. Shaftesbury was seeking to prevent the reintroduction of ceremonies excluded from the Prayer Book. The lay people had looked to the clergy and then to the bishops for protection. Nothing had been done. The laity he said was now taking matters into its own hands. Convocation, he said, was to be distrusted because it was purely a clerical body. This bill was to protect the laity; vestments were not merely a clerical matter. His speech occupied some twenty-two columns in Hansard. Shaftesbury probably knew his bill was heading for defeat. He noted in his diary:

> *Much time and trouble on Vestments Bill. It is right, and it is hopeless, to undertake this cause. There are many open, and more secret, sympathisers with the Ritualists; defeat is certain; success would not bring much, for the abomination is but a symptom of a deep and incurable disease, a disease quite unreachable by anything short of God's Spirit...* [5]

The bill was defeated by 61 votes to 40. The next day he reflected in his diary that the bill, even if passed, would have been destroyed piecemeal. The victory was the Royal Commission on Ritual. He was invited to be a member, but declined. He acknowledged his own strong feelings but did not place much hope in the Commission.

The Commission's reports, in August 1867 and April 1868, were unsatisfactory to Evangelical eyes in not passing judgment upon the contentious issues. To Shaftesbury, more action was needed. Thus the Earl introduced to the Lords, the Uniformity of Public Worship Bill, which was read a second time on 9 July 1868. This time he sought to legislate on vestments, incense, and candles. The Commissioners had also pointed out that the use of candles and incense in parish churches was a very recent innovation. The bill was intended to give legal force to the Commissioners' call for restraint in all these areas. For the avoidance of doubt (the issue being whether the matters were already illegal), the use of candles on the communion table, except where necessary for the purposes of light, and of incense were to be declared illegal, along with vestments. Shaftesbury argued that ritualism was an occupation of the more well-to-do class and held little attraction for working people. He drew a contrast between the ornate worship of St Alban's and the simple services at Field Lane School, just 150 yards away, attended by 800 to 1,000 of the poor. He similarly highlighted the attraction of simple theatre services to the poor. Shaftesbury stated that his strong feelings on the matter had not diminished at all. The bill was opposed by the Archbishop of Canterbury and failed without a vote being taken.

Had Shaftesbury lost perspective? Perhaps he had become obsessed by the Protestant crusade to such an extent that he became distracted from the wider mission in which he did so much good. Certainly it was a doubtful judgment to seek to bring the law to bear as the arbiter of church vestments and practices. Shaftesbury himself acknowledged that much in recognizing that an Act of Parliament which was disregarded in practice would soon fall apart. Regrettably, as we will see shortly, Shaftesbury appears not to have learnt that lesson. In his defence, Protestantism was not only the Evangelical faith, it was also the faith of the Church of England and, indeed, of the state of England. In these circumstances Shaftesbury saw it as his duty, whether he liked it or not, to ensure church and state remained faithful to that which had been entrusted to them.

Bible revision and domestic matters

In 1869 Minny took Constance, the couple's eighth child, to Cannes to aid her recovery from illness. As usual the Earl lamented the separation. The weight of debt and lawsuits related to the estates continued to bear heavily. He even objected that Jesus had borne all the sorrows of humanity – except for debt! Now in his late sixties, he was still very busy. In May of that year he led 100,000 people in the unveiling of a statue in Bradford to the factory campaigner, Richard Oastler. It was a whole week of visits and speeches before returning to London. In July he commented, "no end of chairs, speeches, committees".[6] In September, Lady Palmerston died.

The year 1870 saw Shaftesbury in battle alongside his cousin, Pusey, over the proposed revision of the Bible. Shaftesbury wrote to *The Times* on 14 February 1870 in his capacity as President of the Bible Society opposing any revision of the Authorized Version. The letter generated much heat and correspondence. A few days later Shaftesbury wrote to Gladstone. He stated that the Authorized Version had "passed into universal acceptance and there has nestled in the hearts of men for 250 years".[7] However, by writing as he did in his role as President, Shaftesbury potentially compromised the Society's neutrality on the matter. The Society's Editorial Superintendent, R. B. Girdlestone, wrote to Shaftesbury stating that the role of the Society was to print the Bible, not critique it, adding: "we are not called upon as a Society to hinder the work of revision or to pronounce judgement on the motives of those who have organised it".[8]

Shaftesbury responded that he had not realized that the Society was favourably disposed to a new translation and said he did not understand the "print, not critique" position. Further correspondence ensued. It was pointed out that the matter had not been discussed in the committee. Shaftesbury made clear that the issue should indeed be debated by the committee and was likely to be raised at meetings. He added: "I will not disguise from you that so far as I am concerned I cannot keep silent."[9]

However, under pressure from officials of the Society he wrote again to *The Times* to make clear that his previous letter had been written in a personal rather than official capacity. He made clear in a further letter to the committee that he would remain neither silent nor neutral. He went on to spell out the obvious implication:

It rests with you to decide how far this course is consistent with the position of your President. It will be my duty whatever be the result to accept your judgement.[10]

To have Lord Shaftesbury occupying such a prominent place in the life of the Society was a great and significant honour. It was not necessarily comfortable. Wisely the committee rejected the proposed resignation. The Bible Society was twice a focus for doctrinal disputes within Evangelicalism during Shaftesbury's lifetime. They illustrate the tension within such societies that gather around a single objective.

The same year was, as already noted, the year of the Education Act. Shaftesbury was fully aware of the implications. The freedom to teach the Bible in schools and indeed the future of the Ragged Schools themselves were at stake.

Shaftesbury gained support from the prominent Baptist minister Charles Haddon Spurgeon who wrote to Shaftesbury, stating that "the Word itself must not be shut out".[11] Despite Anglicans and Dissenters joining together, the prime minister, Gladstone, would not budge.

In 1871 Shaftesbury celebrated his wedding anniversary with praise and thanks to God for his wife. The same summer saw the family needing to spend time on the Riviera because of Constance's poor health and then Cecil, the youngest son, fell ill, as did Minny. In 1872 Shaftesbury was battling against the Ballot Act – the introduction of the secret ballot in elections. Shaftesbury took the view that people of principle should declare their positions openly. Correspondence with Minny, who was still in the south of France, revealed that Conty was improving: the Earl missed his wife, despite being surrounded by his grandchildren, for whom he had nicknames – Gigas, the Dwarf, Rover.

Minny had not always enjoyed the best of health. In his diary on his wedding anniversary (10 June 1872) he poured out his feelings, despite being a year out as to the date of his anniversary.

To-day my wedding day! Forty-one years ago was I united to that dear, beautiful, true, and affectionate darling, my blessed Minny. What a faithful, devoted, simple-hearted, and captivating

wife she has been, and is, to me! And what a mother! Ah, Lord,
give me grace to thank Thee evermore, and rejoice in Thy
goodness. Send forth Thy Holy Spirit on us, and lead us yet in
the way of service, obedience, and of love! But still she is absent!
God, in Thy mercy, bring her home speedily and safely, and with
her, my poor, precious, suffering Conty![12]

Mother and daughter did return, but a little over four months later
Minny was dead. At the end of September he wrote to the Golden
Lane Costers' Mission asking for prayer. On 15 October Minny
died. He lamented his dear wife. "Minny, my own Minny, is gone.
God took her soul to Himself at about twelve o'clock this morning.
She has entered into her rest and has left us to feel the loss of the
purest, gentlest, kindest, sweetest and most confiding spirit that
ever lived. Oh, my God, what a blow! But we bow before Thee
in resignation and sorrow. Almost her last words were, 'None but
Christ, none but Christ'."[13] The Queen wrote to him, as did many
others. There was a great deal of personal sadness in Shaftesbury's
long life. Before the year was out, Conty his daughter had also
passed away.

In the aftermath of the debacle of the Uniformity of Public
Worship Bill Shaftesbury turned his attention to the reform of the
ecclesiastical courts and to Convocation. This latter body was the
meeting of clergy representatives from the Province of Canterbury.
Shaftesbury had generally opposed its revival for two reasons. First,
it was purely a clerical body; and second, it excluded the Province
of York. In 1872 he sought to prevent Convocation from sitting,
or at the very least that major reform should be instituted, as
ordinary clergy and the laity were being alienated. He sought an
extended franchise, but nothing was done. Ritualism continued,
conflict remained, and Shaftesbury was at the heart of it. Attempts
to provide for auricular confession within the church provoked his
wrath. He presided over a meeting at Exeter Hall, sided with the
Church Association, and threatened further attempts at legislation.

Archbishop Tait was not only under pressure from the Evangelical leadership but also from the Queen who disliked ritualism as un-English.

Sweeps again

The fifth report of the Children's Employment Commission in 1866 gave evidence of the continued evasion of the amended Act regulating sweeps. However, problems remained. The matter had now been laid before Parliament by the Earl of Shaftesbury for over a quarter of a century. The matter stirred again in late 1872 when a climbing boy, Christopher Drummond, died in a flue at Washington Hall near Gateshead. The boy was about eight years old and had been sent up to remove an obstruction and suffocated. Shaftesbury was prompted to write to *The Times*. He wrote in his diary that he was "yesterday stirred, after a long period, by my poor climbing boys... Years of oppression and cruelty have rolled on, and now a death has given me the power of one more appeal to the public".[14] After reporting the case and noting his own attempts to bring protection, he went on:

> *This system still prevails to a frightful extent in cities that plume themselves on their liberality and civilization – in Manchester, Nottingham, and Sheffield. It is simply a disgrace to England.*[15]

He had lost none of his fire. However, the public and the press remained unmoved. Then three years later in 1875 a boy of fourteen, George Brewster, died in a flue in Cambridge. The master sweep was convicted and sentenced to six months' hard labour. On this occasion *The Times* thundered in an editorial that the time had come for a final review of the system. Shaftesbury asked a question in the Lords as to whether the government would institute an inquiry. This boy had suffocated from the soot in his lungs despite having been in the flue for only a few minutes. The request for an inquiry was denied. Shaftesbury gave notice to the House of Lords on 20 April 1875 of his intention to bring in a new bill. The second reading was to be on 11 May. Shaftesbury lamented that the misery of the climbing boys had been before the public eye for over a century, "yet in many parts of England and Ireland it still prevails, with the full knowledge and consent of thousands of all classes".[16]

The bill proposed a system of annual licensing of chimney sweeps under the jurisdiction of the local police. A register had to be maintained and it would not be lawful to carry on business without a certificate or to fail to provide name and address to an officer of the crown. Certificates were non-transferable. Offences under the Acts of 1864 and 1840 would result in suspension of the certificate.

On the second reading in the Lords Shaftesbury adopted the pattern he had long used for his major speeches. He stated that the bill "concerned the temporal and eternal welfare of some thousands of children, the most oppressed, degraded, and tortured creatures on the face of the earth". He set out the history of regulation. He reminded the House, in graphic detail, of the evidence submitted to various committees and commissions. He went on to state that "he had given them but a sample of the atrocities perpetrated under this Satanic system".[17] The bill passed unscathed and quickly progressed through its remaining stages in both Lords and Commons to become law.

This Act effectively ended a century of oppression. Shaftesbury had pioneered and championed the campaign for protection for thirty-five years. The Earl was seventy-four years old when the Act finally passed. Despite the ups and downs of the legislative process over the years Shaftesbury had shown remarkable perseverance and long-term commitment to this cause. It was a characteristic of his campaigns and a reason for his success. Throughout he had been meticulous in the gathering and presenting of evidence. He had placed his trust in his faith both for himself but also as the key motivating factor for his work. For Shaftesbury the eternal destiny and welfare of a chimney sweep or factory worker was equally but no less essential to their temporal and bodily welfare. These campaigns were remarkable. Perhaps Parliament would eventually have legislated in these matters. However, without doubt, the character, tenacity, and skill of the Earl of Shaftesbury ensured that the need for, evidence, and follow-up of the necessary legislation was always before Parliament and indeed the nation at large. He turned down office and honour in order to keep his life and mind focused on all of those for whom Jesus died.

Spurgeon and others

Shaftesbury drew sustenance in this time of distress from his friendship with Spurgeon, minister of the Metropolitan Tabernacle just south of the River Thames. He regarded Spurgeon with great favour – "few men have preached so much and so well, and few men have combined so practically their words and their actions. I deeply admire and love him…"[18] In June 1870 Spurgeon asked Shaftesbury to chair the annual meeting of his orphanage in Stockwell, "to serve the cause of the fatherless,"[19] showing the warmth of the relationship. Spurgeon wrote to Shaftesbury the next month:

> *I was deeply saddened when I saw you last to find you so depressed. The Lord is with us yet. I do not believe he will let your spirits sink. Your trials have been seven fold.*[20]

The Earl visited Spurgeon three years later to review Spurgeon's institutions of social welfare. He was, said Shaftesbury, "a wonderful man, full of zeal, affection, faith, abounding in reputation and authority, and yet perfectly humble".[21] Even at eighty years old, Shaftesbury was still visiting Spurgeon and his wife at home – finding him on 10 July 1881 "still full of perseverance, faith, and joy, in the service of our blessed lord".[22] Spurgeon wrote to Shaftesbury bemoaning that "men in whom I had confidence are turning aside.

They undermine the foundations by casting doubt upon the canon of inspiration".[23] In 1884, just a year before he died, Spurgeon requested Shaftesbury to preside over the preacher's fiftieth birthday celebrations:

> *If we are spared till then, will you take the Chair? You shall be allowed to go in one hour if you feel at all tired… You are a truly wonderful man to work as you do, but I do not like to see you worried and I fear you are at this time… I should like you to come because I want <u>old-fashioned Evangelical Doctrine</u> to be identified with the event. I am a fair representative of the old faith, even as you are, and I shall ask only men of our own order of belief, as far as I can be sure of anybody.*[24]

Shaftesbury did not embrace all new players on the scene. He lamented towards the end of his life that he once knew what an Evangelical was, but had no clear notion as to what constituted one now. He was, perhaps surprisingly, critical of the Salvation Army, finding no scriptural warrant for their method of organization. They were also, of course, providing some competition in the field. The American revivalists Moody and Sankey also aroused his suspicions, but he revised his opinion. He went to one of the meetings in 1875 and was impressed by the humility, the simplicity of the gospel message, and the effect on the ordinary people. Shaftesbury was not a revivalist, more committed to the constant, hard, steady work of the gospel. His nuanced understanding of the "end times" preserved him from over-emphasis on secondary matters and kept him focused on the life of "faithful discipleship".

The Public Worship Regulation Act 1874

The final part of the story of Lord Shaftesbury and the ritualist controversies concerns another piece of legislation, closely linked to his name, though he was not the initial instigator, the ill-fated

Public Worship Regulation Act of 1874. This was actually put forward by Archbishop Tait in response to the pressures upon him. It was, at this point, a rather modest measure which in Shaftesbury's view left too much power in the hands of the bishops themselves. Shaftesbury commented on one occasion to CPAS that "I am not such a lover of episcopacy as to think it necessary to salvation".[25] However, Shaftesbury was persuaded by the Evangelical Lord Chancellor, Lord Cairns, to seek to improve and strengthen the bill. Shaftesbury spoke in the second reading debate on 11 May 1874 but his main move came in committee on 4 June. The essential scope of the bill was to regulate all matters to do with ornaments, vesture, and the directions of the Book of Common Prayer. The issue was who would pass judgment – the bishop or an independent judge. Shaftesbury feared numerous contradictory opinions from the bishops and probably a lack of will on the part of many. Shaftesbury moved an amendment that jurisdiction should be exercised by a single judge for the Provinces of Canterbury and York. This would lead to better procedure and demonstrate independence. It was a master stroke. The ability of the bishops to frustrate or to give contradictory judgments was removed. There would be a senior lay judge to sit in all cases. Tait was in a quandary but, wary of more drastic moves from the Church Association, threw his lot in with Shaftesbury. Although Shaftesbury was not the originator of the bill he had transformed its application. He compromised to allow a bishop some discretion in deciding whether or not a case should go ahead, but he also headed off an attempt to legalize the eastward-facing position of the priest at communion – a high church practice. Much of Shaftesbury's work was related to what he had previously sought to enact in seeking the reform of the ecclesiastical courts. The high church party resisted civil judges (as they had in the Gorham case and more widely in the origins of the Oxford Movement); to a lay national Protestant, it was entirely right. Shaftesbury endured much abuse from the press and the bill was not yet securely on the statute book.

The bill then moved to the Commons, facilitated by Disraeli's government, but opposed by Gladstone. The latter overplayed his hand. Shaftesbury described Gladstone's speech as florid and fallacious. Gladstone set out a viewpoint that even Disraeli described as subverting the country's religious system. This gave Disraeli the opportunity to provide more time for the bill and to demand a decision from the House. Shaftesbury noted in his diary that there were nearly 600 members present for the second reading which was carried without a division. In committee the key clause of a lay judge was carried. The Earl noted that the "finger of God has been manifest all through".[26] There remained some tricky negotiations which involved Shaftesbury seeking to persuade MPs to accept the Lords' rejection of a Commons amendment to give right of appeal to the Archbishop against a bishop's decision not to place a case before the judge. Shaftesbury's political and negotiating skills should not be underestimated. Rivalry between the two Houses was intense. The amendment had been introduced on behalf of the Church Association. Shaftesbury, whatever his weaknesses and failings on the matter, could see that to press the point would lose the whole bill. So the Public Worship Regulation Act received the Royal Assent on 7 August 1874.

The application of the Act proved problematic. The compromise on the episcopal veto meant few cases came before the judge, Lord Penzance, sitting in the Court of Arches. This entailed what Shaftesbury had sought to avoid – disparity in decisions over the determination of cases. There were other problems as well. The basic weapon in the hands of the court was an injunction to desist. However, Anglo-Catholic clergy were unlikely to acquiesce. The outcome was disaster. In 1876 Arthur Tooth, vicar of the London parish of St James Hatcham, was charged under the Act with the use of vestments, incense, and candles. He refused to attend the hearings and ignored the court's injunctions. In January 1877 he was jailed for contempt of court. The charges against Sydney Fairthorne Green were extensive. They included the use of the mixed chalice, making the sign of the cross, the eastward position, and elevating the bread, as well as the usual matters of vestments and candles. Refusing the injunctions of the court, Green was jailed for contempt in March 1880. Three other clergy, Thomas Pelham Dale, Richard William Enraght, and James Bell Cox were also imprisoned for contempt. The last case, that of Bell Cox, was in Liverpool, the diocese presided over by the leading Evangelical J. C. Ryle. The bishop consistently refused to intervene to exercise his veto or discretion to prevent Bell Cox's imprisonment.

The key issue was that once a cleric had refused to recognize the court's injunctions, the individual came into contempt of court, the sanction for which was imprisonment until the contempt was purged. The Public Worship Regulation Act was falling quickly into disrepute. The jailing of clergy for liturgical practice and the continued persecutions by the Church Association increased public sympathy for the Anglo-Catholics and severely damaged Evangelical standing. Indeed it proved a considerable distraction for Evangelicals from their core purposes. This was not what Shaftesbury desired or intended. However, his judgment in supporting these various Acts of Parliament, bringing the statute book to the communion table, were suspect. Although his position was consistent and understandable he failed to appreciate the nature of the consequences and indeed the changing scene of Protestantism in Britain. Principled as he was, he never regretted these actions, but the damage to the Evangelical cause was serious. If in his Christian social work Shaftesbury showed himself to be a man ahead of his times, in his battle against ritualism he demonstrated his ability to stick so rigidly to his Protestant principles that he lost sight of the wider cause of the gospel.

The later years
In 1876 Shaftesbury was urging the Queen not to accept the title of Empress of India. To him it was simply vulgar and detracted

from the regard due to God. The same year he showed his breadth
of interests by opposing vivisection. Speaking on it in the Lords
he bemoaned the fact that the bishops all disappeared from the
chamber at dinner-time – "of what use are the Bishops in the
House of Lords".[27] He added the following month: "The thought
of this diabolical system disturbs me night and day. God remember
Thy poor, humble, useful creatures..."[28] In 1879, speaking in the
parliamentary debate on the Cruelty to Animals Bill, he appealed
to the principles of stewardship, biblical authority, and creation.
He referred to experiments on the brain of a dog conducted by a
German Professor:

> And that was the use they made of the creatures committed
> to their charge – that the account they would render of their
> stewardship. All he could say was – and he said it truly and
> conscientiously – that, in every respect, he would definitely
> rather be the dog than be the Professor. But whether the law
> was efficient or inefficient, whether vivisection was conducive to
> science, or the reverse, there was one great primary consideration.
> On what authority of Scripture, or any other form of Revelation,
> he asked most solemnly, did they rest their right to subject God's
> creatures to such unspeakable sufferings?... The animals were
> His creatures as much as we were His creatures; and "His tender
> mercies", so the Bible told us, "were over all His works."[29]

In his later years Shaftesbury lost none of his zeal or passion for
the truth. He had a low view of poorly performing clergy and
shallowness of faith.

> He preaches very smooth things. In a long sermon about
> forgiveness and God's mercy, he mentioned "sin" once... What
> is belief? What does it contain? What does it demand? Does
> it demand conviction of sin, confession of sin, repentance and
> faith? All these things, except faith, are dropped now-a-days... it

is in fact reduced to an easy, agreeable acceptance of a pleasant invitation, to be had at any time that is convenient to you.[30]

In March 1879 the Earl was reporting himself, "heavily pressed and heavily oppressed. Have lost all my former buoyancy, and contemplate effort with something akin to terror. Lie down very much for short intervals; and so get strength and a whiff of courage... Heartily pray to God, hour by hour, that I may have power to discharge the 'few things that remain'."[31]

Shaftesbury was ill, he was burdened by money troubles, and Cecil was suffering from a second dangerous illness. Nevertheless, in 1880, Shaftesbury was able to unveil a statue to Robert Raikes in Gloucester in commemoration of the centenary of Sunday Schools, of which Raikes was the pioneer. He attended a similar event at Carisbrooke Castle on the Isle of Wight a few days later at the request of his son, Evelyn, the MP for the island. In 1881 Shaftesbury was still chairing meetings but his health was becoming more difficult, describing himself as in very bad heart. He spent much time reading Scripture but was able on 14 June 1882 to attend the anniversary of the One Tun Ragged School. In July his close friend Alexander Haldane died. Christmas was spent with the family at St Giles. He continued his exertions in 1883. In June of 1884 he received the freedom of the City of London.

CHAPTER 14

A PASSIONATE FAITH: UNDERSTANDING SHAFTESBURY'S MOTIVATION

Why did Shaftesbury act as he did? What were the factors which motivated his life's work and commitments? Various elements of his purpose, his intellectual and religious rationale have emerged during the review of his life. To complete the biography of "the great reformer", we need to understand the inspiration for his work.

The religious, indeed theological, factors were central. To Shaftesbury the idea of mission was an essential part of his Evangelical faith. His understanding, however, of the Christian imperative embraced evangelistic initiative, social welfare concern, government intervention, and voluntary action. This combination made him somewhat unusual. He saw the established Church of England as being uniquely placed to exercise this responsibility through its parish system. He encouraged flexibility. This included the reform of Sunday evening services and, as we have seen, the holding of services in theatres and the open air. According to Shaftesbury no one at home or overseas should be left bereft of the message of the Christian gospel.

Shaftesbury's beliefs placed him in the mainstream of the Evangelical tradition. He believed humanity to be corrupt and flawed. Forgiveness could be obtained only through the death of Jesus on the cross. In his notes of religious reflections which Ashley kept in the 1830s this theme was prominent. Any idea of human perfection he held in absolute horror. The heart was deceitful and wicked. Perhaps this reflected the dark side of his own character as well as Christianity. He commented that the "best act that the best man ever did, contains in it that which is worthy of condemnation".[1] This pessimistic view of humanity was contrasted with an optimistic view of God. The message of salvation needed to be carried afar. The preaching of the gospel was both a means of conversion and a witness to the truth. The Christian message would be preached through thick and thin, success and failure – the early missionary movement had a good deal of the latter to contend with.

The role of the voluntary society

Shaftesbury's life calling revolved around a dual commitment. The first of these was to legislative action and intervention on behalf of those most in need of the protection of the state. This was affected significantly by his "national Protestantism", a belief in the Christian state and its responsibilities. The second was to the principle of the voluntary society. In Victorian England a wide spectrum of such societies developed. These ranged from visiting societies and working men's organizations to Evangelical social missionary societies. Although such voluntary associations were not new there was a significant expansion in the nineteenth century. They were characterized by an independence from state aid and formed part of middle-class identity.

These general features also fitted well the increasing number of societies advancing Evangelical aims. Early Evangelical societies often represented the voluntary work for God of the middle class. The industrialization of society tended to reinforce paternalistic attitudes with the working classes becoming objects of pity and activity. Some critics argued that this represented the middle classes working out their salvation. Effectively the voluntary society, even the Christian one, was a response to middle-class guilt over socio-economic conditions. Many secular groups formed for the benefit of the working classes such as building societies, savings clubs, and clothing clubs were aimed at the industrious working class rather than the poorest sections of society. However much of the work supported and encouraged by Shaftesbury reached to the very underbelly of society. Although the bigger organizations such as the LCM and the CPAS employed paid agents, most workers in the voluntary societies were unpaid. This included many of the Evangelical societies including all teachers in ragged schools. Women were prominent.

Many secular voluntary societies distinguished between "deserving" and "undeserving" poverty. This was especially so under the influence of utilitarianism and political economy (the standard terminology for the "free market"). The draw of the voluntary society to proponents of these philosophies was that it kept social welfare separate from state intervention. Poverty was assessed by the visitor and concern for the poor was shown. However, there was little structural attempt to deal with the conditions and the assumption was always that the industrious could lift themselves out of their poverty.

Shaftesbury, however, represents an entirely different outlook. The voluntary society was a place for social relationships to be worked out in the new industrial age. It was here where the old rural paternalism and mutual responsibility could be put into practice. Critics today might view this as institutionalized paternalism or a form of social control that allowed middle-class elites to continue to exercise their authority and power, even to legitimize such power.

There was a remarkable increase in the number of voluntary societies after 1850. Much of the reason for this rests with the Evangelical societies. Kathleen Heasman carried out a comprehensive study of this phenomenon and concluded that "as many as three-quarters of the total number of voluntary charitable organizations in the second half of the nineteenth century can be regarded as Evangelical in character and control".[2] There is an obvious connection between the sociological development of the voluntary society and the use of such mechanisms by Evangelicals for their work. Nevertheless, the parallels are not exact. For Evangelicals there were also deeply theological reasons. For the Christian there was a concern to make the world a more suitable place to which Christ should return. Revivalist campaigns such as those of the American Dwight Moody (who visited the United Kingdom in 1867, 1873–75, 1881–84 and 1891) led to significant recruitment of workers for Evangelical voluntary societies.

The dominance of Evangelical Christian voluntary societies within the sector may help explain why secular reformers looked toward a more exclusive role for the state. Government was seen as neutral and there was a reluctance to embrace models or approaches driven by Christian conviction. For a national Protestant the state was neither neutral nor secular so it was an entirely appropriate response to allocate a role to the state. However, for Shaftesbury there were also limits upon the state's power and capability. Sin meant that the government could not be completely relied upon. The activities of the state removed the essential requirement of personal relationships in care and action in society. So for Shaftesbury the answer lay in both state and Christian voluntary action. For him also the latter could not divide the social and evangelistic. This was a dynamic position which recognized the failures of over-reliance upon the state, while giving a genuine role to both state and voluntary action.

The practical effect of all of this can be gauged from the impact of the 1870 Education Act. This piece of legislation was a watershed in the history of social thought. As the state became more secular the dynamic of the Christian voluntary society was diluted. The Act itself effectively introduced compulsory state education. The legislation established school boards with the responsibility for the provision of schooling in each area. The rationale was entirely understandable. The coverage of the ragged schools and the other charitable schools was patchy and standards variable. It is unfair to say that the Act removed the Bible from schools. The die, however, was cast. The ragged schools declined quickly. Once government was in charge the place of the Bible in schooling was likely to decline, not least because professional teachers rather than volunteers were less at ease in handling the material. It was only a matter of time before the state began to dominate in other areas of voluntary provision. The main losers were the Evangelical societies.

Shaftesbury's position was thus considerably more nuanced and vibrant than the critical epitaph of "Tory paternalism". The bringing together of a state with Protestant and Christian responsibilities into partnership with both social and evangelistic voluntary agencies produced a dynamic that has not since been repeated. The reasons behind his approach were, of course, complex, but were deeply affected by his Christian thinking.

Sin and Paternalism

Sin is non-negotiable for Evangelicals. Exactly what constitutes sin is another matter. Shaftesbury, like all good Evangelicals, was against sin. In traditional theology sin constituted a personal moral failing. Evangelicals extended this understanding to include a person's whole attitude towards God, but in practice sin remained a personal moral matter. It was rarely extended into the social sphere. Shaftesbury was also influenced by the paternalistic norm accepted for a high Tory of his times. Aristocratic duty was a responsibility to be exercised for which account would be given to God. Shaftesbury's paternalism led him to apply Evangelical concepts of sin to breaches of the covenant between the various groups in society. This had two implications. First, sin was moved from merely personal into the realm of wider social relationships. Second, it allowed for a more corporate understanding of sin as it related to the ills of society. The essence of Shaftesbury's understanding was holding the dynamic between the individual and the corporate, not allowing them to be separated. His agrarian paternalism affected how he expressed these views, but the key elements were clear.

> *Avarice and cruelty are not the peculiar and inherent qualities*
> *of any one class or occupation – they will ever be found*
> *where means of profit are combined with great, and, virtually*
> *irresponsible power – they will be found wherever interest*
> *and selfishness have a purpose to serve, and a favourable*
> *opportunity.*[3]

The underlying principle could be equally applied in the contemporary age. In fact Ashley was speaking in the debate on the Factories Bill in 1844. He had earlier told the House in the 1840 debate on the Employment of Children that the poor tended to think "capital odious, for wealth is known to them only by its oppressions".[4] He warned against those "who erect capital into a divinity and worship it with ten times more intensity than the God who created them".[5] He went on to denounce in the 1840 debate the legalized slavery of children – a child effectively being used as security for a loan the parents could never pay off. His *Quarterly Review* article on the Factory System, four years earlier, as noted in Chapter 6, had been equally clear. Humanity was being treated as a machine, children seen as of less value than cattle, valued only for the amount of work they produced. He maintained that it was impossible for the nation to claim to be a Christian country when the wealthy preferred climbing boys to machines and magistrates connived at breaches of the law. He came very close to a concept of corporate sin: "… But their guilt is our guilt; we incur it by conniving at it."[6] Remarkable words for a Tory who despised socialism and trade unionism!

From this starting point Shaftesbury denounced the sinful breakdown of social and domestic relationships. Perhaps the paternalism is too strong here for the modern mind but it was a logical extension of his powerful critique. Shaftesbury did not use the language of rights, more that of responsibility and duty. The wealthy, the landowners, the proprietors of factories all had obligations to those they employed or had some form of relationship with. Breach of those responsibilities or violation of duty constituted sin. This ranged from the quest for profit, excessive labour, beatings, and starvation through to factory owners sitting as magistrates on cases concerning their own factories. This idea of sin was then extended to domestic life, including the relationship of parents and children. The question was not only the behaviour of children, but also the neglect of duty by parents under the pressures of work. Although Shaftesbury advocated traditional paternalistic responsibilities in the home it is too simplistic to see his views as prejudicial and irrelevant. He extended his analysis across the whole range of relationships and responsibilities. Crucially for Shaftesbury the analysis was always linked to Evangelical Christianity. It was only possible to understand the nature of sin and its social remedy if one first understood the nature of sin and its eternal remedy. It was, in his view, impossible to teach the precepts of the Good Samaritan or any other parable apart from the doctrines of Christianity and the centrality of the atonement. When this is added to his stress on stewardship and accountability at the day of judgment, something of the Evangelical basis of Shaftesbury's social views begins to emerge.

The Bible and Protestantism

Shaftesbury's understanding of the Bible and the Protestant faith formed a bedrock for his life and actions. His views on the Bible were uncompromising. He believed it was all that was needed for a relationship with God, that it was word for word from God and contained no errors (in technical terms the ideas of the sufficiency, plenary inspiration, and inerrancy of Scripture). His basic maxim was to "let the Bible tell its own story, use its own language, make its own appeals. Enforce all these, but add nothing of your own".[7] He told CPAS:

> *There is no security whatever except in standing upon the faith of our fathers, and saying with them that the blessed old Book is "God's Word written", from the very first syllable down to the very last, and from the last back to the first.*[8]

Liberal rationalism was challenging the authenticity of many aspects of the Bible. Shaftesbury was quite explicit that the key contested parts of the Old Testament would be proved. This included the literal creation, the flood and Noah's Ark. Every syllable would become clear, he wrote in his diary on 29 August 1863. He followed the sixteenth-century Reformer, John Calvin, in adopting one basic approach to interpretation, "nothing but Scripture can interpret Scripture".[9] He deeply appreciated Calvin's *Commentaries*.

In *The Record* Ashley declared: "Let us then, as Protestants, stand by that which alone was the pillar and ground of truth – the Bible, the whole Bible and nothing but the Bible."[10] Scripture was to Shaftesbury a crucial component of the Christian life. It was to be studied privately and devotionally, guiding the whole of life and being, equally applicable in both private and public domains. He argued that Second Chronicles should be studied, prayed over, and weighed by every person in public life. The Bible was the Word of God and he considered himself firmly under its authority. The Scriptures spoke not only to the intellect but also to the heart. Shaftesbury also argued, speaking to the Bible Society, that the Bible was its own missionary.

> *Tens of thousands have thrown off their corrupt and ignorant faith, not in consequence of the efforts of preachers, or teachers, or lecturers, but simply and solely from reading the Word of God, pure and unadulterated, without note or comment, without any teaching except the blessed teaching of God's Holy Spirit.* [11]

Shaftesbury believed in the rights of access of the ordinary person to the Scriptures and their ability to understand its message. He stated, responding to the liberal rationalism of *Essays and Reviews*, published in 1860:

> *I maintain, that if their principles of interpretation be true, the Bible is not the Book for the poor man, the Bible is not the Book for general and universal circulation. If it be true that the Bible can be comprehended only by the learned, only after long and prolonged thought, by great acquisitions in classical and ancient knowledge, – if that be true, do you not at once, by that admission, shut out the right [of circulating the Scriptures] because you shut out the possibility of private judgement?* [12]

The challenge to the place of Scripture came not only from rationalism but also from Tractarianism. He saw the CPAS as the main bulwark.[13] He commented: "The constitution of this Society is essentially Protestant. It is Protestant in its principles. It is Protestant in its character. It is Protestant in its action. It is Protestant in its organisation."[14]

Christian unity

Shaftesbury was passionately committed to the cooperation of Christians across denominational boundaries – the concept of Evangelical catholicity. This principle was expressed in his work and support for many of the great missionary societies. For the Earl the twin evils to be resisted, as he told the Bible Society, in an association very clear to nineteenth-century Evangelical eyes, even if not to contemporary ones, were Satan and Popery. Evangelical unity would bring immeasurable benefits to the people. This was true of both their eternal salvation and their temporal welfare. The supreme requirement of imparting the gospel to others was the higher and superior object to all others. So he regarded the Bible Society as "a solemn league and covenant of all those who 'love the Lord Jesus Christ with sincerity'; that it shows how, members of the Church of England and Nonconformists may band together in one great effort".[15]

Shaftesbury believed that such interdenominational cooperation could bring immense benefit to the masses of the metropolis. In 1845 he noted in his diary a meeting at a ragged school:

Last night Broadwall Infant Ragged School; very humble, but very useful; well received... Many Dissenters; but it is high time to be thinking where we agree, not where we differ. Tens of thousands of untaught heathens in the heart of a Christian metropolis cry aloud for vengeance.[16]

In 1862 Shaftesbury advocated the same line with the RSU.

All who care for the advancement of Christ's kingdom, to whatever church they may belong, must join together, heart and soul, for the purpose of bringing to completion this great, this mighty undertaking.[17]

Shaftesbury was something of an enigma in pan-Evangelical

cooperation. He was both an Evangelical and committed to the established church. He loved the liturgy and was critical of Dissent. Yet at the same time he was committed to united action, working together for the greater good. He was an idealist. Nothing must get in the way of the gospel. Nothing must be allowed to hold back practical Christian action.

In a remarkable speech for its time Shaftesbury told the 1863 annual meeting of the LCM:

Put all that aside, and let all establishments and all distinctive churches sink into the ground, compared with the one great effort to preach the doctrine of Christ crucified to every creature on the earth, to every creature that can be reached on this habitable globe.[18]

The volunteer laity

The term "lay agency" referred to the use of non-ordained workers, whether voluntary or paid. The principle bound Shaftesbury to several missionary societies. In his view lay agency was "absolutely and essentially necessary".[19] He was, of course, himself the prime example. It was a principle to be stood for and never departed from, the biblical basis of mission and indispensable to its practice. Shaftesbury defended and advocated lay agency both as a theological position and also as a pragmatic method for mission. Both the CPAS and the LCM were based upon the view espoused by Shaftesbury "that if you wish to win working men, you must enlist for that service a vast body of the working men themselves".[20] He commented on the LCM's lay workers that "not a few of them [are] drawn from the very ranks they are enlisted to assail".[21] He added in his diary that lay agency provided a means "to penetrate and percolate those large masses to which access [was] very often denied to the ordained minister".[22] In similar vein he commented on the voluntary teachers in ragged schools: "Ragged Schools reach a depth below them, and occupy a field which can only be occupied by volunteer agents."[23]

The privileged ranks of the established church had been unable to respond to the challenge of mission to the emerging working classes. The necessary and appropriate response required a much wider view of ministry than ordained ministry. To Shaftesbury the lay agency principle was a much more effective way of meeting both the social and spiritual needs of the people.

Shaftesbury always preferred the option of supporting and supplying living agents for mission and was highly sceptical of the fashion for church building (often known as church extension).

"We want men, not churches". How true! I have known many churches without congregations, but I never knew a pious congregation which did not desire, and soon obtain, a place of worship.[24]

Six years later, in 1879, he had not lost the sharp sting that his tongue could carry.

I will only say that I retain all my strong feelings of the great importance of a living agent over and above the material edifice. A living agent may save the Church; the multiplication of cathedrals will rather tend to sink it.[25]

He described the obsession with church building in the midst of spiritual destitution as monstrous and idolatrous.

The Earl demonstrated a long-standing passion and commitment to the principle of lay agency. It was these lay workers who conducted most of the visiting so they were in the best position to deal with the social need. In 1881, speaking to the LCM, Shaftesbury pointed out that the success of lay agency had been proved by its practice over the previous forty years. In 1882 he recalled the scale of early opposition to lay agency, and noted the more recent calls for lay workers to operate under close guidelines and supervision, akin in some ways to ordination vows. Such a narrowing of the view of ministry was anathema to Shaftesbury, damaging both mission and social welfare. He insisted that for lay agency to be effective among the masses the agents had to be trusted.

Keeping body and soul together

The unity of body and soul was a linchpin of Shaftesbury's social and evangelistic attitudes, a guiding and motivating principle in his work. It related to his beliefs about the end of time when body and soul would again be reunited in the final resurrection. This led logically to having as much concern for the body, physically, socially, and materially, as for the soul and its eternal and final destiny. Shaftesbury expressed this view frequently before the various missionary societies and in his parliamentary speeches. To him a concern for body and soul was equally the work of the gospel. Earthly matters could not be separated from heavenly.[26] This was, of course, exemplified in his beloved societies. Shaftesbury paid tribute to the teachers of the RSU who devoted so much to "the advancement of the temporal and eternal welfare of the neglected children".[27] For himself, he declared his determination to labour, "so long as there is a soul to be saved, misery to be relieved, and ignorance to be enlightened".[28]

In his work through the CPAS the social element has not previously been recognized. Shaftesbury set out before the CPAS the dual responsibility.[29] Although strictly speaking temporal welfare was not part of the society's objectives, the spiritual and the temporal were closely linked in its work. Shaftesbury urged the agents of the CPAS to give temporal as well as spiritual assistance. On one occasion, in 1873, the noble Lord even went so far as to make a direct link between the CPAS and the movement for the reform of factory hours.[30] This was perhaps less fanciful than might be imagined. Somewhat surprisingly the CPAS made a number of interventions on the need for legislation in matters of social need. In 1862 it demanded legislative action for the protection of miners. In 1868 it welcomed the extension of the Factory Acts to cover all trades and occupations. In 1871 the society praised "the wise provisions of the Legislature for promoting the health and comfort of the labouring classes".[31]

The end times

Shaftesbury's understanding of "the end times" (eschatology) is crucial for understanding his motivation and purpose. The manner in which the various understandings of the millennium and the end times related to attitudes to evangelism and social welfare are complex.[32]

Shaftesbury's diaries are full of references to the second coming, although rarely do they expand on his understanding of the associated events. He was clear that Christ would return in person and reign on the earth. He said that he could not understand the Scriptures in any other way. The return of Christ was also a matter of personal devotion. The doctrine provided him with much comfort especially after the death of Minny and the final illness of his daughter, Constance. The hope was of being re-united with loved ones. The Second Advent was an event to be prayed for and the only real basis of hope for humanity.

Every hour of reading, every hour of reflection, strengthens me more and more, God be praised, in the conviction that the Second Advent is the hope for all the ends of the earth.[33]

Thus this momentous event was to be soon, but no date could, or indeed, should be set. Shaftesbury was committed to preaching...

*... the Second Advent of our Blessed Lord. Pay no attention
to excited and angry critics, who charge such a scheme with all
the extravagancies of the fifth monarchy, and the millennial
inventions. The Second Advent, as an all-sufficient remedy,
should be prayed for; and as a promise, should be looked for.
The mode, form, and manner of that event are not revealed, and
therefore no business of ours.*[34]

This outlook is very important in building up the reasons how
and why this thinking led Shaftesbury to his position of uniting
social and evangelistic outreach. Many of those who adopted
millennial schemes spent a great deal of time and effort on the
minute details of chronology and timing. This included setting a
date for the return of Christ (despite the injunctions of the Bible
to the contrary).

The day of judgment also played an important part in the
Evangelical understanding of the end times. To Shaftesbury
judgment involved not only eternal destiny but also accountability
and responsibility for actions on earth. This day would "exhibit
some fearful reckonings", including Herod for the murder of
the innocents, and Louis XIV for his massacres in Germany.[35]
Shaftesbury was intensely practical. The God he believed in did
not just act in ancient times but throughout history to the present.
Sins were not to remain unpunished, a point which Shaftesbury
made in relation to Britain's unholy role in the Opium War against
China. The day of judgment was to be a day of reckoning for
the stewardship of the gifts of God. Inevitably, for Shaftesbury
the Tory paternalist, the account to be given to God included the
responsible exercise of the gifts of rank and station.

Those concerned with the end, especially those who adopted the
outlook of premillennialism (in which the return of Christ would
inaugurate the period of the millennium), were also concerned for
the "signs of the times" – the matching of contemporary events
to the chronology of the book of Revelation. Shaftesbury offered

several instances. These included references to gathering clouds, the frequency of meteors and earthquakes and the persecution of the Florentine shopkeepers for their Protestantism in 1852.[36] He even saw the meetings of the London Society bringing the end "nearer and nearer" and notwithstanding the rhetoric of the May meetings, he firmly asserted the hope of many that "the last days are at hand".[37]

Some commentators placed particular emphasis on the return of "speaking in tongues", the ecstatic utterances associated with the day of pentecost in Acts 2. Although there were several instances many Evangelical commentators became increasingly disillusioned with the prophetic movement and its concentration on the gifts. To Shaftesbury the revelation of the Bible could never be replaced by that of a latter-day prophet. Thus, "in no one place are we told of a *true* Prophet as a *new* Revelation to instruct us in the latter days", and "many false prophets have arisen since Christ, but all have fallen and… away; and the Holy Bible, by the blessing of God, remains, as it was, seventeen hundred years ago". Shaftesbury's Protestantism was not going to be overturned by current Evangelical fashion".[38]

The obsession with the minute details of the hoped-for millennium proved to be an enormous distraction from the tasks and responsibilities of the present. Shaftesbury's discipleship was based on living in the constant, yet unknown, expectation of the second coming. He refused to set a date for this, nor did he speculate on the details of the millennium. He pursued an understanding that demanded that the Christian life be lived out in expectation of Christ's imminent return. This allowed him to emphasize the duties and responsibilities of Christians for which account would be required at the day of judgment. This included the duties of the nation – a Christian nation would also be held to account. The nearness of the second advent and judgment was to Shaftesbury an impulse to action, not withdrawal. He referred to the natural tendency to "repose in present security", rather than being "active to avert a distant peril".[39] If the Lord's people, he told the CPAS in 1845, are found sitting down and waiting for peace on the day of judgment, they will be surprised that there will be no such peace. Neglect of duty in the period leading up to the second advent would bring directly the judgment of God. The duty of God's people was "to look at the interval that may elapse between the present period and the final and glorious consummation".[40] The key was faithful discipleship in the light of the coming judgment:

> *The time is short, that the period of the great conflict for all nations is coming on; and that that nation and Church alone will stand upright which are found engaged in the service of their Master. Therefore, let us pray, that in the great day of account we may be an acceptable, ay, and an accepted people.*[41]

The time was coming, he added, "when matters will not be measured by the talent, or the ability, or by fine clothes, or by power to speak, or by being on platforms, or by listening to those upon platforms", but "when matters will be measured by those who have the truest faith, the deepest love, and the most sincere acts of obedience to their Lord and Saviour, and most devoted and strong imitation of his blessed example".[42]

Faithful and obedient discipleship in the period before the return of Christ lay at the root of Shaftesbury's work. It was this which animated his labour as legislator, missionary activist, and supporter of voluntary societies. It also motivated his passion as the defender of Protestant and Evangelical truth. Speaking to the annual meeting of the CPAS in 1876 he showed that he had lost none of his zeal half a century after first embracing the Evangelical faith.

> *I am now looking, not to the great end, but to the interval. I know, my friends, how great and glorious that end will be; but while I find so many persons looking to no end, and others*

rejoicing in that great end, and thinking nothing about the interval, I confess that my own sympathies and fears dwell much with what must take place before that great consummation.[43]

CONCLUSION

Shaftesbury was sprightly and active until his final illness. In May 1884 he had presided at the annual meetings of the Bible Society and the London Society and a special celebration for the LCM. He had also made a speech to the Young Men's Christian Association and been involved with both the commemoration of John Wycliffe the Bible translator and early English Reformer and a statue to William Tyndale, Bible translator and martyr. In the midst of all of that he had met with representatives of the Great Northern Railway to ensure the interests of the working classes were being protected. It was in June 1884 that he had presided over Spurgeon's fiftieth birthday celebrations at the Metropolitan Tabernacle. However, Shaftesbury was weakening and becoming weary. He continued to make diary entries for the rest of that year and the beginning of the next but now they were fewer. In April 1885 he celebrated his eighty-fourth birthday. In May he struggled to Exeter Hall and presided at the Bible Society only to fall ill the next day. On 19 May he managed to attend the annual meeting of the RSU where he was honoured. At St Giles on 22 May he received holy communion for the last time. He was taken back to London in an invalid carriage on 4 June – and managed to chair a meeting at a refuge. He met on 24 June the Flower Girls' Mission, and on 10 July City Missionaries. He announced his depression to his diary: his last entries were on 25 and 28 July. He left London for the last time, and arrived in Folkestone on 25 July. He suffered a fall and a lung infection. His children and his valet read to him from Scripture, including every morning the twenty-third Psalm. He received a letter from the Dean of Westminster offering him a final resting place in the Abbey, but he preferred St Giles. He died peacefully on 1 October.

How can we assess Shaftesbury and his impact?

Shaftesbury stands as a towering figure not just of the nineteenth century but of the whole of history. His impact was enormous. His character, tenacity, and Christian commitment served him for some sixty years of public service. He was courted by all. Even at the beginning of his career he noted in his diary that he was probably unsuited to Cabinet office. Despite being offered Cabinet posts by various prime ministers he resisted. In doing so he probably ensured a greater legacy than if he had accepted. It would have been impossible, for example, for him to sustain his long-term commitment to the reform of the lunacy laws if he had been in and out of the Cabinet. In many of his other campaigns he would not have been able to stand against the government. Shaftesbury's independence was something he rightly highly prized. In character and temperament he was also unsuited to high government office. The impact of his long public service came from his painstaking commitment to evidence, to detail and above all to vision.

Shaftesbury had a vision for God in society. This came from his uncompromising Protestantism, a conclusion that some might find uncomfortable. As a campaigner for some "party" causes he was unyielding in his adherence to the Protestant faith. Undoubtedly he made errors and misjudgments. However, his clear understanding of Protestantism also gave him the clarity of vision that there was a role for God in the public domain. It was because the nation was Christian that the state carried responsibilities for God's creatures.

Shaftesbury saw the role of God in society as a partnership between a Christian state and the Christian voluntary society. In this way he also developed a unique Evangelical vision for mission. Evangelicals have always struggled with the relationship of the eternal welfare and destiny of individuals and the responsibility to provide and care for people on earth. Shaftesbury's ability to bridge this gap was not just a consequence of an excessive paternalism. His vision rather reflected deep Christian and Evangelical thought. His position within the spectrum of Evangelical beliefs about the end of time was a carefully worked out belief which turned on its head the classic application of such views to social welfare. He saw the Evangelical voluntary societies as instruments used by God in preparation for the judgment, practical expressions of faithful discipleship. He saw a definite, albeit limited, role for the state. This set of beliefs and their application in practice gave Shaftesbury a vision that combined spiritual and earthly destinies, state intervention and voluntary societies, responsibility and faithfulness, commitment to the Word of God, and also the Christian nation. The Second Advent was not simply a consoling doctrine, but an impulse to action.

In some ways Shaftesbury was well ahead of his time. This includes his passion for Christian unity, a state founded on Christian principles and a life of unstinting public service. In other ways he remained an old-fashioned paternalistic high Tory. He preferred rural to urban, village to city, land to capital. His utopian vision was probably not shared by many of those he campaigned for. He always opposed political reform. As late as 1872 he was opposing the proposed secret ballot – he viewed it as dishonest and cowardly not to vote in public. Socialism was anathema to him.

Shaftesbury inspired and exacerbated in equal measure. The same man who fought to save the children from the horrors of the mines and the chimneys tried also to legislate to prevent clergy from wearing particular vestments. What might seem incongruous to the modern onlooker was to him all of a piece; the motivation was the same Christian faith, Protestant and Evangelical commitment.

Shaftesbury achieved more than any government could ever have done. He was an intelligent and skilful operator. He never gave up. He was also not influenced by the manoeuvrings of political parties and alliances. It allowed him to press for the principles for which he was campaigning year in, year out until the necessary provisions were achieved. The only offices he really sought were the chairs of the Evangelical societies. These were his love and to him they were a central part of the whole package of Christian mission alongside his parliamentary campaigns.

Depressive, sometimes rigid, certainly not moderate. Without his happy marriage to Minny he would never have survived so long. Yet he was also full of surprises. His resignation from Parliament because he had changed his views on the Corn Laws was simply highly principled. It contrasted with Peel's own government which had succeeded in blocking factory legislation under threat of resignation. At the end of his life he became very concerned for the welfare of animals – including that remarkable speech to the Lords on vivisection in which he said that he would in every respect rather be the dog than the professor. He demanded to know the scriptural authority for causing such suffering.

Shaftesbury was more than simply a nation's conscience, though he was certainly able to stir that conscience. He was in essence a man, flawed, but also one of courage, integrity, consistency and persistence: in short a man of passion. He showed to the nation true Christian leadership, discipleship, and service. His legacy is on the statute books, in the voluntary Evangelical mission societies and their work, evangelistic and social, and in the vision for a Christian nation and public policy.

We have much to thank him for.

APPENDIX: THE MILLENNIUM

The variations and differences within the millennial tradition have rarely been recognized and are frequently subsumed within generalized categories, even in histories of Evangelicalism. The usual division of post-millennial and premillennial is unhelpful and inadequate in understanding the range of views within the Evangelical movement and their implications. There were in fact a whole plethora of voices from professional exegetes to self-proclaimed messiahs.

The millennium

The basic ideas of the millennium were set out in chapter 4. Post-millennialism emphasized the return of Christ at the end of the period of blessing. Premillennialism was based on the idea of the second coming or second advent inaugurating the millennium.

The post-millennial tradition stressed continuity with the world, whereby the millennium represented a progressively achieved improvement upon the present. The premillennialists emphasized discontinuity, revolutionary change, and the complete reversal of worldly fortunes. Christ would return in person and the millennial era would commence with Jesus and his saints reigning on earth. This would include both those who had already died, who would rise from the dead, and those living at the time of the advent. The ungodly would be overthrown, the Jews restored, and the world converted. There would be a final resurgence of evil followed by the general resurrection, the day of judgment, and then the end. Hence there were three important stresses in the premillennial tradition: firstly, on divine agency – it was God's initiative;

secondly, on the material – the Lord's reign was on earth; thirdly, on the "signs of the times" – where the world was in the divine chronology.

The signs of the times

The book of Daniel (along with Revelation a key book in this methodology) refers to a spiritual despotism which would arise and last, according to Daniel 7:25, "a time, times and half a time". The question was what this meant. The first step was to link "a time" to a year. Hence the verse was seen as referring to a year ("time"), plus two years ("times") and half a year. This totalled three and a half years or 1,260 days. Exegetes used the principle of the "year-day" theory based on Numbers 14:33 to equate a day to a year. This led to the conclusion that this spiritual bondage would last 1,260 years. Further references to 1,260 days in Revelation 11:3 and 12:6 were seen as confirming this reference. The question remained of exactly how these time periods were to be applied to the history of the church. There were alternative schema put forward (one was provided by the seven seals and seven trumpets of the book of Revelation) but the principle was the same. These symbols covered the whole of history. The only issue was the precise identification of events to match the symbols. The papacy became associated with the imagery from the book of Revelation of the Whore of Babylon or the Beast. England, it was argued, had turned from being an elect nation to Laodicea (the church in Revelation 3 which was "lukewarm"). The 1,260 years was seen, at least by the Protestants of the nineteenth century, as beginning around 533 AD – the emergence of the Papacy and Roman Catholic Church – and ending around the time of the French Revolution, 1793 being the year of the execution of Louis XVI. Hence, the end must be near.

A number of problems arose – even beyond the basic issue of whether the very first steps of year–day linkages were justifiable.

Some attached different interpretations to the imagery. Was the beast the Pope (the traditional Protestant position) or Napoleon (in the light of the Revolution)? There was much competition and variety over the symbolism. Then there was the problem of the time periods. The book of Daniel also refers to two other time periods, 1,290 days and 1,335 days – when the person who has waited will be blessed. Different millennial schemes adopted different starting points for measuring the passage of time. However, given the general acceptance that the end was imminent this led to a tendency to look for a date for the great event. Several millennial commentators saw the year 1867–68 as the one which most obviously brought together the several pieces of the prophetic jigsaw – the numbers worked! The neatness also illustrates the problems.

The millennium and social welfare

It remains to summarize how the different millennial traditions responded to both mission and social welfare. It was the combination of optimism and pessimism, of imminent judgment and present duty, and of the individual and the corporate which provided the millennial framework for evangelistic mission and social action in the nineteenth century. This particular combination of the eschatological details differs from the traditional divisions in a number of key ways. This outlook, adopted by both Bickersteth and Shaftesbury, can perhaps be best described as "contemporary premillennialism". The details of the main divisions and how they relate to social welfare are summarized in the table opposite.

	Post-millennial	Futurist Premillennial	Historicist Premillennial	Contemporary Premillennial
Return of Christ	Future	Future	Imminent	Near
Day of Judgment	Future	Future	Imminent	Near
Signs of the times	Moderate, optimistic	Moderate, neither pessimistic nor optimistic	Detailed, pessimistic	Moderate, pessimistic
Details of millennium	Vague	Moderate	Detailed	Moderate
Pentecostal gifts	Sceptical	Yes, future	Yes, now	Sceptical
Reason for preaching the gospel	Means	Witness	Witness	Means and witness
Role of social welfare	Quietist – dealt with in future	Quietist – dealt with in future	Quietist – reversal of fortunes imminent	Activist – present duty in light of pending advent and judgment

Post-millennialism tended to be optimistic about human progress and even the human condition. As the gospel gradually spread and the world was converted so that would, in time, lead to an improvement in the social condition of the poor. Futurist premillennialism also projected the second coming and the day of judgment far into the future, hence lessening the current impact. The classic historicist premillennial position so strongly reflected a loss of confidence in human means and human ability to bring about change that proponents became quietists in respect of social welfare needs. Indeed, there was no need to worry, the Lord was returning soon, and fortunes would be reversed. There was enormous distraction in this outlook caused by over concentration on the details of the millennium, the pentecostal gifts, and discerning the signs of the times. In contemporary premillennialism the emphasis remains upon the second coming and day of judgment but without the obsessions with signs, dates, gifts, and other details. The concentration in this case is on responsibility and duty, on giving account for current life and discipleship at the judgment, which will be soon but at an unknown juncture. Until that point there is a fundamental responsibility for both the witness of preaching the gospel and social activism. The Lord's disciples should be found doing his work when he returns, rather than simply awaiting his glorious arrival. Ignorance of the date of the second advent gave the church a permanent state of expectation which should stir up the sense of present duty and activism. This led to great emphasis on the unity of body and soul and the duties and responsibilities of the present in the light of Christ's expected return. It is this dynamic which explains the combination of evangelistic and social action with equal vigour, together with the association of state and voluntary action.

NOTES

Introduction

1. *The Times*, 9 October 1885, p. 12, column A.

2. Edwin Hodder, *The Life and Work of the Seventh Earl of Shaftesbury*, London: Cassell and Company Limited, 1886, volume 3, p. 517.

3. Hodder, *Shaftesbury*, volume 3, p. 518.

4. George M. Young, *Portrait of An Age*, London: Oxford University Press, 1960, p. 79.

5. Letter from Lord Shaftesbury to the Earl of Derby, 29 June 1866, in Hodder, *Shaftesbury*, volume 3, pp. 211–12.

6. Journal of Henry Fox, quoted in Georgina Battiscombe, *Shaftesbury*, London: Constable, 1974, p. 16.

7. Geoffrey B.A.M. Finlayson, *The Seventh Earl of Shaftesbury,* London: Eyre Methuen, 1981, p. 600.

8. *The Times,* 2 October 1885, p. 9, column A; p. 10, column A; 9 October 1885, p. 9, column C.

Chapter 1

1. The title "Lord Ashley" will be used for the period before his succession to the earldom in 1851 when referring to his specific actions and speeches. "Shaftesbury" will be used for the period after 1851 and also for generic description and assessment throughout the book.

2. David Roberts, *Paternalism in Early Victorian England*, London: Croom Helm, 1979, p. 3.

3. Lord Ashley, Mines and Collieries Bill, *Hansard*, House of Commons, 16 May 1843, column 467.

4. Shaftesbury, Masters and Operatives Bill, *Hansard*, House of Lords, 19 July 1866, column 1061.

5. Hodder, *Shaftesbury,* volume 1, p. 51.

6. Lord Ashley, Diaries, 18–23 September 1825.

7. Lord Ashley, Diaries, 28 April 1826.

8. Lord Ashley, Diaries, 13 November 1828.

9. Finlayson, *Shaftesbury*, p. 15.

10. Hodder, *Shaftesbury*, volume 1, pp. 50–51.

11. Southampton University Library, Broadlands Papers, SHA/MIS/73.

12. Hodder, *Shaftesbury,* volume 1, p. 51.

13. Hodder, *Shaftesbury,* volume 1, pp. 47–49.

14. Hodder, *Shaftesbury,* volume 1, p. 51.

Chapter 2

1. Lord Ashley, Diaries, 28 April, 1826.

2. A. N. Wilson, *The Victorians*, London: Arrow, 2003, p. 84.

3. Lord Ashley, Diaries, 28 April 1826.

4. Ibid.

5. Lord Ashley, Diaries, 8 September 1825.

6. Lord Ashley, Diaries, 13 October 1825.

7. Lord Ashley, Diaries, 28 April 1826.

8. Ibid.

9. Lord Ashley, Diaries, 16 November 1826.

10. Lord Ashley, Diaries, 12 December 1826.

11. Lord Ashley, Diaries, 17 April 1827.

12. Lord Ashley, Diaries, 18 April 1827.

13. Ibid.

14. Lord Ashley, Diaries, 22 April 1827.

15. Lord Ashley, Diaries, 22 Feb 1827.

16. Lord Ashley, Diaries, 25 Jan 1828.

17. Lord Ashley, Diaries 3 July 1829.

18. Boyd Hilton, *A Mad, Bad, & Dangerous People?* Clarendon Press: Oxford, 2006, p. 380.

19. Hodder, *Shaftesbury*, volume 1, p. 86.

20. Hodder, *Shaftesbury*, volume 1, p. 105.

Chapter 3

1. William Wilberforce, *A Practical View of the Prevailing Religious System of Professed Christians in the Higher and Middle Classes in This Country Contrasted with Real Christianity*, London: Thomas Cadell, 1797, chapter 6, p. 422.

2. Wilberforce, *Practical View*, chapter 4, p. 197.

3. John Wolffe, *The Protestant Crusade in Great Britain 1829–1860*, Oxford: Clarendon Press, 1991, p. 22ff.

4. Hodder, *Shaftesbury*, volume 1, p. 197.

5. Hodder, *Shaftesbury,* volume 1, p. 44.
6. Lord Ashley, Diaries, 11 February 1827.
7. Lord Ashley, Diaries, 28 April 1826.
8. Lord Ashley, Diaries, 22 April 1827.

Chapter 4

1. Hodder, *Shaftesbury,* volume 1, p. 116.
2. Battiscombe, *Shaftesbury,* p. 51.
3. Lord Ashley, Diaries, 2 August 1829.
4. Ibid.
5. Lord Ashley, Diaries, 3 August 1829.
6. Lord Ashley, Diaries, 11 August 1829.
7. Hodder, *Shaftesbury,* volume 1, p. 116.
8. Lord Ashley to the Duke of Wellington, 30 November, 1831, in Hodder, *Shaftesbury*, volume 1, p. 121.
9. Southampton University Library, Broadlands Papers, BR 35.
10. Southampton University Library, Broadlands Papers, SHA/PC/130.
11. Hodder, *Shaftesbury*, volume 1, p. 125.
12. Hodder, *Shaftesbury*, volume 1, p. 173.
13. Hodder, *Shaftesbury*, volume 1, p. 174.
14. Lord Ashley, Diaries, 25 December 1833.
15. Lord Ashley, Diaries, 1 October 1843.
16. Hodder, *Shaftesbury*, volume 1, p. 175.
17. Hodder, *Shaftesbury*, volume 1, p. 176.
18. Hodder, *Shaftesbury*, volume 1, p. 177.
19. Hodder, *Shaftesbury*, volume 1, p. 184.
20. Lord Ashley, Diaries, 8 February 1834.
21. Lord Ashley, Diaries, 13 February 1834.
22. Hodder, *Shaftesbury*, volume 1, p. 193.
23. Lord Ashley, Diaries, 9 June 1834.
24. Lord Ashley, Diaries, 12 July 1834.
25. Lord Ashley, Diaries, 14 October 1835.
26. T. R. Birks, *Memoir of Edward Bickersteth*, 2 volumes, London: Seeley,1851, p. 42.
27. Birks, *Bickersteth*, p. 43.
28. CPAS, *Fourth Annual Report*, 1839, p. 25.

29. Lord Ashley, CPAS *Abstract*, 1848.

30. Lord Ashley, CPAS, *Abstract*, 1850.

31. Lord Ashley, Diaries, 4 October 1838.

32. Shaftesbury, CPAS *Abstract*, 1860.

Chapter 5

1. Report from Select Committee on Pauper Lunatics in the County of Middlesex, and on Lunatic Asylums, *Parliamentary Papers 1826–27 (557)*, p. 15.

2. *Parliamentary Papers* 1826–27 (557), p. 19.

3. *Parliamentary Papers* 1826–27 (557), pp. 33, 37.

4. Robert Gordon, Lunatic Asylums, *Hansard*, House of Commons, 19 February 1828, column 578.

5. Lord Ashley, Lunatic Asylums, *Hansard*, House of Commons, 19 February 1828, columns 583–584.

6. Lord Ashley, Diaries, 20 February 1828.

7. Lord Ashley, Diaries, 13 November 1828.

8. Lord Ashley, Diaries, 7 February 1829.

9. Lord Ashley, Diaries, 3 October 1838.

10. Ibid.

11. Thomas Wakley, Lunatics Bill, *Hansard*, House of Commons, 21 September 1841, column 695.

12. Sir Robert Inglis, Lunatics Bill, *Hansard*, House of Commons, 21 September 1841, column 699.

13. Lord Ashley, Diaries, 17 May 1842.

14. Lord Ashley, Diaries, 18 November 1844.

15. Lord Ashley, Diaries, 15 May 1849.

16. Lord Ashley, Diaries, 9 November 1842.

17. Lord Ashley, Diaries, 2 July 1844.

18. Lord Ashley, Lunatics Bill, *Hansard*, House of Commons, 11 July 1845, columns 402, 404.

19. Report of the Metropolitan Commissioners in Lunacy, to the Lord Chancellor, *Parliamentary Papers 1844 (001)*, p. 6.

20. Lord Ashley, Treatment of Lunatics, *Hansard*, House of Commons, 23 July 1844, columns 1258.

21. *Hansard,* House of Commons, 23 July 1844, columns 1263, 1269.

22. *Hansard*, House of Commons, 23 July 1844, column 1271.

23. Lord Ashley, Diaries, 30 July 1845.

Chapter 6

1. "The Factory System", *Quarterly Review*, volume 57, December 1836, p. 409.

2. Robert Southey to Lord Ashley, 13 January 1833, quoted in Hodder, *Shaftesbury*, volume 1, p. 143.

3. Letter from Rev G. S. Bull to Short-Time Committees, 6 February 1833, quoted in Hodder, *Shaftesbury*, volume 1, pp. 148–149.

4. Hodder, *Shaftesbury*, volume 1, p. 149.

5. Robert Southey to Lord Ashley, in Hodder, *Shaftesbury*, volume 1, p. 143.

6. Lord Ashley, Factories Commission, *Hansard*, House of Commons, 3 April 1833, columns 86, 88.

7. *Quarterly Review*, volume 57, December 1836, pp. 397–98.

8. *Quarterly Review*, volume 57, December 1836, p. 413.

9. *Quarterly Review*, volume 57, December 1836, p. 423.

10. *The Times*, 25 June 1838, p. 4, column B.

11. *The Times*, 6 October 1840, p. 4, column C.

12. Children's Employment Commission, First Report of the Commissioners: Mines, *Parliamentary Papers*, 1842 (380, 381, 382), p. 51.

13. *Parliamentary Papers*, 1842 (380, 381, 382), p. 94.

14. Lord Ashley, Employment of Women and Children in Mines and Collieries, *Hansard*, House of Commons, 7 June 1842, columns 1321, 1326–27, 1336–37.

15. Lord Ashley, Diaries, 9 June 1842.

16. Lord Ashley, Diaries, 8 July 1842.

17. Lord Ashley, Diaries, 8 August 1842.

18. Lord Ashley, Diaries, 29 September 1842.

19. Lord Ashley, Diaries, 16 March 1844.

20. Lord Ashley, Diaries, 19 March 1844.

21. Lord Ashley, Diaries, 23 March 1844.

Chapter 7

1. Lord Ashley, Diaries, 29 September 1838.

2. Lord Ashley, Diaries, 4 October 1838.

3. Lord Ashley, Diaries 15 October 1838.

4. Lord Ashley, Diaries, 19 October 1838.

5. Lord Ashley, Diaries, 23 November 1839.

6. Lord Ashley, Diaries, 6 March 1840.

7. Lord Ashley, Diaries, 1 July 1840.

8. Lord Ashley, Diaries, 8 October 1838.

9. *Quarterly Review*, volume 63 January 1839, p. 186.

10. Lord Ashley, Diaries, 12 October 1841.

11. Hodder, *Shaftesbury*, volume 1, p. 380.

12. Letter from Lord Ashley to Lord Selborne, December 1841, in Hodder, *Shaftesbury*, volume 1, pp. 389–390.

13. Lord Ashley, Diaries 2 January 1844.

14. Lord Ashley, Diaries 23 August 1844.

15. Lord Ashley, Maynooth College Debate, *Hansard*, House of Commons, 16 April 1845, column 776.

16. *Hansard*, House of Commons,16 April 1845, column 781.

17. Lord Ashley, Diaries 7 April 1845.

18. Lord Ashley, Diaries 3 May 1845.

19. Shaftesbury, The College of Maynooth, *Hansard*, House of Lords, 18 April 1853, column 1329.

Chapter 8

1. Report from the Committee on Employment of Boys in Sweeping of Chimnies, *Parliamentary Papers* 1817 (400).

2. Lord Ashley, Chimney Sweeps – Climbing Boys, *Hansard*, House of Commons, 14 April 1840, column 1093.

3. Lord Ashley, Climbing Boys, *Hansard*, House of Commons, 25 June 1840, column 108.

4. Lord Ashley, Diaries, 19 September 1840.

5. *The Times*, 14 August 1847, p. 6, column E.

6. Report on an Inquiry into the Sanitary Condition of the Labouring Population of Great Britain, *Parliamentary Papers* 1842 (006), p. 279.

7. Lord Ashley, Diaries, 27 September 1841.

8. Lord Ashley, Diaries, 24 November 1845.

9. Lord Ashley, Diaries, 23 December 1845.

10. Lord Ashley, Diaries, 27 January 1846.

11. Lord Ashley, Public Health Bill, *Hansard*, House of Commons, 8 May 1848, column 781.

12. Lord Ashley, Diaries, 26 September 1848.

13. Lord Ashley, Diaries, 13 April 1848.

14. Lord Ashley, Diaries, 2 June 1849.

15. Lord Ashley, Diaries, 7 June 1849.

16. Lord Ashley, Diaries, 11 October 1849.

17. Lord Ashley, Diaries, 6 October 1849.

18. Lord Ashley, Post Office, *Hansard*, House of Commons, 30 May 1850, column 475.

19. Hodder, *Shaftesbury*, volume 2, p. 306.

20. Hodder, *Shaftesbury*, volume 2, pp. 331–334.

21. Shaftesbury, London Necropolis and National Mausoleum Bill, 8 June 1852, *Hansard*, House of Lords, columns 190–91.

Chapter 9

1. London City Mission, Minute Book 1, 16 May 1835 – 3 January 1837, Minutes of First Meeting, London, 16 May 1835.

2. London City Mission, Minutes, 20 May 1835.

3. London City Mission, *Second Annual Report*, 1837, p. 1.

4. Revd J. M. Rodwell, Second Public Meeting of the London City Mission, *LCM Magazine*, June 1836, p. 77.

5. *LCM Magazine*, August 1845, p. 175.

6. *LCM Magazine*, August 1845, p. 179.

7. *LCM Magazine*, volume 1, number 1, January 1836, p. 1.

8. Revd E. Bickersteth, Proceedings of the Eighth Annual Meeting, *LCM Magazine*, June 1843, p. 84.

9. Hon. and Revd B.W. Noel, Second Public Meeting, *LCM Magazine*, June 1836, p. 65.

10. *LCM Magazine*, February 1845, volume 10, p. 24.

11. Shaftesbury, Proceedings at Annual Meeting, *LCM Magazine*, June 1879, p. 129.

12. *LCM Magazine*, June 1879, pp. 127, 129.

13. Shaftesbury at the Mansion House, *LCM Magazine*, April 1881, p. 65.

14. Lord Ashley, Proceedings of the Thirteenth Annual Meeting, *LCM Magazine*, June 1848, p. 128.

15. *LCM Magazine*, June 1879, p. 130.

16. *LCM Magazine*, June 1879, p. 129.

17. Shaftesbury, Proceedings at the Thirty-First Annual Meeting of the LCM, *LCM Magazine*, June 1866, pp. 132, 134.

18. Shaftesbury, Proceedings at Annual Meeting, *LCM Magazine*, June 1863, p. 126.

19. *LCM Magazine*, July 1874, p. 147.

20. Shaftesbury, Proceedings at Annual Meeting, *LCM Magazine*, June 1848, p. 126.

21. Shaftesbury, Introduction to J. M. Weylland, *Our Veterans*, London 1881.

22. *LCM Magazine*, January 1884, p. 2.

23. Shaftesbury, Proceedings at Annual Meeting, *LCM Magazine*, June 1848, p. 127.

24. *LCM Magazine*, November 1885, p. 232.

25. *LCM Magazine*, June 1848, p. 126.

Chapter 10

1. Ragged School Union Minutes, Minutes of First Meeting, 11 April 1844.

2. Ragged School Union Minutes, Special Meeting of the Managing Committee, 1 November 1844.

3. *RSU Magazine*, January 1849, p. 1.

4. *RSU Magazine*, March 1849, p. 5.

5. RSU, *Second Annual Report*, 1846, p. 35.

6. *RSU Magazine*, volume 18, November 1866, pp. 252–53.

7. Lord Ashley, *RSU Second Annual Report*, 1846, p. 6f.

8. J. Stuart, *Fifty Years of the Costers Mission*, Hunter and Longhurst, London, 1911, p. 92.

9. RSU, *Twenty-Seventh Annual Report*, 1871.

10. RSU, *Eighth Annual Report*, 1852.

11. *RSU Quarterly Record*, volume 2, April 1877, p. 44.

12. Shaftesbury, Diaries, 18 May 1870.

13. RSU, *Thirty-Third Annual Report*, 1877.

14. Shaftesbury, Proceedings, RSU, *Twenty-Ninth Annual Report*, 1873.

15. RSU, *Thirty-Third Annual Report*, 1877.

16. Shaftesbury, Proceedings, *RSU Twenty-Seventh Annual Meeting*, 1871.

17. Shaftesbury, Prize Scholars Meeting, *RSU Magazine*, New Series, volume 19, April 1867, p. 84.

18. Shaftesbury, Proceedings, RSU, *Twenty-Third Annual Report*, 1867.

19. Shaftesbury, Scholars Prize Meeting, *RSU Magazine*, volume 13, April 1861, p. 87.

20. Lord Ashley, Diaries, 11 December 1845.

21. Shaftesbury, Proceedings, RSU, *Twenty-Eighth Annual Report*, 1872.

22. Shaftesbury, Testimonial to Joseph Gent, *RSU Magazine*, volume 18, March 1866, p. 62.

23. Shaftesbury, Diaries, 16 March 1870.

Chapter 11

1. Shaftesbury, Diaries, 17 May 1851.

2. Ibid.

3. Ibid.

4. Shaftesbury, Diaries, 25 December 1851.

5. Ashley, Lodging-Houses, *Hansard*, House of Commons, 8 April 1851, columns 1259–60.

6. Lord Ashley, Diaries, 12 December 1850.

7. Lord Ashley, Diaries, 31 January 1851.

8. Shaftesbury, Sanitary State of the Metropolis, *Hansard*, House of Lords, 29 April 1852, column 1288.

9. Shaftesbury, Sanitary State of the Metropolis, *Hansard*, House of Lords, 29 April 1852, column 1295.

10. Shaftesbury, Diaries, 24 September 1852.

11. Shaftesbury, Diaries, 7 April 1853.

12. Shaftesbury, Diaries, 12 June 1853.

13. Shaftesbury, Diaries, 29 June 1853.

14. Shaftesbury, Diaries, 24 May 1853.

15. Shaftesbury, Diaries, 28 May 1853.

16. Shaftesbury, Chimney Sweepers Regulation Act Amendment Bill, *Hansard*, House of Lords, 12 May 1853, columns 198–99.

17. Shaftesbury, Chimney Sweepers Bill, *Hansard*, House of Lords, 4 April 1854, columns 364–67.

18. Shaftesbury, Diaries, 2 May 1854.

19. Shaftesbury, Diaries, 20 May 1854.

20. Shaftesbury, Diaries, 21 May 1854.

21. Letter from Lord Aberdeen to Lord Shaftesbury, 4 May 1854, in Hodder, *Shaftesbury*, volume 1, p. 474.

22. Shaftesbury, Diaries, 10 May 1854.

23. Shaftesbury, Diaries, 21 May 1854.

24. Shaftesbury, Diaries, 31 July 1854.

25. Shaftesbury, *Hansard*, House of Lords, 17 August 1871, column 1762.

26. Liza Pickard, *Victorian London*, London: Weidenfeld & Nicolson, 2005, p. 34.

27. Shaftesbury, Metropolitan Railways – Displacement of Labourers, *Hansard*, House of Lords, 28 February 1861, column 1069.

28. *Hansard*, House of Lords, 28 February 1861, column 1072.

29. Shaftesbury, Dwellings for the Labouring Classes, *Hansard*, House of Lords,

21 March 1861, column 148.

30. Shaftesbury, Great Eastern Railway Bill, *Hansard*, House of Lords, 12 March 1863, column 1323.

Chapter 12

1. Shaftesbury, Diaries 8 May 1855.

2. Letter from Lord Shaftesbury to Lord Palmerston, 7 February 1855 in Hodder, *Shaftesbury*, volume 2, p. 492.

3. Hodder, *Shaftesbury*, volume 2, p. 508.

4. Shaftesbury, Diaries, 16 June 1855.

5. Shaftesbury, Diaries, 7 July 1855.

6. Letter from Shaftesbury to Hon Evelyn Ashley, 28 February 1855, in Hodder, *Shaftesbury*, volume 2, p. 505.

7. Shaftesbury, Diaries, 1 November 1865.

8. Shaftesbury, Diaries, 6 February 1855.

9. Shaftesbury, Diaries, 1 November 1865.

10. Ibid.

11. Hodder, *Shaftesbury*, volume 3, p. 200.

12. *The Times*, 4 November 1856, p. 9, column F.

13. Shaftesbury, Diaries, 28 March 1857.

14. Shaftesbury, Diaries, 31 May 1857

15. Shaftesbury, Divine Service in Theatres, *Hansard*, House of Lords, 24 February 1860, columns 1686–87.

16. Shaftesbury, Diaries, 22 October 1867.

17. Shaftesbury, Diaries, 20 December 1860.

18. Shaftesbury, Diaries, 3 February 1861.

19. Shaftesbury, Diaries, 11 December 1861.

20. Southampton University Library, Broadlands Papers, BR 37/2.

21. Shaftesbury, Diaries, 29 June 1862.

22. Southampton University Library, Broadlands Papers, SHA/EST/8.

23. Shaftesbury, Diaries, 20 August 1863.

24. Southampton University Library, Broadlands Papers, BR 37/3.

25. Children's Employment Commission (1862), First Report, *Parliamentary Papers*, 1863 (3170).

26. Shaftesbury, Chimney-Sweepers and Chimneys Regulation Bill, *Hansard*, House of Lords, 3 June 1864, column 1130.

Chapter 13

1. Shaftesbury, Diaries, 23 July 1866.

2. Shaftesbury, Clerical Vestments Bill, *Hansard*, House of Lords, 11 March 1867, column 1624.

3. Shaftesbury, Clerical Vestments Bill, *Hansard*, House of Lords, 14 May 1867, columns 488, 492.

4. Ibid., column 493.

5. Shaftesbury, Diaries, 9 May 1867.

6. Shaftesbury, Diaries, 11 July 1869.

7. Southampton University Library, Broadlands Papers, BR 36/2.

8. Ibid.

9. Ibid.

10. Ibid.

11. Southampton University Library, Broadlands Papers, SHA/PC/92.

12. Shaftesbury, Diaries, 10 June 1872.

13. Shaftesbury, Diaries, 15 October 1872.

14. Shaftesbury, Diaries, 9 October 1872.

15. *The Times*, 7 October 1872, p. 12, column E.

16. Shaftesbury, Diaries, 28 April 1875.

17. Shaftesbury, Chimney Sweepers Bill, *Hansard*, House of Lords, 11 May 1875, columns 437, 442.

18. Hodder, *Shaftesbury*, volume 3, p. 397–98.

19. Southampton University Library, Broadlands Papers, SHA/PC/90.

20. Southampton University Library, Broadlands Papers, SHA/PC/93.

21. Shaftesbury, Diaries, 12 June 1875.

22. Shaftesbury, Diaries, 10 July, 1881.

23. Southampton University Library, Broadlands Papers, SHA/PC/100.

24. Southampton University Library, Broadlands Papers, SHA/PC/101.

25. Shaftesbury, CPAS *Abstract* 1873, p. 268.

26. Shaftesbury, Diaries, 18 July 1874.

27. Shaftesbury, Diaries, 21 June 1876.

28. Shaftesbury, Diaries, 12 August 1876.

29. Cruelty to Animals Bill, *Hansard*, House of Lords, volume 248, 15 July 1879, column 430.

30. Shaftesbury, Diaries, 14 May 1878.

31. Shaftesbury, Diaries, 29 March 1879.

Chapter 14

1. Hodder, *Shaftesbury*, volume 3, p. 6.

2. Kathleen Heasman, *Evangelicals in Action*, Bles, London, 1962, p. 8.

3. Lord Ashley, Hours of Labour in Factories, *Hansard*, House of Commons, 15 March 1844, column 1075.

4. Lord Ashley, Employment of Children, *Hansard*, House of Commons, 4 August 1840, column 1270.

5. Shaftesbury, Speeches, 1868, quoted in J. Wesley Bready, *Lord Shaftesbury and Social Industrial Progress*, London 1926, p. 34.

6. Lord Ashley, Employment of Children in Calico Print Works, *Hansard*, House of Commons, 18 February 1845, column 655.

7. Shaftesbury, Diaries, 31 January 1871.

8. Shaftesbury, Address to CPAS, 8 May 1862, quoted in Hodder, *Shaftesbury*, volume 3, p. 7.

9. Shaftesbury, Diaries, Christmas Day 1852.

10. *The Record*, 16 May 1839.

11. Shaftesbury, Bible Society, 56th Anniversary Meeting, *Monthly Reporter*, June 1860, p. 373.

12. Shaftesbury, Bible Society, 57th Anniversary Meeting, *Monthly Reporter*, June 1861, p. 494.

13. Lord Ashley, CPAS *Abstract*, 1842.

14. Shaftesbury, CPAS *Abstract*, 1854.

15. Shaftesbury, Bible Society, 47th Anniversary Meeting, *Monthly Reporter*, May 1851, p. 27.

16. Lord Ashley, Diaries, 27 November 1845.

17. Shaftesbury, RSU, Proceedings of the 18th Anniversary Meeting, *RSU Magazine*, volume 14, June 1862, p. 130.

18. Shaftesbury, Proceedings at Annual Meeting, *LCM Magazine*, June 1863, p. 127.

19. Lord Ashley, CPAS *Abstract*, 1850.

20. Shaftesbury, CPAS *Abstract*, 1873.

21. Shaftesbury, Introduction to *The Man with the Book*, by J.M. Weylland, London 1878.

22. Lord Ashley, Diaries, 10 May 1850.

23. Shaftesbury, RSU, Proceedings of the 39th Annual Meeting, *Quarterly Record*, vol 8, July 1883, p. 107.

24. Shaftesbury, CPAS *Abstract*, 1873.

25. Shaftesbury, CPAS *Abstract*, 1879.

26. Shaftesbury, RSU, Proceedings of the 39th Annual Meeting, *Quarterly*

Record, volume 8, July 1883, p. 107.

27. Ibid.

28. Shaftesbury, RSU, Proceedings of the 29th Annual Meeting, *RSU Magazine*, volume 25, June 1873, p. 139.

29. Shaftesbury, CPAS *Abstract*, 1858.

30. Shaftesbury, CPAS *Abstract*, 1873.

31. CPAS, *Thirty-Sixth Annual Report*, 1871, pp. 20–21.

32. A more detailed, technical account has been included in an appendix for those who wish to pursue the matter in more depth.

33. Lord Ashley, Diaries, 26 December 18475.

34. Letter from Shaftesbury to Joseph Angus, 27 January 1870, in Hodder, *Shaftesbury*, volume 3, p. 261.

35. Lord Ashley, Diaries, 11 October 1843.

36. Shaftesbury, Diaries, 12 November 1852.

37. Shaftesbury, London Society, Proceedings at 56th Anniversary, *Jewish Intelligence*, June 1864, p. 126.

38. Lord Ashley, Religious Notes, 1835–37, Southampton University Library, Broadlands Papers, SHA/MIS/1.

39. Lord Ashley, Diaries, 19 January 1846.

40. Shaftesbury, CPAS *Abstract*, 1868.

41. Shaftesbury, CPAS *Abstract*, 1857.

42. Shaftesbury, RSU, Prize Scholars Meeting, *RSU Magazine*, April 1867, p. 84.

43. Shaftesbury, CPAS *Abstract*, 1876.

SELECT BIBLIOGRAPHY

Ackroyd, P., *London*, London: Vintage, 2001

Battiscombe, G., *Shaftesbury*, London: Constable, 1974

Bebbington, D. W., *The Dominance of Evangelicalism*, Leicester: IVP, 2005

Best, G. F. A., *Shaftesbury*, London: Batsford, 1964

Birks, T. R., *Memoir of Edward Bickersteth*, 2 volumes, London: Seeley, 1851

Bradley, I., *The Call to Seriousness*, London: Cape, 1976

Brown, F. K., *Fathers of the Victorians*, Cambridge: Cambridge University Press, 1961

Chadwick, O., *The Victorian Church*, 2 volumes, London: A. & C. Black, 1966–70

Clark, J. C. D., *English Society 1688–1832*, Cambridge: Cambridge University Press, 1985

Finlayson, G. B. A. M., *The Seventh Earl of Shaftesbury*, London: Eyre Methuen, 1981

Harrison, J. F. C., *The Second Coming*, New Brunswick: Rutgers University Press, 1979

Heasman, K. J., *Evangelicals in Action*, London: Bles, 1962

Hennell, M., *Sons of the Prophets*, London: SPCK, 1979

Hilton, B., *A Mad, Bad, & Dangerous People?*, Oxford: Clarendon Press, 2006

——— *The Age of Atonement*, Oxford: Clarendon Press, 1988

Hodder, E., *The Life and Work of the Seventh Earl of Shaftesbury*, 3 volumes, London: Cassell & Company, 1886–1887

Hunt, T., *Building Jerusalem*, London: Weidenfeld & Nicolson, 2004

Lewis, D. M., *Lighten their Darkness: the Evangelical Mission to Working-Class London, 1828–1860*, New York: Greenwood Press, 1986

Martin, R. H., *Evangelicals United*, Metuchen, New Jersey and London: Rowman & Littlefield, 1983

Noll, M. A., *The Rise of Evangelicalism*, Leicester: Apollos, 2004

Oliver, W. H., *Prophets and Millennialists*, Auckland: Auckland University Press, 1978

Pickard, L., *Victorian London*, London: Weidenfeld & Nicolson, 2005

Porter, R., *English Society in the Eighteenth Century*, London: Penguin, 1991

Roberts, D., *Paternalism in Early Victorian England*, London: Croom Helm, 1979

Toon, P., *Evangelical Theology, 1833–1856*, London: Marshall, Morgan & Scott, 1979

Turnbull, R. D., *Anglican and Evangelical?*, London: Continuum, 2007

Wesley Bready, J., *Lord Shaftesbury and Social Industrial Progress*, London: Allen and Unwin, 1926

Wilberforce, W. *A Practical View of the Prevailing Religious System of Professed Christians in the Higher and Middle Classes in this Country Contrasted with Real Christianity*, London: Thomas Cadell, 1797

Wilson, A. N., *The Victorians*, London: Arrow, 2002

Wolffe, J., *The Protestant Crusade in Great Britain 1829–1860*, Oxford: Clarendon Press, 1991

Young, G. M., *Portrait of an Age*, London: Oxford University Press, 1960 edition

Ziegler, P. R., *Palmerston*, Basingstoke: Palgrave MacMillan, 2003

Manuscripts and other sources

Birmingham University Library

Archives of the Church Pastoral Aid Society

Minutes of the General Committee

Annual Reports (including *Sermons* before Annual Meeting)

Abstract of Report and Speeches at the Annual Meeting

Miscellaneous Papers

Cambridge University Library

Archives of the British and Foreign Bible Society

Minutes of the General Committee

Annual Reports, 1804–86

Monthly Extracts

Monthly Reporter

Miscellaneous Papers

Hansard Parliamentary Debates

London: London City Mission

Archives of the London City Mission

Minutes of the General Committee

Annual Reports

The London City Mission Magazine

London: Shaftesbury Society

Archives of the Ragged School Union

Minutes of the Ragged School Union, 1844–85

Annual Reports, 1845–86

The Ragged School Union Magazine, 1849–75

The Ragged School Union Quarterly Record, 1876–84
Miscellaneous Papers
Oxford University: Bodleian Library
Archives of the London Society for the Promotion of Christianity
Amongst the Jews
Minutes of the General Committee and sub-committees
Anniversary Sermons
Annual Reports
The Jewish Advocate
The Jewish Expositor
The Jewish Intelligence (including *Proceedings at Annual Meetings*)
Miscellaneous Papers
Parliamentary Papers
Quarterly Review, The
Southampton University Library
Broadlands Papers
Diaries of the Seventh Earl of Shaftesbury (fourteen volumes)
Miscellaneous Papers
Times, The

INDEX